SOCCER GRANNIES

The South African Women Who Inspire the World

JEAN DUFFY

ROWMAN & LITTLEFIELD
Lanham • Boulder • New York • London

Published by Rowman & Littlefield
An imprint of The Rowman & Littlefield Publishing Group, Inc.
4501 Forbes Boulevard, Suite 200, Lanham, Maryland 20706
www.rowman.com

86-90 Paul Street, London EC2A 4NE, United Kingdom

British Library Cataloguing in Publication Information Available

Library of Congress Cataloging-in-Publication Data

Names: Duffy, Jean, 1958– author.
Title: Soccer grannies : the South African women who inspire the world / Jean Duffy.
Description: Lanham, Maryland : Rowman & Littlefield Publishing Group, [2023] | Includes bibliographical references and index. | Summary: "The inspirational story of an amazing group of soccer-playing South African 'grannies' and their journey to the United States. These women play together despite resistance from their communities to improve their health and socialize—and for a brief respite from the injustices and struggles they face on a daily basis"—Provided by publisher.
Identifiers: LCCN 2022039787 (print) | LCCN 2022039788 (ebook) | ISBN 9781538170175 (cloth) | ISBN 9781538170182 (epub)
Subjects: LCSH: Women soccer players—South Africa—Biography. | Women, Black—South Africa—Biography. | Women, Black—South Africa—Social conditions. | Soccer—Social aspects—South Africa. | South Africa—Social conditions.
Classification: LCC GV942.7.A1 D84 2023 (print) | LCC GV942.7.A1 (ebook) | DDC 796.334092/2—dc23/eng/20221013
LC record available at https://lccn.loc.gov/2022039787
LC ebook record available at https://lccn.loc.gov/2022039788

To Beka,
without whom there would be no story

Hail the mighty baobab!
Hail the mothering love
Peerless in height and size
Great in aid and shade.
Defiant in the parched land
Neither the drought nor the flood fears.
But the mighty Harmattan mocks
And the fierce blazing sun scoffs.
Blooming or shedding the greenery
At her own sweet will and time
And her fruit are constant in season.
Anger or malice she knows not
Neither a grumble nor a wail she utters
But within her big beating heart keeps
All the pain and scars of a harassed land.
If we but learn her ways,
We should be twice blest over
In this harsh and remorseless world![1]

CONTENTS

Foreword

My name is Rebecca "Beka" Ntsanwisi. People call me "Mama Beka," and some call me the "Mother Teresa of Limpopo." The Mother Teresa name was given to me by a radio personality who I highly respect, Dlayiseta Abbie Baloyi. One day he and I were with the former Tzaneen mayor, O. J. Mushwana, touring one of the communities where I do my work helping the residents. At the third house we visited that day, they were afraid to go in. Dlayiseta saw the tough work I was doing and told me I was "like Mother Teresa." That's how I got that nickname.

I am proud that I have won so many awards for my community work. I was the Shoprite Checkers/SABC2 Woman of the Year finalist in 2004 and winner in 2005. I also won the regional award and was the national overall winner for Community Builder of the Year. But the award that made me realize that God is with me was the 2008 Order of the Baobab, presented by the then president of South Africa, Thabo Mbeki. Just touching his hand and the award itself meant so much to me. National orders are the highest honors, given only by the president of a country.

When Jean told me she was writing a book about me and the Grannies soccer team I founded, in my heart I did not take it seriously, as so many people have promised so many things that have never come to pass. When she persisted, I then realized it was true. I still can't believe that my work is being recognized internationally. Jean, Catherine, and their soccer teammates, the Lexpressas, have become good friends of mine. They support me in moving forward and wish me well in so many ways.

This book is important because it will help people around the world understand the challenges the Grannies face every day. I arranged for Jean to have interviews with the Grannies so these women have a voice to share their stories and so you can get to know them like I do. The

Grannies deserve understanding and care. I give them love and help when they need it. My hope is that this book will help others see the need to care for the aged. I hope *Soccer Grannies* inspires readers to support my plans to build a home for the elderly of South Africa. My dream is to have it staffed with retired professionals and people who love to work with older people and give them the love and special care they deserve.

Jean and I have been friends and worked together since early 2010, when she first heard about our team and was inspired by us. We even traveled to meet each other—me to America with the Grannies and her to South Africa with the Lexpressas. Our friendship thrives, and Jean and I are always in contact. Her teammates have become my sisters, supporting my vision of changing the world through love. I want to thank Jean for understanding me and always telling me that I'm a strong woman.

It feels like quite an achievement that Jean has written this book about my work, helping it gain recognition internationally. *Soccer Grannies* will open doors for us. When people read it, they will understand that it wasn't so easy convincing the Grannies to play soccer and helping them put aside for a time the worries in their heads. Today the Grannies are famous and travel the world. Besides South Africa, I have helped form Grannies teams in Togo, Benin, France, and Malawi. I'm so proud of this. My dream is to impact the world and inspire Grannies teams in every single country.

Even when I'm facing my own challenges, people don't stop asking for help. I've become a shoulder to cry on for many. But before I can help anyone else, I always first ask the Lord to help *me*.

Reading this book, you will get to know the Grannies and me. But first I want you to meet some of the people who have helped me become who I am. Their belief in me has made my work possible and inspired me. These people will always have my gratitude.

One young lady, Criseldah Ndlovu, from Mpumalanga province, follows the community work I'm doing. Once when she was going through a hard time, she called me for encouragement. I told her that God would bring new people into her life, people who would be there with her. Today she is a successful businesswoman. We are still in frequent contact, still helping each other. Thank you, Criseldah, for believing in me.

Pastor Ruddock Ndou and his wife have counseled me through some difficult personal times. With the help of my friend Christine DuPree from Hoedspruit I have been able to help other women grow from my experiences.

When I was a twelve-year-old pianist, my mentor and friend Dr. Elijah Maswanganyi told everyone that one day I'd go far and change the world. His words were a prophecy. This man has inspired me. He's always told me I'm the best, even when life has me down. I appreciate his encouragement.

I call Dr. N. M. Shipalana "Mukutsuri," which means "Redeemer" in Xitsonga. When he sings, you see Heaven even though you're still on earth. His voice also speaks volumes. Many friends through the years have fallen by the wayside, but Mukutsuri is still here, standing beside me and supporting my projects.

Richard Chauke is so humble. A long time ago he and I began pooling our salaries to help a few students in need, and we are still doing it today. I respect him with all my heart. When times are tough, he encourages me, telling me that I'm a strong woman.

My friend Phindile Maringa worked with me at SABC Limpopo, where I had my radio show. She believed in me then, and now we are still friends. I love her so much.

Topman Ngonyama is a geologist and pastor of a church in Mtititi Village. During a very dark period of my life, he offered me love and respect. We are like family. Now I call him my son. When I left my radio show at SABC, he told me that I had to keep doing my community work. I took his advice, and today his company, GeoPoint Africa, is supporting the 2023 Grannies International Football Tournament I'm organizing with his help.

A colleague at SABC, Happiness Thomo Maake, has motivated and strengthened me to unleash my talents on large projects like the tournament. His encouragement and respect for my abilities has been so uplifting and I look forward to being a partner with him for the rest of my life.

My family's support keeps me going and their prayers make me strong.

My daughter Nkhensani Sannie watched her busy mother always leaving home to help other people. Today she works alongside me. Together we've come to understand that loving people is from the heart. I salute you, girl, from the bottom of my heart.

Reneilwe Madibana, my second-born, fills me with love. To her I say, you must follow your heart.

To my grandson, Amukelani Ntsanwisi: Granny loves you.

I thank my younger sister, Lydia Tutu, for her prayers and encouragement.

My brothers, Ephraim, Vusi, and Sam, have always shown me respect and prayed for me. Thank you.

To my other son, Pastor Gift Mashele: You are so amazing, dear.

And finally, I'm so grateful to my parents, Rene Pondo and Julia Ntsanwisi. Dad, thank you for supporting my vision and work, even giving me your bakkie with petrol without complaining. Mama, you are a prayer warrior. Even when we have problems, you guide us to believe in prayer and read books. Thanks, Mama.

Now you know a little bit about some of the many people who have helped me along my way. Here, now, is part of my story—the book written in America. Thanks for your support, dear Jean. And thank you, readers.

Rebecca "Beka" Ntsanwisi
Polokwane, Limpopo
June 24, 2022

Author's Note

THIS IS A TRUE STORY.

It's been collated, teased apart, woven back together, marked up, and reformulated, only for the process to start all over again. I have penned my story during a span of seven long years from a veritable library of carefully saved personal text messages, email correspondence, Facebook posts, photographs, notes on napkins, informal recollections retold over coffee, formal interviews conducted on tape, documentaries, clipped newspaper articles, archived news videos, conference footage, and, of course, my own memories.

I have also relied on the scholarship of many historians, anthropologists, and sociologists to better inform my understanding of South African history, women's issues, the origins of soccer, and the cultural context of the Tsonga people. Please see the bibliography for a complete sourcing.

In the interest of narrative harmony, I have on occasion slightly altered the time frame of minor events or reconstructed actual dialogue from multiple sources. In a very few instances I have changed an individual's name upon request to protect their privacy.

I have taken great pains to tell this story truthfully. "Truth," however, is so often in the eye of the beholder. To that end, I have compared memories and viewpoints with many individuals who lived this story along with me; sometimes their recollections diverged from mine. I thank them for their honesty and generosity, which have only made this book stronger.

Any errors or omissions are, of course, my own.

For the women whose stories you will read in these pages, I have only humble gratitude that they have trusted me with the telling. May this narrative honor them.

Jean Duffy
Somerville, Massachusetts
July 1, 2022

PROLOGUE

A People United

Sport has the power to change the world. It has the power to inspire. It has the power to unite people in a way that little else does. It speaks to youth in a language they understand. Sport can create hope where once there was only despair. It is more powerful than governments in breaking down racial barriers. It laughs in the face of all types of discrimination.—Nelson Mandela[1]

THE CLOUDS WAFT ABOVE THE JOHANNESBURG ARENA ON JUNE 11, 2010, as if buoyed by the waves of enthusiasm coming off the packed crowd. Vuvuzela horns have been toted from rural towns, where once their drone invited distant villagers to community gatherings. Today in Soccer City Stadium, they buzz like a swarm of crazed bees, without ceasing, vibrating to a deafening crescendo during moments of suspense and celebration.

The excitement cannot be contained. Today South Africa becomes the first nation on the continent to host a FIFA World Cup.

In the years since the 2004 announcement that South Africa would host the World Cup, stadiums have been readied in nine host cities across the Rainbow Nation. The first high-speed train in all of Africa now glides on gleaming tracks, shuttling fans painted in team colors from city to city. Staff have learned to say "Welcome!" in hundreds of languages to the visitors now pouring in from Mexico, France, Uruguay,

Nigeria, Greece—scores of nations the globe over. South African flags have sprouted from balconies, office windows, taxi antennas. Billboard-sized screens erected in parks across the country broadcast the match for throngs of local residents brightly dressed in yellow and green, eager to cheer along with the millions who will tune in on their own TV sets over the coming weeks.

In the stadium, no less colorful, Black arms link with Brown arms link with White arms—and then shoot up, almost in unison, as their beloved Bafana Bafana take to the field. "Boys Boys," the crowd cries.

The band strikes the first notes, and the roar lowers to a charged hum. They stand shoulder to shoulder, flags waving high above their heads. Embodying the promise of the moment, fifty thousand voices unite in singing the national anthem.

> Sounds the call to come together
> And united we shall stand;
> Let us live and strive for freedom
> In South Africa, our land![2]

As the sixteen-year-young democracy celebrates on the global stage, the revelry radiates well beyond the stadium walls. The rush of national pride extends across the parks, over mountains, beyond high plateaus and rolling grasslands . . . into a modest home of concrete, where the TV—deeper than it is wide—blasts the match at full volume.

Tensely perched on the edge of an upholstered loveseat, a Bafana Bafana superfan closely follows the gameplay with a critical eye that has been trained by hours upon hours on the pitch, dribbling the ball and running drills.

"Eeeeeeee!"

The sudden outburst is startling.

"He was offsides"—to no one, everyone. Hands to head, now softly tsking the TV screen. Then, catching the eye of her youngest grandchild: "You never want to overanticipate the attack," explains the wizened Granny. "Everyone knows that."

This grandmother is not just another football fan; her knowledge of the game comes from her own time on the field, her foot on the ball, setting up plays with her fellow grandmother teammates. She's one tough Soccer Granny.

Part I

The Dream

After climbing a great hill, one only finds that there are many more hills to climb.—*Nelson Mandela*[1]

Vakhegula Vakhegula FC

I always say to the Granny Lizzy that any coach who might come to take over Vakhegula Vakhegula—it will be tough for that coach! [Laughs]

The Grannies know that when they come here, this is where they find their joy; they find their happiness; they talk and they laugh. At the end of the day, when I am going home, I too am leaving with something. —Abraham Sevor Kwabena, Soccer Grannies coach[1]

SOMETIMES YOU GO LOOKING FOR INSPIRATION, AND SOMETIMES IT JUST hits you in the face.

Like when you're on an early morning run and suddenly you're awash in clarity about that thorny work problem that's been plaguing you for weeks. Or maybe a total stranger makes a passing comment that pushes you to see yourself a little bit differently. Once in a while these gifts of insight motivate you to change course, act in a big way—and your life takes a major left turn.

For me, it came down to some uncharacteristic procrastinating at the start of a workday: I couldn't know it then, but that morning my carefully charted path veered upon a seemingly chance encounter with a group of older women playing recreational soccer halfway around the world.

Go back all the way to early 2010—a cold February morning. I was seated at my desk in a seven-story building outside of Boston, early as usual so I could get a head start on the day's work. So it was still silent, a good hour yet before my coworkers would arrive for the day and with them the chatter of greetings and the clink of coffee mugs bringing our department to life. But on this particular Tuesday morning, my best intentions were derailed by a news story emailed to me—something about a soccer team in South Africa.

Opening ceremonies for the FIFA World Cup were still a good four months away at that point, yet my anticipatory excitement was already stirring. A self-proclaimed soccer freak, then fifty-one years of age, I had only recently switched from soccer momming on the sidelines to chasing the ball myself. I've always been a sucker for human-interest stories—the soft, meaningful narratives that tug heartstrings—and in 2010, I was particularly charmed by any features on the upcoming World Cup. The link before me had been emailed by my friend Heather, who played keeper on my soccer team. The story was about a football club in rural South Africa made up entirely of grandmothers.

I scrolled down to the embedded video and clicked *play*.

On my computer screen appeared an older woman with a round brown face and several missing teeth. She was wearing a saffron shirt and a paisley bandana. She was staring into the camera. "If I were to run with you, I would *beat* you."[2]

I didn't doubt her; she spoke with confidence and had the fierce eye of a competitor.

"—even though I am eighty-three-years-old and have had six strokes."

Whaaaaaaat?

"But soccer has really changed my life," she continued. "It's improved because of the football."

Work temporarily forgotten, I brushed my papers aside—neatly placing my color-coded to-do list atop—and leaned forward to take in the scene as the camera zoomed out.

The reporter explained that this grand dame with the swagger of a seasoned footballer was part of a team of thirty-five women in rural South Africa, in their late forties to early eighties. They were affectionately called the Soccer Grannies.

I saw a dusty, sunbaked field on which the women moved through their warm-up exercises. Shoulder to shoulder they worked their way up the field—shuffle-shuffle, kick to the right, handclap; shuffle-shuffle, kick to the left, handclap. Loose-fitting shirts and below-the-knee skirts gave them freedom of movement. Beyond the dirt field, a few short trees and tufts of yellow scrub grass grew.

Another Granny with close-cropped hair came into focus.

"I like to play soccer because it helps us. We were sick, but now our cholesterol, our blood pressures, have gone down. Even our doctors are amazed when we go for a checkup. God bless the person that came up with this glorious idea."

With that, the Grannies were off and running. They chased the leather ball, kicking wildly and sending knee-high clouds of dust into the air. Caught up in the excitement, they paid no attention to the positions they were supposed to be playing.

I knew this feeling well. I wasn't the only newbie on my Massachusetts team; like the Grannies, we were drawn to the ball like kids at a birthday party descending on a bludgeoned piñata.

The camera followed a few heftier Grannies who had slowed to catch their breath. Most of these women, I had to imagine, were not sitting all day in ergonomically designed desk chairs like mine. Yet here they were, after a full day of work, showing up for afternoon practice, tearing down the field on well-worn joints. Other Grannies were skinny, nothing but bones and muscle, racing toward the ball. Their dark skin accentuated the rainbow of colors of their headscarves and skirts.

The ball was kicked again and again and finally found the net. Smiles blossomed across Grannies' faces as they embraced nearby players. Cheers erupted on the sidelines from the cluster of fans huddled in the limited shade. One blew on a three-foot-long plastic horn that sounded like an elephant trumpeting.

The news reporter relayed that not everyone is supportive of the Grannies' football club, and yet the women play on despite resistance from community members. *Your place is at home watching the grandchildren*, they've been chided by townsmen.

The local churches frown upon women wearing trousers, on or off the field, so at first the Grannies played in skirts. Over time, as their confidence grew—and as their neighbors grew used to seeing them play—the Grannies pushed back on what had traditionally been deemed "acceptable" sports attire for women. Today they play in shorts. But even some of the Grannies' friends still disapprove. "It's undignified, squeezing into short pants."

A few of their own grandchildren are among the naysayers: "Grandma, you can't play soccer; you're too old."

But not everyone feels that way. The camera panned to a teenager on the sidelines, bursting with pride. "I feel good when the Grannies play soccer so that they can be fit and strong," he says with a smile.

The video ended, and I noticed the clock with a start. It was going on 7 a.m. I *really* should be getting to work . . . and yet . . . I couldn't help myself.

I went back and immediately replayed the video—two more times.

The outside observer might conclude that these ladies and I had little in common. Me: White suburban professional. Them: Black rural grandmas. But I knew better; my own time on a cherished team told me of the camaraderie and support they must be getting from their own teammates, the feeling of confidence that grows from flubbing shot after shot on goal, and then one day there's a little more oomph behind your kick, directed with just a little more finesse, and suddenly your teammates are slapping you on the back. We weren't so different, these Grannies and I.

Sighhhhh. Unable to ignore the towering pile of paperwork any longer, I grudgingly turned my attention away from the Grannies.

But they had unpacked their bags and taken up residence in my brain. That day, as I scrolled through endless spreadsheets, I couldn't have imagined that in fewer than six months the 7,875 miles would be bridged between my home in Lexington, Massachusetts, and the Grannies' in Nkowankowa, Limpopo, and I would be joining them on the field.

The ref blew his whistle, signaling the halftime break. It was our regular Thursday evening game, and the faces of my teammates matched our pink team jerseys as we headed to the sideline and reached for water bottles. Heather, our fearless goalie with a strawberry-blonde ponytail, interrupted the chatter. "Did you guys see the video I sent? The one about the Soccer Grannies?"

"I saw it!" I enthused. "I just loved that they haven't stopped playing just because they're older."

"Ladies," Catherine broke in with her French accent, "we can do what they are doing. We can keep playing as we age, *just* like the Grannies." She'd been born in France and had played soccer with her brothers as a young girl. Now she coached and played on our amateur team—the Lexpressas, an assemblage of middle-aged women of all abilities.

"We need all the inspiration we can get," said Allison, a midfielder gazelle who excelled at sprinting up the sidelines. "Those dang birthdays just keep coming . . ."

Our lively conversation had caught the attention of Anne, a player from the opposing team. I knew her as a skilled defender who had stolen the ball from me countless times. "You know," she said, "the Veterans Cup will be held in Massachusetts this July." Every year a different state hosted the national tournament for adult soccer teams. I'd never attended but had heard lots of stories. "Heck," Anne continued, "we can invite the Soccer Grannies to come play. A Japanese men's team plays every year."

Thus sparked an idea in my brain.

If there were other suggestions made that day, I missed them, for I had already burrowed deep into thought, thoroughly enchanted at the prospect of meeting these women.

"Catherine," I piped up, "I'd like to try to contact the Soccer Grannies."

"*Bon,*" she said with a sharp nod, "you do that. We will see what we learn."

7

Granny fever, I saw, had proven contagious. The original NTV Kenya video I'd seen only days before had led to articles from Reuters, the BBC, and CNN. I pored over the reportage, trying to figure out how to reach the Grannies.

The official name of their football club, I learned, was Vakhegula Vakhegula—vah-KAY-goo-lah, vah-KAY-goo-lah, they pronounced it. It means "Grannies Grannies" in their native Xitsonga, in homage to South Africa's beloved national men's team, Bafana Bafana.

I scanned another article and found what I was looking for: *The team was set up in 2006 by cancer survivor Beka Ntsanwisi.* I scribbled her name on a piece of paper and eagerly read on.

"Most of the time I have to use my salary to buy kit for them and organize events. It is not easy for me. I hope as more people get to know about the league, we will get sponsors," she said.[3]

I searched, and her name popped up as the recipient of dozens of community awards. Lovingly known as "Mama Beka," she hosted a religious radio show on Sunday mornings, reading Bible verses and interviewing guest pastors. Beka would invite listeners to call in and share their problems on the air. One such caller, it seems, had been mourning a relative's death for months but still was unable to bury the body, which remained in the mortuary because the family could not afford the funeral expenses. Moved by their plight, Beka sought donations from listeners and local businesses, which she then used to purchase a coffin and provide a tent and food for a proper funeral service.

Other listeners would share details about their physical woes; many, many were in need of medical interventions they simply could not afford. Beka to the rescue: she would contact healthcare providers on their behalf and seek financial assistance. On multiple occasions she had found donated wheelchairs and gotten them to callers in need.

One more Google search, and I found Beka's email address at the radio station.

Suddenly shy, I didn't want to seem pushy—just friendly; I decided in this first message to not mention Anne's idea about the Grannies attending the Veterans Cup. I lowered my eyes to the computer screen and typed.

Dear Ms. Beka Ntsanwisi,

Good day!
I play soccer with a women's group in Lexington, Massachusetts, in the United States. The women are 35 years and older, but as time marches on, more of us are in our 50s. We were delighted to see the video and articles about South Africa's football Grannies. The Vakhegula Vakhegula Football Club with players in their 60s, 70s, and 80s is an inspiration to us!
Perhaps we could be sister teams?

Best regards,
Jean Duffy

Good enough. I took a deep breath and hit *send*, uncertain if I'd ever hear back.

Mama, We Can Try This

Eish! I love football and our team so much. Actually, I get crazy whenever it is time to go for soccer practice. I joined this team when it started, and I have been with it ever since. Soccer changed my life so enormously. I don't know what my mates say when they look at me. Most of them do not even believe that I am eighty-six years old; they think I am just exaggerating. It is because of soccer and exercises. Even now, I am telling you, if I can start running or make exercises, you will not believe your eyes.—Gingirikani Mirriam Mushwana, Soccer Granny[1]

Morning Jean

I am so happy to receive a message from you. I can't believe this is happening to me.

She'd written back! My to-do list for that morning vaporized.

I do not have a sponsor yet but I believe with people like you I will have.

   I have colon cancer. When I die I would like to leave a legacy. That is my main aim.

We are invited to play with the American veteran teams in jolly.
I know I will be able to see you.

Beka[2]

I COULD HARDLY BELIEVE THAT AWARD WINNER, COMMUNITY ACTIVIST extraordinaire, radio station host, Soccer Grannies founder Rebecca Ntsanwisi had responded to *me*. I reread her message several times. The casual mention of colon cancer sobered me, and the reference to the "American veteran teams in jolly" was perplexing. Had she already been invited to the Veterans Cup this July in Massachusetts? Maybe Anne had already written her . . .

I didn't want to respond to Beka's note until I'd first checked in with Anne. But I was so excited to have made contact! This prompted an even deeper Internet dive into Beka's connection to the Grannies.

Back in 2003, at the age of thirty-five, Beka had felt pains in her stomach. A visit with her doctor provided a shocking diagnosis: colon cancer. She immediately began a course of chemotherapy and tried to remain optimistic. But at times the pain was unbearable, and she began to fear death was approaching.

But Rebecca Ntsanwisi had never been one to lay down when faced with life's troubles. She focused her discomfort and dread and pulled from them inspiration for her next great endeavor.

While in the hospital for her chemotherapy drips, her fellow patients had made quite the impression on her. "Each time I went to the clinic, I saw large numbers of grandmothers with diseases," she recalled. Arthritis, diabetes, hypertension, rheumatism—an armlong list of ailments was robbing South Africa's women of their twilight years. "I knew I had to do something."

Weakened by the harsh medical treatment, Beka was told by her doctor that she must exercise in order to get her strength back. *But what about these women*, Beka asked—always thinking of others. *Yes, exercise would ease their conditions too*, the doctor said. She recognized the cycle these elderly women had been caught in: Their sickness left them unable to cope with the responsibilities they faced; the stress left them lonely and depressed. So, as Beka began exercising to slowly gain back her own physical fitness, she began sweet-talking some of the older women she'd befriended at the hospital. With a mix of cajoling and cheerleading, she formed an exercise program for ladies who were out of shape and wanted to do something about it.

One day in 2006, the women were exercising in a field when some local boys accidentally kicked a soccer ball toward them. One of the ladies ran forward, booted the ball, and sent it flying while the others howled with laughter. Half-jokingly, Beka suggested the women try soccer.

"Mama," they said, "we can try this!"

While the women stood around shyly, Beka talked to the boys, asking them to demonstrate how to kick a ball.

The next day the women came back to Beka. "Mama," they said, "we want to meet for soccer again."

The Soccer Grannies team was born.

That initial group of women encouraged their friends to join Vakhegula Vakhegula. Beka used her radio show to talk up the team, reaching the ears of Granny Rossina, an eighty-year-old blessed with ten grandchildren. "They were looking for grannies to come and play football," Rossina recalled later.

"Mama Beka said that grannies shouldn't stay at home looking after their children's babies; otherwise they would strain themselves by always sitting at one place. She encouraged us to come out and gather so that we could exercise by playing football. So one day I requested my husband to go check the grannies at the soccer playfield to find out what was happening.

"When I arrived there at the playfield, I found women playing football, and I was surprised. To see women playing football was a miracle to me. I was standing under the tree, and someone asked me if I had come to play football, and I just said yes, even though I did not know how I would start to play it."

With the team growing in popularity and numbers, Beka hired a coach from a local boys' team to work with the Grannies. He organized soccer practice three days a week and taught the women basic soccer skills. The team would dress in colorful skirts, standing in a circle around their new coach, laughing as they stretched to touch their toes. Soon the grand-mothers' mobility and strength had increased from the exercise. Beyond the physical benefits, they were also enjoying laughter and friendship—which in turn improved their mental health. They were sleeping better too.

"I am stress-free since I have joined the Grannies' team," says Granny "Brian Mathé," her soccer nickname chosen in homage to the South African soccer idol.

"You may go to the playing field with something bothering your mind, but once you get there, you forget about it because of the jokes we share and laugh about whenever we are together.

"I am so thankful for loving soccer. I thank the Vakhegula Vakhegula soccer team for building me. I had a lot of stress before joining it, but now I am fine."

Beka being Beka, she built on this good deed and recruited a doctor to perform regular medical checkups for the Grannies and to refer specialists as needed; he oversaw the Grannies' hospital care, marveling at the notable improvements to their health after just a few months of playing soccer.

Each Granny who was able paid a modest monthly contribution to the team to cover soccer-related expenses. Some of the money would be reserved for loans available to the Grannies so they could start small income-generating businesses. They might request money to grow crops or buy supplies to make items to sell for profit. This helped them feed their families and grow more financially independent.

The success of the team naturally attracted others eager to join. Granny Florah, a sixty-four-year-old who had left school at age fifteen to train as a nurse, happened upon the team by chance.

"No one told me that there was Vakhegula Vakhegula. I was diag-nosed with arthritis, and as a result I was advised to exercise. One day while I was at work, I had time to run along the hospital wall fence. When I turned the corner, I saw the Grannies gathered some distance ahead of me. I asked myself as to what was happening, and I went to check. When I got there, I was told that those Grannies were a soccer squad, calling themselves Vakhegula Vakhegula, and that I could join them if I wanted to; I was welcomed. From then I started playing with them."

When Beka's work took her to nearby communities, she would talk up the Soccer Grannies. Repeatedly she would be asked to start a new team in their towns. So she would recruit anywhere from thirty to fifty women, ages fifty years or older, to join their friends and form a squad. Team captains were appointed to help coordinate activities.

Soon half a dozen communities across the province of Limpopo had their own Soccer Grannies football clubs. They began meeting for friendly tournaments.

Granny Rossina now celebrates sixteen years playing with the team. "It brought me joy. When time comes for going to the soccer field, you forget everything. You wouldn't even care what the next meal is going to be." She leaves those thoughts for after practice when she gets back home.

"At the soccer field, it is all joy. We talk, jump, laugh, and so on. I am proud of myself that I play football. Maybe I am so proud because I am so old?" she laughs. "Mama Beka has done us a good thing of football, and we are proud of it."

3

We're Not Bimbos

Hold your chest like this if it's bouncing.—Abraham Sevor Kwabena,
Soccer Grannies coach[1]

MY SPECTACLES WERE IN PERIL.

I'd contorted my upper body to insert one arm into my sports bra and then the other but had paused when my readers began to slide precariously down my face. Using my hobbled, half-bound arms, I managed to place my glasses gently on the dresser. With a sharp inhale, I pulled the tight band of elasticized fabric over my head and let go—*snap!*—tugging it down until my breasts were firmly imprisoned. Even though my modest womanly curves were now barely detectable, I appreciated the comfort the compression would provide.

I owed my gratitude to three American women who had lamented the discomfort they endured while jogging, breasts bouncing every which way. It was during the US running craze of the late seventies that one of them asked, "Why isn't there a jockstrap for *women?*"[2] In response, this woman's husband promptly left the room, returning moments later with an athletic cup bound around his chest. Everyone had laughed, but soon it was clear they'd stumbled onto a gem of an idea. Thus was born the modern sports bra, revolutionizing comfort for women athletes.

Speaking of support systems (hey-oh!), this fine spring morning in April 2010 I was on a mission to scrounge up backers for "The Grannies

Take Boston." I was headed to the annual Icebreaker Tournament, a charity series for women players that Anne Strong organized every year to herald the end of winter and the beginning of the outdoor soccer season. As it turned out, she *had* reached out and invited the Grannies to the Veterans Cup—only hours before I'd first emailed Beka—and the two of us had since coordinated our efforts, agreeing to ask today's captive audience for help bringing the Soccer Grannies to Massachusetts this coming July.

My eye on the clock, I downed yet another glass of water—hoping to avoid being sidelined with leg cramps. I grabbed my keys, my wallet, my shin guards—what else? My thoughts kept bouncing back to the countless emails I'd exchanged with Beka in the weeks since our initial contact. She told me she would need an official invitation letter before she could apply for visas, so I'd contacted the organization hosting the Veterans Cup and told them about Vakhegula Vakhegula; I'd even sent them a draft invitation letter. Days passed as I waited, alternating between finger drumming and toe tapping. Their board, it seems, was hung up debating insurance requirements for foreign teams. But after a few weeks they produced the invitation letter and even generously waived the Grannies' tournament entry fee.

Our project was creeping forward, but the slow pace was excruciating.

I was going to be late if I didn't head out now. I quickly checked my bag to make sure I had everything I needed for the day's gameplay and hollered a goodbye behind me. Wishes of good luck echoed back from Karen and Kate, my high school–aged daughters, and I was off.

Less than an hour later I was amid hundreds of women gathered for the tournament's ceremonial welcome. From above we would have looked like a bouquet of spring flowers, teams bunched together in posies of colorful matching shirts. I scanned the crowd eagerly, seeing women from anywhere around their early twenties to their late sixties. Maybe it was because I worked mostly with male engineers, but being with large numbers of women always gave me a thrill. *So many ponytails!*

In today's era of huge amateur sporting events where women comprise more and more of the field with every passing year, our modest, cheerful assemblage that day registered at most a bit of benign rubbernecking from curious passers-by. But we should feel anything but blasé about women's participation in athletics; it wasn't so long ago that sport was severely circumscribed for women and public athleticism was altogether taboo. Over the past few decades, soccer has become one of the most popular sports for girls and women in the United States, and today female athletes proudly call themselves "jocks." But this is a recent phenomenon.

It was back in 1881 that a group of brave ladies took to a field in Scotland to play the first game of women's soccer on record. Their kit would not have included spandex of any kind; knickerbockers, belts, stockings, heeled boots—yes. "Upwards of a thousand witnessed the game primarily out of curiosity," a reporter from the *Glasgow Herald* wrote. "Some of the individual players had a fair idea of the game."[3] (I guess for some people it's just inherently *hilarious* to see women outside of the kitchen.)

With each of the half dozen games the Scottish women played that spring, the attitudes of onlookers rapidly devolved from bemusement into overt hostility. Raucous hecklers in the crowd often disturbed play, and two of the matches had to be halted entirely after disrespectful spectators charged the field. During one particularly harrowing interruption, the women players ran to the safety of their horse-drawn carriages while police constables drew batons against the mob. The general public, it would seem, was not ready for ladies to play soccer.

Fifteen years later, the British Ladies' Football Club was established. Seeing what their sister athletes had gone through and anticipating a negative reaction, these players assumed aliases to protect their identities. The club founder, identifying herself only as "Nettie Honeyball," told the *Daily Sketch* that she wanted to prove women are not the "ornamental and useless creatures men have pictured" and that she looked forward to a time when "ladies may sit in Parliament and have a voice in the direction of affairs, especially those which concern them most."[4] (If you have pearls, you may want to clutch them now.)

It's easy to forget how cultural norms change—how what seems laughably customary, even mundane, today once registered as a revolutionary notion. And that kind of progress too rarely just happens on its own; it requires the brave first steps onto the pitch taken by those women in Scotland, followed by the club in Great Britain, followed by the next group and the next and the next—until today, on a lovely spring morning in Boston, Massachusetts, in 2010 when the tough, perseverant, skilled, focused, joyful athleticism of a group of women could be celebrated—or even ignored for commonplace.

"Good morning, women!" Anne Strong's voice boomed over the loudspeaker. "Welcome to the tenth annual Icebreaker soccer tournament." Cheers resounded from the crowd. "As always, I appreciate your support, with proceeds from today's event helping us bring soccer to Boston middle school girls." The throng applauded, hooted, and whistled, happy to pass their love of the game down to the next generation. When they finally quieted, Anne reviewed rules and safety procedures before calling Heather up to make one last announcement.

"A few months ago," Heather began, "we became aware of a group of women playing soccer in South Africa. An inspiration to all of us, they range in ages from forty-nine to eighty-four." The friendly crowd listened with smiles on their faces as she told them about Beka, the founding of Vakhegula Vakhegula, and how "through soccer they are reaping the benefits of valuable friendship as well as improved health." Whoops followed in appreciative recognition. When Heather explained that we had invited the Grannies to play at the Veterans Cup that July, applause erupted.

Having won hearts, it was now time for the ask.

"Beka is in the process of lining up sponsors," Heather said, "but we could use your help: We're looking for people with connections for discounted lodging or bus transportation for the Grannies." We would need community support to pull this off, but I was confident based on the enthusiastic reception I was seeing that we'd made more than a few friends today.

Four hours and as many games later, I high-fived my teammates after a final win and collapsed onto a blanket, glad to rest my weary legs. Over the last bite of a peanut butter sandwich, I saw Anne stroll over.

"Jean," she said, "this is Lois, my teammate on the Bay State Breakers." I got up—*creeeeak*—quickly wiping my hands on my shorts, and shook the hand of a woman who looked to be in about her mid-fifties, five feet tall, with spiky gray hair and the strong calf muscles of an athlete. Lois worked with the Massachusetts Adult State Soccer Association, Anne explained, the group hosting the Veterans Cup this year.

"I'm excited to meet those ladies from South Africa," Lois said. "My motto is, *Spread soccer, and do the right thing.* I'll help any way I can. I attend all the planning meetings for the Veterans Cup tournament, so I'm sure I can get discounted hotel rooms." What a find! I thanked Lois and assured her we'd appreciate any help she could give us.

"Oh, hey," I said. "I think our teams are playing each other next!"

I swear their smiles flickered from pleasant to predatory and back to pleasant.

As their seasoned play that day attested (they trounced us), Anne and Lois had decades-long soccer histories, much of it spent working and fighting to set up an infrastructure so the rest of us could play the game. Anne's illustrious soccer career had started in third-grade gym class. "I remember this big bully had the ball. I stole it from him. The other boys snickered." Too often a girl's athleticism inspires surprise, then amazement, then amusement. "I might be smaller than everyone else, but soccer proved I could be short and still capable."[5]

As an adult, Anne fostered a passion for the game, which drove her to shift midcareer from attorney to founder of CityKicks!, Boston's first soccer league for grade school–aged girls. She received numerous community awards for helping young athletes find confidence and excellence in all areas of their lives through sport. Personally, that's what I've always found most rewarding about the game, and in all of the videos I'd seen to date, Granny after Granny had expressed the same sentiment: Getting out and moving your body and forging the bonds of a team does more than flex your muscles and build endurance. It creates resilience and calm and a certain self-assurance too often missing in girls of any age.

Back in the 1960s when Anne and Lois had first started playing, they'd thought it unfair that no soccer teams existed for *them*. But girls were about to get a critical assist: In 1972, with passage of Title IX and the Education Amendments, Congress prohibited sex-based discrimination in federally funded educational programs. Though the legislation did not explicitly mention sports, most athletics in the United States are organized and funded by schools. This meant the equal rights of girls on pitches, on courts, and in swim lanes across the United States were now protected by the judicial system. US sports underwent a massive revolution: Within ten years, the number of girls participating in high school sports across the nation had increased tenfold, from two hundred thousand to almost 2 million. Before anyone could level the playing field, Title IX had to *open* the playing field.

For her part, Lois Kessin had grown up a tomboy—that outdated word for any girl who loves running, jumping, climbing, and anything else an active body is inclined to do. As a young adult in the early seventies, she'd joined a men's pickup soccer game, whereupon some of the players told her she should be home cooking dinner for her new husband. Not to be deterred, Lois ignored the jibes and played on; over the years she even developed close friendships with those men. And when eventually they had daughters of their own, they began to think differently about their teammate's unconventional behavior. *You were brave*, they told her. *My daughter plays because I saw you playing.*

Lois laughs thinking about it. "It's nice to hear," she says wryly, "but *oh* the crap I had to put up with in those early days."[6]

When she cofounded the Eastern Massachusetts Women's Soccer League in 1979, the initial planning meeting made it clear a new game was in town. "The women decided the teams would share responsibilities for running the league," inviting the talents and energies of everyone onboard into a collaborative effort. "However, the only man in the room that day declared *no one* ran leagues that way, you need *someone* in charge. Well. I tore him apart. 'We're not bimbos. We'll get it done.' I was right."

In the intervening years, Lois has been inducted three times into the Massachusetts Adult Soccer Hall of Fame and once into the New England Soccer Hall of Fame for her work as a coach and organizer for women's teams.

No bimbo indeed.

In the same period that Lois and Anne were pushing their way onto the soccer fields of Massachusetts, the full stretch of the Atlantic and another hemisphere away, the first documented South African women's soccer team was taking to the pitch in Soweto. This was 1962. Soon after, a team of young girls played in Cape Town, inspiring reporters to comment on their impressive foot skills—whereupon they then proceeded to rate the athletes' sexual attractiveness. Both teams disbanded after a short time.

Thirty years later, the rebirth of South Africa into a democracy coincided with the arrival of global competition in women's soccer. The first *Women's* World Cup was held in 1991. The team from Nigeria was the only African squad to qualify for that first FIFA competition, and South African women eagerly cheered their sisters on, envisioning a future in which women would represent the homeland at international competitions. After the tournament, a surge of Black women joined the sport.

Following FIFA's move, women's soccer was added to the Olympics' slate of events, and by 1993, there were numbers enough to assemble a South African women's national team, composed of players from across the nation. Banyana Banyana—or "Girls Girls"—were cheered on by their largely female fan base as important milestones followed, with qualifications for the Olympics for the first time in 2012 and for the Women's World Cup in 2019.

Even with all this progress, soccer in South Africa largely remains a sport of and for Black men. The women with a passion for the game work together to overcome inequities, forming supportive communities to mentor and care for each other across lines of age, class, and race, fighting battles that in many ways resemble the struggles Lois and Anne have taken on all their adult lives. And in many important ways, the fight is entirely different. These athletes in South Africa bring their experience with activism and resistance to help ease the way onto the pitch and to change minds—sometimes one detractor at a time. In one instance, a fifteen-year-old player went on a hunger strike for four days until her mother relented and let her join the local squad.

It is in this progressive era of not-enough-progress that the Grannies proudly refuse to give up the game they love, defiant in the face of a backward wisdom that still insists girls are weak, women belong in the home, and sport is for the boys. They respond with a pass across the field, a goal, fighting cultural norms and societal expectations, all despite being told that grandmothers should not chase a ball, that it's unseemly for them to dress in shorts, that any woman on the field must be neglecting childcare duties and household chores back at home. In the face of all this, the Grannies play on.

4

A Little Bit of Good

If someone fall [sic], you must try to help out. I always say this. Don't just stand there and look at the person. You understand?—Abraham Sevor Kwabena, Soccer Grannies coach[1]

Jean,

The reason why I am writing this note is I did not sleep yesterday. I received a call from Bochum, 120 km from my place. I did go there to find these kids on their own. The parents dead. They stay with their uncle who is very sick and their aunt who has 3 kids. In a small shack they are 11. The aunt is trying but it is pathetic. See the photos I send.

I decide from the money that I have to build them a house. I bought bricks yesterday. I need cement, concrete, a builder, and roofing. If you can, please try and help out. I am humbling myself unto you. This is for the first and last time, mama. I am not taking this as an advantage.

Beka[2]

I STUDIED THE THREE PHOTOS BEKA HAD SENT ME. THE FIRST SHOWED a small shed, a patchwork of corrugated metal surrounded by bare earth. A colorful striped cloth, pulled aside with a cord, hung in the doorway. A second photo of the interior captured a bony man dressed in loose khaki pants and sandals, sitting on a wooden chair. A woman stood by his side, wearing a long skirt and a bandana tied around her head. I could see the strain and worry reflected in her face. The only furnishings were a small table and shelf displaying a few bowls and a wooden box. I saw no signs of running water or electricity. In the final photo, nine barefoot kids stood outside next to a makeshift fireplace. They were different heights—like weeds sprouting up, competing for the sun. I studied each face as they stared at the camera. I imagined Beka telling them, *Let me take your picture. It will help.*

How could I not be moved by their story? I was learning that a little money could go far in Beka's hands. I also understood, however, that sending money might invite more such requests, and I dreaded getting into a position where I would have to repeatedly decide whether or not to give money and how much. On the other hand, I wanted to help.

What was prudence and what was stinginess? What was generosity and what was condescension? My thoughts and emotions were jumbled when my husband walked into the kitchen.

Mark poured himself a glass of grapefruit juice. Then, tilting his head, topped with the blond curls he had passed on to our daughters, he peered at my laptop screen. "A request for money? Be careful," he said wryly. "You could be communicating with a couple of guys sitting in a café in Lagos, having a laugh while they sucker you in."

My heart sank as I considered the options before me.

Mark, a designer of secure software and computer systems, knew what he was talking about; he frequented security conferences and was up to date on the latest internet fraud schemes. Nigeria, he'd told me, was notorious for their sophisticated scams: Emails would arrive in your inbox that slowly gained your trust, directing you to a website to verify the sender's identity or their cause—when in fact the sites had been created expressly to deceive you. The scammer's skillfully worded appeal would play on your emotions, awaken your compassion . . . and then they'd ask for money, creating a sense of urgency to drive a quick decision.

"I'm not saying this *is* a scam, but you should be careful."

Nigeria is not South Africa, my mind protested. *Beka is a saint, not a con artist.* In the face of Mark's warning, I was surprised to find myself taking Beka's part, a little bit defensively. "But I was the one who reached out to *her* in the first place," I countered, almost pleadingly. Besides, I told him, reputable sources like the BBC had written articles about her and the Grannies. "And Beka is amazing. She's won awards that you can read about on official South African government websites." But even as I said it, I felt the *teensiest* twinge of doubt. I mean, they *looked* like official South African government websites . . .

Mark only shrugged his shoulders. "Just promise me you'll keep your guard up."

I dragged my spoon through my oatmeal, mining for a raisin. I felt ashamed for having doubts about Beka and was insulted to have my judgment questioned; I had cultivated a relationship with her that was already becoming important to me. I had to admit, though, the Grannies *could* be real and at the same time someone could be taking advantage of their appeal. Someone could have stolen Beka's identity; it would be an ingenious scheme. But it just *couldn't* be a fraud.

Was I so doubtful of Beka's request because of my trust in Mark—or had something uglier given me pause? I didn't like to think about it. But . . . would I be agonizing over this if the soccer team were from Germany?

Whether my friends and I could actually manage to fly some twenty-odd women from South Africa to the United States or not, I had to respond to Beka's email. Money is always such an uncomfortable topic. I needed some perspective. I would call upon the wisdom of my fellow Lexpressas—Coach Catherine and Heather. I was glad I wasn't alone in this. Together we could decide how to respond to the request for money.

"Jump in, guys! Sorry I'm late."

It was the day after I'd gotten Beka's email, Thursday night, and a few of us were gathered in the Lexington High parking lot, waiting to carpool to our game. The sunset had painted the underside of the clouds a salmon pink color and Catherine's otherwise-gray car tangerine. She pulled to a stop in front of us, and we piled in. Heather plopped her bulging bag of soccer gear on the floor of the passenger seat and buckled up. "Why does chaos erupt every time I'm ready to leave the house?"

I smiled. "Makes you appreciate your few hours of freedom."

As Catherine headed down the highway, conversation turned to our favorite topic. I'd discovered another Grannies-related video, I told them—Beka being interviewed, in which she'd said she was already raising money to take the team to America. "I nearly fell off my chair!" Since then, I'd found several articles that also mentioned fundraising for the trip, but the amounts they said they'd already raised or had yet to raise varied wildly.

"I just want to say, Jean, you're doing an amazing job with this," Heather gushed. "Your Grannies slideshow for the US Adult Soccer Association was so professional. And that fundraising flyer too. Not to mention all the back-and-forth with Beka."

But there was no way I was accepting all the thanks for the progress we were making. It was Anne who'd found South Africa Partners, a nonprofit with a Boston location that had agreed to collect donations on our behalf—a huge help. Their work to secure equitable access to health care and education made the Soccer Grannies' program a perfect fit. For us, their involvement meant all the donations we scrounged up would be tax-deductible.

Now it was time to broach Beka's request for money. Tentatively, I told my teammates about her email asking for help to build the house for the family in need. Diligently, I made sure to echo Mark's warning. "I mean, our reputation is on the line if we ask anyone for money and it turns out to be a scam." I felt queasy just saying it. And disloyal. "But the odds of it not being legit seem miniscule," I quickly added.

Over the past day since I had gotten Beka's email, I'd chewed over my concerns—and contemplated how we could help Beka: Not long ago, the Lexpressas had gifted Catherine and me with a check for three hundred dollars, to be given to a charity of our choosing in thanks for the work she and I had done as coach and team treasurer, respectively. I offered the suggestion up to my teammates: Wouldn't the Grannies be a perfect fit?

"I like it," said Catherine decidedly. "How often do you get a chance to donate money that goes directly to the cause without some go-between organization siphoning off funds?" But she had taken Mark's caution to heart. "Can you send me the links to recent articles and to the websites documenting Beka's awards? I just want to check them out and make sure I'm comfortable."

As for Heather, she said she was on board.

It was decided! Well, almost decided. In any case, I was relieved to share my burden of doubt with my friends.

During the next few days, while Catherine reviewed the materials, I pressed ahead full bore, working to secure funding for a Granny visit to the States. Despite my introversion and aversion to the spotlight, I sent the fundraising flyer to circles of my family and friends—but not without considerable angst. I had never asked people for money before. Would they relate to the allure of this project, or did you have to be an older woman soccer player to get it? Was I going to make them uncomfortable, torn about how to respond? Holding Beka as a role model, I'd cringed and hit *send*. I'd also asked the Lexpressas to share the fundraising flyer with friends and family.

Together, the team brainstormed possible funding sources and scoured our employers' affiliations. More than once we were told this opportunity would not attract a corporate sponsor because the tournament was not televised and the event had no stadium full of fans. Sure enough, our company asks were either declined or ignored. Even so, I pressed on. It was incredibly stressful—but also weirdly invigorating.

Then one afternoon, the Veterans Cup organizers forwarded an email to me. A woman named Betsy wanted to help get the team to the tournament.[3] She had exchanged emails with Beka and understood $950 was needed to help the women get visas. Betsy wanted to know if this assistance was the best way to help.

I leaned toward my computer screen, the initial disbelief transforming into amazement. Betsy's email ended with a boilerplate description for a company I didn't know, but they sponsored athletic teams.

My fingers danced on the keyboard as I expressed my thanks, asking her to please wire the money, as Beka had visa interviews scheduled. And would she please forward this attached flyer to any other potential supporters?

Evidently I had failed to grasp the magnitude of her interest; she made that clear in the next email.

Thank you, Jean. I would like to know how much is needed—TOTAL—to bring the entire Vakhegula Vakhegula team here for the tournament. Can you give me that information?

Without rising, I propelled my office chair toward the door, slammed it shut, and scooted back to my desk. I misdialed the phone number at the bottom of her email. Twice. I paused and took a deep breath. On the third attempt, I succeeded in connecting to this woman who might well be the miracle we were waiting for.

She and I exchanged quick introductions before getting right down to business. Betsy peppered me with questions about the status of passports, visas, and flights.

"We have a travel quote," I explained. "It's required for the visa application, but the quote is just a placeholder. With so many people returning from the World Cup back to the US, there are hardly any seats available." I told her we had raised about $5,500 but estimated we needed $40,000 to $50,000 for flights.

Silence down the line.

Quietly wincing, I plowed on. "If someone were to appear with a check to pay for the flights, we'd use the money we've raised for hosting them—for hotels near the tournament site and for food and entertainment."

Betsy told me her company had an office in South Africa and she thought they might be able to help with travel arrangements. She could make me no promises about the sponsorship, but she would see what she could do.

I thanked her, and we traded cordial goodbyes.

I hung up the phone, sitting for a moment in stunned silence. Had I just spoken with my fairy godmother? I shook my head in astonishment. Maybe—*just maybe*—we could pull this off.

I phoned Catherine, eager to fill her in on our big break. What she said sobered me up a bit: We would first need to make sure that there were no strings attached to any donations we accepted on the Grannies' behalf.

Sighhhhhhh.

It's not so easy, I was coming to understand, either to be *asked* for money or to *accept* it.

This whole exercise in charity was a fraught endeavor. It wasn't nearly as simple as Beka made it look. Not only were my teammates and I brokering a sizable sponsorship from a US corporation, but we were also asking friends and family for donations. Beyond that, we were contemplating helping Beka build a *house*.

What were we doing? Why exactly were we getting involved? This had all grown so quickly. What was our motivation? Were we trying to help a family in desperate straits? Were we trying to please Beka or make her feel good about helping? Were we giving money to make *ourselves* feel good?

If I was honest with myself, it was likely a combination of all those factors. And what was behind our motivation to help the soccer team in the first place?

I remembered something Heather had once told me about strangers on the street calling her a "White savior" when they'd seen her walking with her son, Tamerat. He's Black and was adopted from Ethiopia. Then I thought about the trips so many Americans take to Africa to volunteer to help build a school or a library—White do-gooders posing for pictures with poor Black children. An ugly discomfort rose up in me.

But it was undeniable that there was work that needed to be done; was it even helpful to criticize a person's motivation for doing a desperately needed thing? I'm sure that these White volunteers felt proud of what they were accomplishing. But was it important whether their hearts were filled with humble service . . . or with self-satisfaction?

With this, further doubts arose: What about the actual work they'd done? Was the project sustainable? Did the volunteers have reasonable skills for the job? Were they taking work from local people? Redistributing wealth and donating time are worthy endeavors, sure. But maybe asking questions and understanding the specific circumstances are important too. Why is it, I thought, that so many White Americans are quick to volunteer at villages throughout Africa but ignore people back home who are struggling with food insecurity and inadequate housing?

And me. And the Lexpressas. We were putting an awful lot of effort into bringing the Soccer Grannies to the States. Were we just some wealthy White American ladies condescending to help poor Black South Africans?

No, that wasn't it—not quite a true representation of what was going on here. On the surface, sure, we were White women with more money paying for Black women from Africa to come visit. But our connection with the Grannies was more personal—it was rooted in a shared love for soccer and a desire for sisterhood. We were creating a bond with these women that we meant to be a long-term relationship, not just a one-off vacation adventure for the Grannies. We were following Beka's lead; *she* was clearly invested in the value of this trip, and I had to trust her. Pushing past the lingering questions, I would hear Beka when she told me what she needed, and I would believe her.

Do your little bit of good where you are, a wise man had once said. *It's those little bits of good put together that overwhelm the world.*[4]

Okay, then! If Beka wanted to build a house for this aunt and uncle and those nine children, we were going to help her do it. We would give her the money we could and trust her judgment to spend it in a way that would be most beneficial and sustainable. She'd proven what she could accomplish when people put their faith in her, and we could help her do this little bit of good.

It was only natural that our relationship with Beka would evolve and expand, I decided. I didn't want to be afraid and suspicious; I wanted to support my new friend and be a part of her broader mission, *following* her lead, relying on her wisdom and experience.

As soon as Catherine completed her review of the materials I had sent and gave her full blessing, I wired three hundred dollars to Beka.

Almost two weeks passed after I sent the money to Beka with no response. Nothing. I would be lying if I said zero doubts reemerged. But I just kept reminding myself, *Trust Beka to tell you what she needs.*

Sitting on the back porch with my morning coffee, laptop open, I'd begun scanning my emails when I yelped with delight. *It was a message from Beka.* She'd gotten the wire transfer and was thanking us for our help!

Relief flooded over me.

She had bought the needed building materials for the house, along with thirty chairs for a local high school where there were more students than seats. This was wonderful.

As I read on, my stomach clenched.

Jean, I decided to write this message to tell you that I am in a lot of pain. Sorry to tell you that I was in hospital and things were bad. I thought they send me home to die but I am some better now. Next week when I get my salary I will go back to the specialist doctor the oncologist. I will go for radiation next week. Life is not easy but I know I will make it, like before. My stomach is swollen and my feet. Remember life is short but since 2003 being sick it was on remission. Now back. The grannies will come whether I come or not. They will be there.

Beka was fighting for her life, I realized. This relapse must have hit shortly after we'd wired the money. I kicked myself for my ignorance, sitting here in my suburban Cape house in America, waiting for a thank-you note. Meanwhile, Beka was hospitalized with advanced cancer yet somehow had still found the strength to buy chairs for high school students who had been sitting on the floor.

Shaking my head, I printed the email and headed out to my morning soccer scrimmage.

"*Zut!*" Catherine exclaimed, reading the printout as the team gathered around. "*Zut alors!*" She tsked as she finished reading. "A swollen stomach is bad. I've seen it before in hospice."

It took about thirty seconds for the Lexpressas to decide to send a second donation. We would ask Beka to use it as she saw fit—for medical treatment, pain medication, or whatever project made her feel better.

But the fact that Beka's cancer had emerged from remission now cast new uncertainty on the Grannies' trip to the States. I had to believe that her strong will and positive attitude had helped her get through prior bouts and that she could do it again.

I just hated to think of her in pain. I didn't know what more I could do for my friend, and this distressed me. South Africa felt very far away as I channeled positive healing thoughts her way.

5

Vusiwana I Vuloyi

My father's work was to manufacture boxes for carrying or packaging tomatoes. He worked until he became a pensioner. The only tough thing at home was that my father was not paid enough, and that made my parents to always have financial problems. My life situation was different from those of my peers, and that made them laugh at me. During lunchtime at school, my peers would eat bread and other delicious things; but as for me, I always carried lunch box of porridge and wild spinach, to the laughter of my peers.—Makoma Selina Matwalane, Soccer Granny[1]

A FEW DAYS LATER, I RECEIVED AN EMAIL FROM BEKA THANKING US FOR our second gift. She'd attached the photo of a man she'd met at the hospital who was sicker than she was; she'd given the money to him (because of course she had). Lacking any real information about her cancer remission and prognosis, I was forced to take comfort in the fact that her spirit of caring and generosity still thrived.

We were now a mere two and a half months away from the Veterans Cup. And while Beka said the passports were in hand, none of my requests for actual passport *numbers* had yielded any response. Meanwhile, I knew she was scrambling to secure the Grannies' visas—a task, I suspected, akin to herding cats. And yet with every email, she exuded confidence. "We are coming," she would reassure me. "We'll see you soon, my friend."[2] I very much wanted to believe her; with every passing day, it was becoming more and more important to me to make this happen.

Part of the difficulty completing the travel paperwork, Beka had told me, was that many of the Grannies had received only limited schooling and were thus illiterate, a reality in South Africa that is more likely among Blacks, women, and rural residents—a triple whammy for our Grannies.

The dearth of education, coupled with the stranglehold White employers long held on job opportunities in South Africa, meant the limited jobs available were low paying. And most were clustered around Johannesburg, easily four hundred or more kilometers from where most of the Grannies lived with their families. Many Black South Africans without reliable income had been left vulnerable to a life of poverty—*especially* the women who tended to the homestead.

At issue, I was beginning to understand, was not the mere difficulty of securing sufficient funding to bring twenty old ladies to the States on soccer holiday. Any inefficiencies, confusion, or lack of organization compounding an already complicated task were born of more than two centuries of targeted destabilization.

The Tsonga people first settled in southeastern Africa around 1300, where they lived comfortably off the land through carefully managed herding and farming practices, and community life found meaning and cohesion in a tradition of strong family structure. There the Tsonga thrived for almost five hundred years—until their way of life began to crack under the strain of external events.

It started back in the early 1800s, with an influx of Europeans to the continent in search of land to support large farming operations. Some of these White landowners provided the Tsonga residence and use of the acreage—provided half of every harvest was paid in rent. Other landowners forced the Tsonga off the land entirely.

The discovery of gold and diamonds at midcentury further intensified European interest in this part of the world, especially among immigrants from the Netherlands and England. Dutch settlers, known as the Boers or Afrikaners, claimed all current-day Limpopo as an independent country—the Transvaal. The colonizing British challenged the Boers in two bloody wars in the late nineteenth and early twentieth centuries, each side fighting to secure gold and diamond deposits for their own people. In 1903, the two powers signed a treaty, forming the White-minority-ruled Union of South Africa, into which were incorporated the Transvaal and several other provinces. With this, the Tsonga were now South African.

In 1913, the newly formed Union of South Africa passed the Natives Land Act, designating 90 percent of all land for White ownership—even though Whites comprised only 20 percent of the population. The remaining 10 percent of the less-arable land was set aside as Black homelands. "All it took was a stroke of the pen," editorialized one South African newspaper on the Land Act's centennial, and "Black families were made landless in the country of their birth."[3]

Sharecropping was now forbidden, and Tsonga farmers were handed eviction notices unless they secured formal employment with the landowners. Families were forced to relocate to the undeveloped and scarcely cultivatable Black homelands.

In addition to the forced migrations born of the 1913 act, the challenge of feeding their families without the actual means to do so led to voluntary departures from traditional Tsonga lands; well over half of all Tsonga men left home seeking employment in the mines or the cities. The once-strong Tsonga family structure was fracturing under the pressure of the Natives Land Act.

And so began a period of rigid racial segregation and gross poverty, inequality, unemployment, and high migration rates—problems that have persisted among South African Blacks to the present day.

Even with the fall of apartheid and the first free democratic elections in 1994, South Africa has struggled over the intervening decades to raise the standard of living in rural provinces. Here Beka and I were clinging to the dream of jetting the Grannies over to the United States while a staggering *half* of all South Africans lived below the poverty line—and unemployment in Limpopo, the Grannies' province, was the highest in the entire nation.

Increasingly, working-age women have been making the difficult choice to leave home in search of jobs in the city. With both mother and father gone, in search of employment, families have begun turning to their grandmothers for childcare. "Maybe they are thirteen or fourteen in a small house," Beka says, which contributes to "a lot of stress. For some, the parents work far from home, and the granny looks after the grandchildren. When they are working far from home, some of them don't even send money."

These grandmothers wring their hands, fretting over whether or not they have enough money to feed their grandchildren this month; many rely on growing their own food for subsistence. Poverty and unstable employment meant that instead of being cared for and doted on in their twilight years, these women have once again become care-takers of a new generation, weaving the tattered fabric of the family together.

The dire situation only worsened with the AIDS epidemic of the late 1990s and early 2000s, which left many young and middle-aged South Africans sick and dying. "Their kids are left behind," Beka explains. "Maybe a daughter had three kids, a son four, another four. Now the granny has *eleven grandchildren* to care for." The fragile point on which household survival depends, these grandmothers are caring for their sick, burying their dead, and then raising the grandchildren left behind. It has been a crippling financial and emotional burden.

As they age, these women have prioritized providing for the family, often forgoing their own necessary medical care. "When you think about it," Beka says of her Grannies, "you can understand that she is so stressed. With the little money the government gives them, I understand their depression." Stress-related ailments—like hypertension, obesity, heart disease, asthma—have become common among the grandmothers of rural Limpopo, only exacerbated by a lack of understanding about disease and limited access to modern health care.

When faced with severe illness, a large majority of South Africans consult with traditional healers, often in combination with modern physicians. Traditional cultures have a long-held, deeply rooted belief in ancestral spirits and interactions between the spirit world and the physical world. In this environment, life has grown even more precarious for the aging and ill of rural South Africa. Witchcraft is accepted, practiced, and feared, creating a dangerous alchemy in a population without adequate education or stable income to pay for doctors' care and with insufficient healthcare resources and pervasive misogyny. Seeking to understand unexplained illnesses or a downturn of luck, many consult with diviners and healers, who often attribute the misfortune to witchcraft. *Vusiwana i vuloyi*, it is said—"Poverty is witchcraft."

Simply raising the suspicion that a witch lurks in the community drives gossip and rumors, which then unite and amplify a collective anxiety and even dread. Fear is hardwired into humans; is critical to protecting us against threats—both real and perceived. But misplaced fear can be deadly. Idle speculation deteriorates into allegations and then into outright accusations of witchcraft. Particularly vulnerable are aged women, especially the mentally ill and those suffering from dementia with erratic behavior.

Why would anyone believe an old lady—likely someone they've known all their life—would use her powers to hurt her community? In an environment ravaged by generations of inequality, the answer too often is *jealousy*. To raise herself up, it is easy to imagine, a woman might push others down, even if unintentionally. Where everyone risks being called a witch, it's a short jump to believing that anyone with jealous bitterness in her heart can muster her ability to do harm. After all, *vusiwana i vuloyi*.

And when intense fear and distrust of accused witches begin to run rampant, the usual social cohesion breaks down. Community members mobilize against the perceived threat. Mobs have been known to burn the homes of suspected witches and even assault the accused and her family. Victims might be bullied, ostracized, beaten, or even stoned. These same grandmothers who have become the lynchpins in so many South African families have also become the targets of discrimination and brutal violence.

Vigilantism played an important role in South Africa's revolution for democracy, where officialdom could not be counted on to act impartially or even at all. Today this reliance on "justice by the people" remains central to a cultural sense of fairness and keeping the peace. Violent mobs see themselves as crusaders for justice. When they attack a presumed witch, they see not a defenseless old woman but a dangerous foe.

As Black women age and lose their faculties, they are increasingly vulnerable to mob lynching. Beka worries, worries, worries over her Grannies.

Sometimes all her worrying, all her efforts, are not enough to keep them safe. All the dollars collected to improve access to schooling, all the bags of cement used to erect homes for the indigent, all the squads of Vakhegula Vakhegula dotting the South African countryside to get these overworked, overtired grannies out of their homes and into the sunshine for community and healthful movement—sometimes even that is not enough.

One day, I woke to a text message from Beka. She was writing about a grandmother she knew in Limpopo.

Accused of witchcraft. They hung a tire around her neck. She died on the spot. She was not a witch. Her problem was dementia. One of our grannies. That is why I'm fighting to protect them. I'm traumatized. I can't sleep.

Mama Beka

The Mother Teresa of Limpopo

"Okay. I am Rebecca 'Beka' Ntsanwisi from South Africa."[1] Beka zips up her jacket and perches on the edge of her chair. As well as being a nickname for Rebecca, *Beka* is Zulu for "Hawk-eyed" or "One who watches." Indeed, where so many look away, Beka looks forward, recognizing the inherent dignity in everyone around her.

"I do things for the community. I am proud of building houses for poverty-stricken families. I need to build two more houses now. I am happy because of what I do in South Africa."

Beka was born in 1968, the eldest of five children. Her father was a school inspector and her mother a principal who later worked at the University of Venda. Even from a young age Beka was moved by the poverty and want around her: When she saw a child was hungry, she would share the bread from her lunch box; when classmates did not have the money to buy school uniforms, she pleaded with her parents to provide them.

Beka has always understood the value of education—how it can create opportunity where there is none. As both of her

Rebecca "Beka" Ntsanwisi. Nkowankowa, Limpopo, October 2020. *Photo by Tessa Frootko Gordon*

parents were educators, it comes as no surprise that Beka, along with all of her siblings, pursued higher education. Upon earning a degree in music, Beka, a talented electronic keyboard player and singer, was hired by Radio Tsonga, where she assembled playlists of country, traditional, gospel, and jazz music.

But she wasn't content to live a life behind the scenes, and those childhood images of poverty and want hadn't faded from her memory. So she set out to change the world, starting by tackling nothing less than the state of public health in South Africa. All around her, she saw the devastation caused by unmanaged disease. "You know, from my province in South Africa where I come from, HIV/AIDS is rife. Cancer also is rife." In response, she partnered with South Africa's Department of Health to form support groups for the ailing. Then she took it upon herself to assemble teams of volunteers to wash clothes and feed the terminally ill.

"Many people die of AIDS. Children are left in the care of a grandparent or uncles and aunts. Also, people there, they believe in witchcraft. You know, if you are sick, they think that it has to do with witchcraft. So I go around to the villages, teaching them how to look after themselves—especially the women. They must go to hospital early. With cancer when they detect it early, then they can get help."

Here Beka takes a deep breath. "In 2003, I was very, very sick. I was told that I have colon cancer. I remember the doctors and care providers, they used to tell me, *You have to prepare your will, because you are about to die.* I was surprised to hear that." Her brow furrows with the memory. "I had many things to do because I was building houses for the destitute. I have kids that I have to pay for their school fees. And it was difficult for me. What I did, you ask? I tell you: I did not listen to those doctors. You know, when you are told that you have cancer, the only thing you think of is death. But to me I thought, *How can I die before I finish building these houses?*"

Even facing her own health crisis, Beka was compelled to relieve the suffering of others. "Let me ask you this: How can I die while an eighty-five-year-old woman is being raped by her grandson? How can I rest while a father is raping his daughter? These things happened, and I fought hard. I remember: This father didn't go to work, and he'd tell his daughter not to go to school. I decided to come up with a plan. I said, *I will fight this*."

She leans in and shakes her index finger. "What I did, I went there with my friends to protect that child. We were three women. You must remember, African men are tough; when you see him, you would say that he can beat you. But we decided to go there. I knew this man will come to that child during the night. We decided to hide in the room."

She settles into the story. "He came at around half past twelve during the night. Let me tell you what we did to him—I don't think he'll forget. We beat him. And then I called—I mean, I *personally* called—the police. He was arrested. He's now serving life sentence. And I am proud of that. You might have read about this in the newspapers. It was on national TV in South Africa."

Where others would falter, Beka charges ahead. "I decided in my life, in a short space of time, I have to give my best. Whatever I do, I make sure I give love. I remember in 2005, when I received the Shoprite Checkers SABC Woman of the Year award, it was bad. I was in a wheelchair. My doctor had to attend the award ceremony to help me." But she holds herself to a vow to work for her community until the day she dies.

Being confined to a wheelchair didn't stop Beka; driven by her belief in the power of education, she brought technology to village schools through arranged computer donations and organized assistance for talented students who could not afford tuition fees. More than fifty students from rural areas have attended university thanks to her intervention. But even this is not enough for Beka. "I have a dream to build a school."

Where she sees more immediate need, Beka does not look away. Upon meeting a family without decent housing, she collected bricks and mortar and built them a new home. When she saw that villagers did not have enough to eat, she acquired a plot of farmland for a community garden; now they are able to sell their excess at the market.

Being surrounded by such constant need would drive many inward; it galvanizes Beka, even as she continues to battle cancer recurrences. "When

I go to chemotherapy, it is hard. It comes with many problems. I had so many surgeries. People would say to me, *You're dying.* But here I am." Beka has gained back some of the weight she lost at her sickest, and her hair has grown in after courses of chemotherapy; these days she no longer wears a wig or relies on a wheelchair. "I still don't know how I survived this terrible monster, cancer. It's very painful. Do not wish anyone to go through that. I still have some pain, but I am alive and kicking."

In 2008, she was awarded one of South Africa's highest honors, the Order of the Baobab, named for the ancient, sacred, and stately baobab tree, which predates humankind and the splitting of continents. It has evolved to survive dry savannas, where it provides shelter, food, and water for those in need. Throughout African folklore, the baobab is a symbol of life, strength, power, and positivity.

Beka's award was inscribed to read, *A woman of courage and unsurpassed love for people, Rebecca Beka Ntsanwisi is a role model and community builder with total dedication to the upliftment of impoverished people.*

"I am proud," she says simply. "Former president Thabo Mbeki gave the award to me."

Indeed, for her decades of care and loving service Beka has become beloved throughout the country. "They call me 'Mama Beka.' Some people call me Mother Teresa, but I don't want people to say that, because I cannot compare myself with Mother Teresa." Beka has been named Community Builder of the Year and a Woman of Excellence, and among her many recognitions are an Achiever's Award and a Premier's Award.

Without a doubt one of her best-known and most celebrated projects, her work with the Soccer Grannies has garnered international attention. "I'm the founder of Vakhegula Vakhegula Football Club. I formed this team in 2006 so these women—ages ranging from fifty to the oldest in their eighties—can be fit and healthy."

She is fond of pointing out that "grandmothers are always at home. All the time they are sitting, watching, and cooking for the kids. They don't have time to rest. They don't have time to enjoy. They don't have time to find happiness. That's what worries me. I tell them, *No, no, come exercise and enjoy.*"

And come they have. By 2010, throughout South Africa she was already running seven Vakhegula Vakhegula squads. "Some of them come to the soccer field with their grandchildren on their back. I say, *No, no, no. At your age, more than sixty* . . . I ask them, *Why are you looking after these children? Take them to preschool.* Remember, the government gives money to help look after children. Too many times the teenage grandchildren are having infants, great-grandchildren." She encourages her Grannies to push back on the teenagers to accept accountability for their actions. "If you have a child at a young age, you have to learn responsibility."

Beka believes that soccer makes these women better grandmothers and better people. "After the Grannies go to soccer, they go home and give the grandchildren the best love. When you are stressed, how can you give love? If they sit at home and worry about food, nothing can make them happy. But after soccer, when the Grannies get home, the kids say, *Play with us!* They kick the ball; they laugh and sing together. It's much better."

Beka also knows that staying physically active can help stave off dementia and blunt the worst effects of mental illness. "In my country, when you are there, at that age, when you have problems like that, they say you are a witch." Her face darkens. "They put a tire around you and burn you alive."

She is not speaking in hypotheticals. "Twice grannies were burnt like this. I have seen it for myself. A crowd of people from the village circles. They say the old woman practices witchcraft. She screams. She stumbles and falls, writhing on the ground. The crowd jeers. They throw cardboard and other flammable objects." She closes her eyes, squeezing them tight.

"It's a painful death. If you see it, you will not be able to sleep. You will not be able to eat. I witnessed that, and it took me a month to begin to forget." But rather than freeze with anguish and horror, Beka sees an opportunity for change. "This is why I'm fighting for the elderly in South Africa. I couldn't stand that. I had to protect old people. That is why I have seven Grannies soccer teams now."

It is a heavy responsibility Beka has taken upon herself, but she believes it's the only way. "If you want to succeed in life, you have to suffer; you cannot just climb a mountain without struggling. I always teach people to believe in themselves. If you are going to climb a mountain, you must make sure you are prepared and fight until you reach the top of Kilimanjaro."

Few who have seen this much need have responded with such warmth, immediacy, and efficiency. "Helping people is a God-given talent. Sometimes I think of quitting because I have no money. I have to pay for rides to the villages where I do my work; they are far apart, so I need a car to drive me from one village to another."

But these details will not stop her.

"When I see people suffering, I just want to help, and that makes me feel better. When the Grannies are happy, that makes me very happy."

6

The Grannies Are Coming!
The Grannies Are Coming!

By pounding the dough, the bread will rise.—African proverb[1]

IT WAS JUNE 6, 2010, FIVE WEEKS BEFORE THE TOURNAMENT START. I LEANED forward, eyes wide with surprise. The first hit of my daily internet search for "Soccer Grannies" and "Beka Ntsanwisi" had returned a link to this morning's edition of the *New York Times*. Pictured at the top of the article were eight Grannies, standing with arms stretched skyward, fingers interlaced, in front of a goal with no netting. They were dressed in matching yellow kerchiefs, white shirts, and long black skirts. Two worn soccer balls, a pair of keeper's gloves, and a discarded vuvuzela horn lay on the bare dirt that was their playing field. Above the photo, in bold, italicized serif, read "FOR THE LOVE OF SOCCER AND A LASTING SISTERHOOD."[2]

The Grannies, it seems, had been invited to play an exhibition game for President Jacob Zuma's visit to their hometown, where he'd be attending ceremonies commemorating the life of a local antiapartheid activist. Despite Vakhegula Vakhegula's meager beginnings, the article continued, news of the team's existence had spread to the United States, and *they had been invited to compete in a tournament in Massachusetts next month.*

We'd made it into the *New York Times*!

Beka, ever resourceful, had taken advantage of the state visit to request a favor of President Zuma: "We voted for you, and now we need your support in our fundraising effort for travel expenses, because we will be representing South Africa."

"Oh, my goodness," I said, my hands resting atop my head, as if to hold in my racing thoughts. "*I'm so excited!*"

By midafternoon, it was clear the *Times* article had garnered a lot of attention. I had begun receiving emails from potential donors in Connecticut and New York, all of whom had gone to the effort of finding contacts for the tournament.

I forwarded the article to Beka, trying to convey the significance of this news coverage and the responses it would bring.

"Thanks so much, my sister," she wrote back almost immediately. "I read the article."

Jean, I am waiting for the confirmation from the premier, executive major, the department of arts and culture. I will update you only that people promise and do not deliver. I will tell you by Friday. I will see what to do. See you when we come. Next year you must come to South Africa.[3]

Her obvious doubt quelled a bit of my enthusiasm.

"They Kick like Grannies, Proudly," announced the *Los Angeles Times* two weeks later. Just below it, "Frail, elderly women in South Africa started playing soccer as a joke. Now they are running and competing on the field, leaving cultural expectations in the dust." The reporter had captured the essence of the Grannies.[4]

I was amused to read that when Vakhegula Vakhegula had first started playing, car drivers nearly collided as they craned their necks at the sight of these grandmothers on the soccer field.

"It's not all fluid, magical movement," the reporter wrote, eloquently capturing the allure of the Grannies. "Sometimes the players look a little stiff. Yet on the field, the women transcend the boundaries that hem them in: the opinions of what a grandmother should and shouldn't do; the lives of poverty and deprivation."

These women, I realized, were providing inspiration across the world. And you didn't have to be a soccer player to feel it. I was confident this new article would raise even more donations.

In the months since I had watched that first Grannies video, I had been mesmerized by Beka's forceful, calming influence, thrilled to do what I could to help. But now, with mere weeks until the tournament, I was suddenly terrified that this could *actually* come to pass. We had no plan for success. Maybe we should get on that. . . . Were there rooms left at the tournament hotel? If not, could we get enough drivers to transport them back and forth from Lexington every day? How would we feed them? Were they vegetarians?

I calmed my racing thoughts and took a deep breath. I wasn't doing this alone; I had a whole team to help me figure it out.

It was June 14, 2010, four weeks before the tournament start. After hundreds of emails pinging back and forth across the Atlantic, I finally had my first phone call with Beka. It was such a delight just to hear her voice. She assured us that this round of cancer treatments was complete, and though she felt tired, she was more energetic with each passing day. We agreed to keep the number of travelers to no more than twenty to help control costs, and she said she would send traveler names and passport numbers "soon." Meanwhile, I told her, Catherine and I were committed to fundraising on both sides of the Atlantic.

"Don't worry," Beka closed our call. "We'll see you soon, my sisters."

A few days later Catherine, Heather, and I met for a heart-to-heart over beers. We discussed visas, fundraising, and flights, each topic landing like a solid punch to the gut. Catherine's friend from South Africa had told her that the process to get a US visa typically took three months. I was responsible for securing finances, yet my previous fundraising experience was limited to selling Girl Scout cookies, and now Betsy, my fairy godmother dangling a corporate sponsorship in front of us, had gone radio silent. And a travel agent had told us our timing couldn't be worse: Tickets were going for $2,500 *each* because of World Cup demand, and even at that price only a few seats remained. Without a miracle, raising $50,000 for a team of twenty loomed impossible.

We briefly discussed setting a give-up-by date before discarding the notion, unable to bear the thought of disappointing Beka and the Grannies. Instead, we would press on, ignoring the rapidly diminishing chance that we could actually pull this off.

It was July 3, 2010, nine days (but who's counting?) *before the tournament start.* Heather had hammered out a detailed budget and a Granny itinerary and had pressed Lexpressas volunteers into service as Granny chauffeurs for the week. Originally, we had envisioned a weeklong visit with a few days in Lexington before the tournament to account for jet lag recovery. But by this point, if we managed to get them here at all, the Grannies would pretty much have to fly over in their soccer kit and run from Logan International straight to the tournament field.

Despite pressures from Veterans Cup organizers, Lois was staunchly refusing to cancel our block of five rooms at the tournament hotel. We were determined to hold this thing together.

Saturday afternoon I finally heard back from Fairy Godmother Betsy. "Hi," she wrote, "I have good news . . . it should be pretty exciting for the Grannies."

Her company had approved $40,000 to get Vakhegula Vakhegula Stateside.

I ran screaming through the house, yanking the family downstairs behind me for a spontaneous dance party, queuing up a playlist fit for the occasion.

"There's still soccer to play," I crooned into a wooden-spoon microphone, "singing, Go on, take the money and run. *Woo-hoo-hoo!*"

It was July 6, 2010, six days before the tournament start. The Veterans Cup was going to happen with or without the Grannies.

A few days ago, Beka had traveled to Pretoria with a few Grannies to get a letter of support for their visa application from the Department of International Relations and Cooperation and had come back feeling upbeat. "Do not stress," she'd written, once again repeating her mantra:

> *We are coming. I decided not to complain, as it will affect my health. I just want to tell you that I know we are with you next week. Rest assured that America will feel us.*

But by today, she'd lost her customary calm assurance. In three messages sent in quick succession, she urgently asked me to send money to pay the travel agent helping with visa applications, to cover travel insurance, and to fund transportation for the Grannies from their village to Johannesburg for visa interviews. My heart sank as I felt her desperation.

Just then, a fourth message arrived.

"My sister," she wrote,

> *For the travel insurance we do not have the money. For the visas I got 32,000 (South African money). I took a loan from a company. I have the receipts. I will apply for the visas.*
>
> *Thanks so much for your support. I know you are trying, but people did promise, and now they are nowhere to be found.*

I was mulling over how to respond when a fifth message arrived, this one containing the final roster of travelers—two coaches, four "officials," and fourteen players—along with their passport numbers (at last). The list appeared to be a mix of first, last, and nicknames, in no particular order. I'd been told that in South Africa the use of nicknames is fluid and creative, accommodating different languages and customs; often for convenience an English name is added to the given name registered at birth. Expecting consistency within all official documentation would be unreasonable, in part given the history of poor literacy in South Africa. However, I also knew that any conflicting information on paperwork would mean delays. But at this point, it was too late for me to question the details.

Catherine took to placing calls to the US consulate in Johannesburg every two hours to find out if the Grannies had the completed visa applications and ask how we could assist. She would wait on hold, only to be told they had no knowledge of the Grannies. When she was finally redirected to someone by the name of Anton who handled visas, she was told that, unfortunately, he had already left for the day.

As Beka's spirits were sinking even further, Catherine tried to rally her. "How much money do you need for visa-related expenses?"

The equivalent of $2,000, "If you can, please, my sister."

We were in a bind: We'd given donors the expectation that they would get all their money back if we didn't manage to bring the Grannies to the States. So it wouldn't be appropriate for us to release their funds to cover the visa applications when we didn't have the assurance that visas, let alone plane tickets, would be secured. Our project felt doomed.

Catherine, Heather, and I had a quick call to debate sending Beka the $2,000 ourselves. I firmly felt it was up to us to cover them. "We've certainly sunk way more than two thousand dollars' worth of energy into this project."

Catherine pointed out that Beka had already put much of her own money toward getting the Grannies here, and it seemed wrong to abandon her. "She said she's already taken out a loan. I'm sure taking those women on a five-hour trip must cost something. I am inclined to wire the money because it's our last chance. Now, this could still fail, even if we send the money. But life comes with risks, and I'm adventurous."

We wired Beka the $2,000.

The high point of my day was a call from a sweet grandmother from Calgary named Isabelle who had read the *Los Angeles Times* article and chased down my phone number. She had spent time in South Africa and told me how moved she'd been by the women there expressing their joys and sorrows through song. "They will touch your lives with an unforgettable experience," she promised me, then offering to send $2,000 as soon as Beka had visas. "Now is the time to push for your dreams," she encouraged. "Reminds me of the Carl Sandburg quote—*Nothing happens unless first we dream.*" This was the message I'd needed to rally my spirits. I thanked Isabelle profusely and promised to send along photos of the Grannies in America.

At the end of the day, a terse message from Beka arrived:

I have tried everything, my sisters.

Just that, nothing more.

Catherine was relentless. On the day the Grannies were to arrive at the US consulate in Johannesburg, she rose at 3 a.m., took to the phone, and insisted on speaking to the supervisor in charge of issuing visas. She explained that the Grannies were role models for women around the world, that they'd been invited to participate in the largest adult soccer tournament in the United States, and that a fairy god-sponsor (my words) had brought about a fundraising miracle. The supervisor listened politely and said she would do her best but that all applicants must have the paperwork completed; the consulate would allow no shortcuts.

Seven or so hours later, Catherine called the consulate again. "Oh, yes," the supervisor reported, "the Grannies were here, but their paperwork was not complete." Beka and the Grannies had been sent away. The good news was that the supervisor had reserved a block of four hours the next day to process visas—provided they had the proper documentation in hand. Beka would be prepared, Catherine assured her.

That night, Beka and the Grannies stayed in Johannesburg in a drafty parish house, as there wasn't time enough to drive back to the village and still make their early morning appointment at the Johannesburg consulate. She'd slept on the floor, and her health was suffering due to the cold. She sounded deflated.

Before collapsing into bed that evening, I ordered two vuvuzelas so we could cheer the Grannies on in proper South African style during gameplay. I hoped this would provide us the good karma we needed.

At 2 a.m., Catherine placed her first call of the day to the consulate. "No Grannies in sight," the officer reported. Catherine reset her alarm for two hours later. The Grannies had arrived! Catherine slept through her 6 a.m. alarm and awoke to an email update from the consulate.

> *The team showed up without applications or photos. By 11:30, they still had not completed the applications. We again made a special exception and asked them to return at 1:30. We don't usually do visa interviews in the afternoon. We will give them every consideration possible under the law when they interview.*

"I wish I was there to help," Catherine wrote back. "I know we are asking you for a miracle."

Impatient for news, Catherine called the consulate at 2 p.m. South African time. "Yes, the Grannies are back. Two aides are helping them with the paperwork." An hour later Catherine was told, "The Grannies are being interviewed."

"Keep those fingers crossed," Catherine emailed Heather and me, as we paced back and forth. On the next call, Catherine was told by the consulate staff that the Grannies had just departed; the supervisor would communicate the outcome.

Minutes later Catherine forwarded the consulate email, adding her own editorial in the subject line.

> *Subject: 19 Visas!*

> *We bent over backwards to assist this group. We provided the infor-mation to them on how to apply for visas and what was required several times to different people at great length. However, the good*

news is most of them (19, all but one) have been issued visas, which
will be printed on Monday. I hope this information is helpful.

I shot up from my chair with a whoop.

Soon, Beka reported they were heading back home to Limpopo; the
Grannies were exhausted, but their spirits were soaring. "I *will* see you
soon, my friend!"

We had the passports, and now we finally had the visas. The only
thing left? Tickets for airline flights.

It was July 9, 2010, three days before the tournament start. By the time I'd
awoken the next morning, Beka had already emailed all the information
we needed to reserve flights. She had been so focused on visas that we
hadn't wanted to worry her about the cost of airfare.

Betsy had also emailed that the best flights their corporate travel
agent had found cost a whopping $4,400 per person. At that price, we
could afford only nine flights. "I'm terribly sorry," she wrote,

> *but the sponsorship is contingent on getting the entire team over. I*
> *really hate to give up, but maybe we try again next year. Is anybody*
> *having better luck with plane tickets?*

I felt like a giant bungee cord had been tied around my waist: For
five months I'd been running, stretching it to its limit, and now, three
days before the tournament start, I had tripped and been sent hurtling
backward. It was agonizing losing all the ground we had fought so hard
to gain.

"I haven't given up yet," Catherine reassured me (her calm thus settling my bungee cord to a gentle bob). "Maybe they can fly into New
York City where there may be cheaper seats. I don't know. My brain won't
rest until this is over."

Her husband traveled every week for work and had premier status
on almost every airline. He had just arrived home from an international

business trip, and after he got some sleep, he told her he'd work on the flights.

"Stand by," she emailed me. "I'm letting him sleep one more hour; then I will greet him in bed with coffee and his laptop."

Just before noon, Catherine called me. "Check your eeee-maaaaail," she sang. *Nineteen tickets had been confirmed, totaling $42,000.*

"We did it!" she wrote Betsy, Heather, Lois, and me. "They will be streaming in on July 14, landing between 11 a.m. and 4 p.m." They would miss the first day of tournament play, but it was a worthwhile exchange for the manageable price of the flights. "Miracles happen when you believe."

Meanwhile, Lois had finally won cooperation from the Veterans Cup committee, who'd reworked the schedule of games for the women's over-sixty teams to accommodate the Grannies' travel, and she'd gotten the tournament host organization to pay for their hotel rooms.

It was all finally coming together!

After a few hours flitting around the house, unable to focus on anything else, I went for a run. I felt like Paul Revere galloping through the streets of Lexington, shouting to everyone, "The Grannies are coming! *The Grannies are coming!*"

It was July 11, 2010, the day of the tournament's opening ceremonies. The thermometer recorded an energy-sapping high of 86 degrees. By evening, when Catherine and I arrived at the tournament soccer fields in Lancaster, cooler temps prevailed.

We strolled toward a cheerful crowd of several hundred people milling around, greeting each other and hugging. Lois, mistress of ceremonies for the night, collared me to introduce Tim, the tournament chair, a gentleman in a polo shirt with a goal-wide smile. She then climbed up on a small stage, and underneath a banner that read "WELCOME TO THE 2010 VETERANS CUP," she pulled the microphone close with one hand, held the other out wide, and shouted, "*Let the games begin!*" (Polite mayhem.)

At her direction, everyone assembled with their teams for the procession. The Japanese men's team, who'd entered under the over-sixty-five category, were waving their colors enthusiastically; it felt like a mini senior Olympics! Massachusetts being the host, a small fife and drum corps dressed as Colonial minutemen marched in first, followed by the teams from youngest (thirty-year-olds) to oldest (sixty-five and up). Catherine and I had lined up as the Grannies' representatives and carried between us the South African flag. I felt both like a total imposter and also immensely proud and excited.

"We have teams representing twenty-two states as well as our returning international participants from Japan," Lois announced. "I am also thrilled to let you know the South African Vakhegula Vakhegula team is in the air, on their way to join us." The crowd gave a rousing cheer, and a few of Lois's teammates circulated through the crowd with black fedoras, collecting last-minute contributions for the Grannies.

Tim-the-chair asked Lois for the microphone. "I'd like to add one thing." The crowd quieted. "This year, as Africa hosts its first-ever World Cup, it's fitting that we host these players from South Africa. I believe soccer is the universal language of our planet. It unites us as human beings in ways few other things do."

I blotted the tear in my eye as the crowd went nuts.

Part II
The Game

It always seems impossible until it's done.—Nelson Mandela[1]

7

A More Perfect (Re)union

As you know, a Black person at that time was not regarded as a person. —*Makoma Selina Matwalane, Soccer Granny*[1]

LOGAN AIRPORT, TERMINAL E, OFTEN JAMMED WITH INTERNATIONAL travelers wheeling refrigerator-sized luggage, was quiet. An expectant crowd of Lexpressas stood together, holding homemade signs at our sides. We eagerly eyed the arrivals board, wondering how long the line for customs snaked and how high the circling carousel of luggage was piled.

Just then, the arrivals door swung open. Out peered a large Black woman capped in a yellow headscarf, wearing a leather jacket over a navy tracksuit. She took a few cautious steps forward, eyes glancing right and left. Another woman wearing a scarf the colors of the South African flag followed, and another woman behind her.

"Welcome, Grannies!" someone in our group hollered, and our hush dissolved into choruses of "Welcome, Vakhegula Vakhegula!" We held our signs high and waved South African flags, their bold yellow, red, blue, black, and white representing the diverse populations united in that land.

More and more of our guests paraded through the arrivals door. I could now see that *all* the women were wearing the yellow headscarves, white polo shirts, and matching blue tracksuits.

Click-click. Tessa, the South African photographer hired by our corporate sponsor, was snapping shot after shot, her face largely obscured by her behemoth camera lens and framed by her wavy blonde bob.

A woman I was to come to know as Granny Chrestina—field nickname "Maradona," in homage to the Argentinian soccer great—pulled a blue vuvuzela from her backpack. The foghorn-like drone underlay cries of welcome, our cacophony echoing through the iceberg-cold air of the airport terminal.

Grateful for my late-night buying spree, I thrust my red and blue vuvuzelas into the air and pumped them up and down. (I didn't dare blow on them, as previous attempts had yielded only embarrassing fart-like sounds; I would ask our visitors for a lesson later.)

Our visitors were smiling widely. I could recognize some of the Grannies from the videos, but live action was so much better. The Soccer Grannies were *here*—really here.

I picked Beka out of the crowd. She too was wearing a tracksuit and had a small bag slung over one shoulder. She stood quietly, hands behind her back. I inhaled and held my breath, temporarily frozen after these months of anticipation. Following her glance, I noticed a Granny spreading a small blanket on the grungy airport floor. Several other Grannies then laid down on their sides atop the blanket; a few who weren't quite as agile kneeled next to it. Then together they began clapping their hands and trilling their tongues, semiprostrate.

"I believe they're expressing their thanks," Tessa whispered to me, leaning in to capture a close-up of the moving scene before us. I knew it had to be a sign of respect, and I was so deeply grateful. But I was also embarrassed, unused to being on the receiving end of such ceremonial display.

As the Grannies carefully rose back to their feet, Coach Catherine led us into an informal reception line. One by one we shook hands and gave each other hugs. Up close, I admired the beaded pouches some of the ladies wore around their necks; one Granny clutched a book titled *Awesome South Africa.*

"I'm so happy to see you, my friend," Catherine said, embracing Beka.

"I'm Jean!" I blurted in a starstruck panic. Recovering my composure, I managed to add, "Wonderful to finally see you in person. I feel like I'm meeting a *rock star*." I erupted into nervous giggles.

One Granny hobbled by with a white bandage wrapped around her right foot. "Oh *no*," exclaimed Allison, one of our Lexpressas cohort. "We have an injury already?"

"Hello," said the youthful-looking Granny. "I'm Beatrice." Her English was crisp and British-accented. She explained that it had been dark when she'd left her house, and "I kicked a rock and broke my toe." We all *aww*-ed in commiseration. "But don't worry—I'm going to play in goal!"

"*Ha!*" Allison cried. "That's exactly what we do when we're injured."

Two men accompanying the Grannies stood back, surveying the scene. I walked over and introduced myself to the young coaches—David and Romeo—shaking their hands in welcome.

Heather came up alongside me. "They must be exhausted," she whispered. "Let's pull the cars up to the door." We made sure the Grannies found the restrooms before beginning our hour-long car ride.

"Ooh it's warm," Beka enthused, emerging outside into the midafternoon warmth. "It feels lovely. It's been such a cold winter at home." Winters in Limpopo, I am told, rarely dip below the forties and are very dry; thank goodness their trip hadn't coincided with a Boston winter.

I noticed Beka placing her hand on her stomach, a brief grimace crossing her face.

"Do you want to sit down?" I offered, motioning to a bench. She hesitated and then took a seat. I glanced around like a mother hen, prepared to head off any straying Grannies.

Just then Catherine pulled her van up to the curb, Allison pulling up behind her. Without waiting for an invitation, one of the older men in the group strolled around to the driver's side and opened the door. Finding the steering wheel, he said, "Oh, I forgot you drive on the wrong side of the road," opting then for the passenger seat instead. Meanwhile, the rest of us helped the Grannies stow their piles of luggage into the vans.

"I'll see you at the game tomorrow morning," Tessa called, hefting her camera bag over her shoulder.

In the van, I grabbed the only empty seat and did a quick head count as the Grannies fussed with their seat belts. We were just entering the Callahan Tunnel, emerging into the city of Boston, when Beka said, rather forcefully, "I need to return to South Africa with a trophy . . . a *big* trophy." She was angry. Evidently the South African government had promised money for the flights only to renege at the last minute, and she wanted a trophy to show *everyone* what the Grannies had accomplished without their help.

Given the team had only formed a few years ago, I privately doubted they would win their age division. But I hated the thought of Beka returning home empty-handed. I'd have to give this some thought.

The car was full of cheerful chatter. The Xitsonga delighted my ears. Once we left Boston city limits, the Grannies pointed and marveled at the hillsides of green trees. The landscape I'd seen in the Grannies' videos was drier, with just a few scrubby brushes—quite a contrast to this forested part of Massachusetts.

"They want to know if there are snakes in the trees," Beka translated for me. "And monkeys?" Nope—no monkeys, I replied, but perhaps a few snakes.

The highway drive lulled more than a few travelers into sleep. It was late afternoon by the time the vans arrived at the hotel in Lancaster—late night at this point in Johannesburg.

As we unloaded, Allison quietly told me that the young coach in her van had been surprised to see a woman driver. She'd explained that most American women learn to drive. "He did say I seemed pretty good at it," she admitted.

Once we'd checked into the hotel, Beka and Catherine organized the women across their shared rooms; the four men would have a room to themselves. I noticed some of the Grannies bickering in the hallway. Were they upset about the room assignments? No doubt they were exhausted and a bit cranky. In a stern tone, Beka quieted them. She was chiding them, young Granny Beatrice whispered to me, reminding them they were guests here and needed to be on their best behavior.

As the women settled in and unpacked their bags, Catherine and I went from room to room with Beatrice translating as needed—showing them how to operate the lights and bathroom fixtures, adjust the air conditioning, and fielding questions about the tournament schedule the kind front desk staff had printed up for each room.

Like a camp director, I carried a clipboard and made notes as I went. One of the Grannies had medication that required refrigeration. A couple of Grannies asked how they might let family members know they'd arrived safely. "We'll get calling cards tomorrow," I assured them.

Corralling them all back into the lobby, we set out piping-hot pizzas and green salads across a few tables. As the Grannies assembled into an orderly line, our four male guests circumvented the queue altogether and descended upon the food. Once everybody had filled their plates and settled onto various couches, the Grannies bowed their heads for a quick prayer of thanks.

It was long past midnight in Johannesburg by the time we finished our simple dinner. Exhausted, the Grannies loaded once again into elevators and then shuffled off to their rooms for the night. I made sure everyone knew I would be sleeping in the room down the hall if they needed any assistance. Beka assured me they were all set.

It was only 8 p.m., too early for bed for me—and besides, I was still wired with adrenaline. I sat on my bed and checked email, scrolling through photos Tessa had already sent, and even fielding a few media requests(!). Heather, I saw, had sent a Lexpressas-wide email request for a check on trophy prices and lead times. (We would *not* let Beka go back empty-handed.)

When I finally turned out the light, I just lay in bed, staring up at the ceiling. Sleep eluded me.

It was so weird, I thought. Only sixteen years ago—sixteen years! about how long my daughters had been alive—it would have been, what, inappropriate? frowned upon? *illegal* for this sort of assembly in South Africa? And now, here we were, White and Black—and beige and brown and cream and jet and cinnamon—hugging, sharing meals, and slowly establishing the elements of friendship that, where the Grannies were from, had systematically been quashed for generations. It was hard to understand how the cultural whiplash might be affecting them. Was it awkward for them being among so many White people? Painful even? My understanding of what they'd had to endure was so sparse, so academic.

At the airport, while we'd been waiting for the Grannies to slowly shuffle through customs, I'd tried to quiz Tessa, the photographer, about her experience as a White person living in South Africa under apartheid. I'd wanted to be sensitive to the difficult topic, but my eagerness to understand emboldened me.

She'd been born in Johannesburg, she told me, and had spent her teen years living in Cape Town.[2] Though her White family was de facto part of the minority elite, her parents wanted their daughter to be aware of what the government was doing. "My mother exposed me early to the inequities of apartheid," Tessa explained. "Once a week she volunteered and taught sewing at a private farm school. She took me out of class to visit on my eighth birthday." Tessa saw Black kids walking to school barefoot, even though the temperatures were freezing. Her mom had told her they'd often sit at their desks hungry, not having eaten anything all day. "She wanted me to see for myself the differences between my school and theirs. It upset me greatly. That experience changed my life forever."

Apartheid, the official state policy of maintaining racial "apartness," ruled all facets of life in South Africa from 1948 to 1994. Building on a legacy of colonialism and slavery, authoritarian architect Hendrik Verwoerd and his National Party rigidly codified separation of the races, all in the name of establishing a White South Africa. Through the 1950s and early 1960s, separate native home territories of barren land were designated for each of the non-White ethnic groups. If the Black majority were separated into smaller groups, Verwoerd reasoned, they would be less likely to rise up and revolt against minority rule—however draconian.

Throughout this fifty-year period, the government strictly limited Black presence in the cities to only what was needed by White employers; this left most Black South Africans back "home" in the villages and small industrial centers that had been assigned to their ethnic groups. The system, of course, was absurd, stubbornly ignoring reality, as by 1948, so many Africans had already become permanent urbanites and many were from ethnically mixed families, with, say, Zulu-Xhosa parents who had met in cities, not to mention the many children of Black and White parents. In point of fact, there *was* no separation between Black and White except what was typed onto government-issued identity cards.

Regardless, crazed with fever dreams of racial purity, the government proceeded to wreak havoc with people's lives, forcibly relocating three and a half million South Africans to the remote territories because it had been decided they were Black, an evaluation so arbitrary that families were often broken up based on the hue of their skin. (Would a pencil stay in your hair when you shook it? You're Black. Would it wriggle free? You're "Coloured," the historical term referring to mixed race South Africans. Would it immediately and easily slide out? You're White.) Given little time to pack, armed police escorted them to their new "homeland," where they might find a collection of one-room prefabricated houses and rations of maize to eat, effectively plunging the majority of South Africans into instant state-induced poverty.

After the Black population was segregated to barren tracts of land, one of the only remaining doors out of poverty—education—was then slammed shut. Verwoerd had quickly passed the Bantu Education Act of 1953, which racially segregated all schools. The new education system provided for Blacks was deliberately inferior; they were taught reading and writing, but only to the extent that it might make them better manual laborers. A curriculum of math and science—which might have led to new employment opportunities for the dispossessed population—was now forbidden.

Apartheid laws also clamped down on physical movement. Black South Africans needed permission to travel outside of the homelands or designated areas of the cities. Passes were issued only when their labor was needed at White businesses. Without a passbook, even travel to seek work was impossible. People caught without the proper credentials were often arrested and threatened by the police. Pervasive separatist policies ensured Whites and Blacks rode in different train cars and visited different parts of the beach. Police patrolled and enforced laws at gunpoint.

To further quash dissent, the government began declaring ongoing states of emergency. These further restricted free assembly, imposing strict curfews and altogether suspending habeas corpus. Perceived "troublemakers" were detained at will, without charge, without trial, and without promise of release from prison. Mention of their names was prohibited, and even funeral services for those who'd died after interactions with the police were circumscribed and their mourners harassed.

Young Tessa had witnessed this disturbing history firsthand. She knew it was incumbent on every South African enjoying the protections and beneficence of the state at the expense of others' persecution to speak up and act out in the name of justice; she aligned herself with grassroots movements and became active in antiapartheid student organizations. "I attended lots of demonstrations during my college days. My husband was a prominent young antiapartheid activist too."

For decades the African National Congress, a prominent social-democratic political party, had risked their freedom and their lives to fight for the rights of Black South Africans. As apartheid began to quash freedoms, the ANC launched their Defiance Campaign—an ongoing multiracial pushback against unjust laws through demonstrations, boycotts, strikes, and acts of civil disobedience. When, in 1976, Black schoolchildren in Soweto protested restrictive education laws, police opened fire on the peaceful marchers, killing many. Tessa and her husband witnessed some of the atrocities firsthand.

This marked a heartbreaking turning point for Tessa and her husband; the situation had become unbearable. "It was a very hard decision, but we packed our bags and fled in search of another country." A steady stream of educated Whites of means began emigrating out of South Africa, mostly to democratic nations like Australia, the United Kingdom, and the United States. "We landed in America."

In self-imposed exile from the country she loved, Tessa looked for ways to support the struggle from a distance.

By 1990, decades of antiapartheid sacrifice were finally beginning to pay off. On February 11, after twenty-seven years of captivity for antiapartheid activity with the ANC, Nelson Mandela was freed from prison. A mere four months after his release, he visited the United States; Tessa helped organize his welcome to Boston. The South African government was under suffocating pressure from the international community and facing increasingly violent unrest at home. Seeing the writing on the wall, they began negotiations with Mandela and the

ANC to end apartheid. In 1994, the first free, democratic elections were held in South Africa in which citizens of all races were finally permitted to participate. Tessa helped organize absentee ballots so that expat South Africans in the Boston area could vote at the Massachusetts State House. "We raised the flag and sang the South African national anthem on the State House steps," she told me. "I remember being dressed in green, yellow, and black—the colors of the ANC—and holding a bouquet of yellow flowers."

With that historic vote, the African National Congress took a majority of seats in the National Assembly and elected Mandela president, elevating him to head of state—a long way from the prison cells where he'd been shackled for the past three decades.

Now poised to forge a path forward, South Africa began drafting a new constitution that would build a future without racial or sexual discrimination, making it one of the most progressive codes of law in the world.

But the new government of a united South Africa faced a country broken down after generations of systematic segregation and oppression. For decades the proapartheid government had purposefully obstructed creation of public infrastructure for the disadvantaged citizens; now everything would have to be built from scratch. "While apartheid is in the past," Tessa said, "complex repercussions continue to manifest in current social problems." It is a legacy that will likely be overcome not in measures of years but of generations.

Today Tessa divides her time between South Africa and the United States, hoping one day to move back home for good. "I would like to lend more of my support to the grassroots efforts battling unemployment, homelessness, hunger." She believes every White South African owes it to themselves to be cognizant of their privilege. "I want to contribute to the growth of my country."

Before now—before this conversation with Tessa and before I'd begun to get to know Beka and the Grannies—I had always considered the horrors of apartheid in small doses, at an emotional remove. But now, when I closed my eyes, I saw the faces of nineteen people I knew personally, people whose names I'd spoken, whose hands I'd held, whose voices

I was coming to recognize—all of whom had suffered under apartheid for the delusions of racial purists.

Troubled, I rolled onto my back and closed my eyes once again. But still sleep did not come.

Granny Rossina
What Happens in the Bush . . .

Although Maka Rossina Mathe was born in 1941, she looks younger than you might expect for someone in her venerable eighties. Maybe it's her sporting lifestyle, thanks to Vakhegula Vakhegula. Maybe it's that all her life she's had access to the freshest of fruits and vegetables, grown right at home. Or could it be divine reward for a life well lived? "I was raised with moral standards," Rossina says. "We were not the kind of girls who roamed all over the place, but we stayed at home. We ran errands for our parents, and we were honest in doing so. I am proud that I grew up being a good child to my parents."[1]

She grew up in a town nestled in the foothills of the Soutpansberg mountain range, a lush strip of land settled by the Venda in the early 1700s that later, in the nineteenth century, was given by a Venda chief to a group of Dutch-speaking White settlers. There sprung up the town of Louis Trichardt, named after the leader of the White expedition, which proved bountiful, yielding crops of bananas, mangoes, lychees, avocadoes, nuts, tea, and coffee. Thus, even when apartheid began strictly segregating the races in 1948, when Rossina would have been only seven, their region remained fairly mixed, with White

Maka Rossina Mathe. Nkowankowa, Limpopo, September 2021. *Photo by Dineo Raolane*

landowners and their Black laborers. This means that while people like Rossina's father could not ever expect to earn a true living wage toiling for the Whites, at least they often didn't have to trek to Johannesburg to find paying work.

He took on several jobs to support his family. "My father was working as a cook for Whites and as a mechanic for their cars," Rossina recalls. In those days, South Africa's pension programs lagged behind much of the rest of the world's, and what structural supports existed were primarily focused on aiding poor Whites. This meant toil well into old age for the majority of Black people. "He was already working when he married my mum, and he continued to work until he became an old man." Meanwhile, her mother's labors were focused on the home, keeping house, raising the children, and farming their homestead.

At harvest time, Rossina would help the family by separating the chaff from the maize and grinding it into flour, which might then be used to make pap, a creamy, hearty porridge they would enjoy throughout the coming year. During other seasons she would hike to the nearby mountain with other girls to collect firewood, feast on fresh lychee fruits—and maybe find a few moments of freedom.

As the girlish chatter ran freely, occasionally a friend would be caught in a lie. But even away from their elders, Rossina would chide her friends to "never repeat those same lies at home." If the girls ever got into an argument, they had an agreement among themselves to not tattle to their parents. "We used the mantra, *Swa nuveni swi helela nuveni*," Rossina says with a laugh—"What happens in the bush stays in the bush."

But even back in town, sometimes trouble found the upright Rossina. Mischievous truant boys would lie in wait to pounce on the schoolchildren walking to their morning lessons.

"These boys used to beat us so that we couldn't go to school. Fierce fights broke out between us and those boys. I was not a fighting type of a girl; I did not like fights. I wouldn't provoke anyone, but whenever I would be dragged into a fight, it became a fierce one. I also beat boys. When I was faced with a boy for a fight, something just told me, *Moer hom.*"

Beat him, the voice inside her would say, and Rossina now raises a fist in remembrance—and then grins. "That's how we grew up." Try to walk in righteousness, but don't take flak from anybody.

On Sundays she and her family would attend the Pentecostal Holiness Church, where she went to Sunday school, eventually becoming a teacher herself. But her formal education at the Catholic school ended abruptly when she was only about twelve years old. Her father had broken his leg, and now that he was unable to earn for the family, Rossina had to find work in his stead.

This meant venturing into the White world as a domestic laborer. The first job she found was babysitting an eight-month-old. It did not go well.

"As soon as I picked up the child, that child started crying hysterically, obviously because she was not used to me. I took the baby to her mum, and she stopped crying. When her mum returned her to me, she started crying again, and I returned her immediately to her mum, and she kept quiet. For the third time when I returned the baby to her mother after she had been shortly given to me, her mother angrily prodded her finger at my chest and said to me in Afrikaans, 'I know you *kaffirs* do not understand our children.'"

That ugly racial slur was tantamount to a slap on the face. Utterly shocked—she had only been trying to keep the baby happy—Rossina just stood there as the woman repeatedly poked her in the chest while screaming angry insults. *Try to walk in righteousness, but don't take flak from anybody.* Finally, unable to stand the degradation one minute longer, young Rossina grabbed the woman by her long hair and pushed her against the wall.

While using the hateful k-word today is a punishable offense under anti–hate speech laws, in 1950s South Africa no White person would have been sympathetic to the Black child, even though she'd been acting in self-defense. The woman screamed for help, dashing to the phone to call the police. Knowing she was in great danger, Rossina made her escape. "I went outside the house, jumped the fence, and fled to the house of the reverend." Waiting, waiting, until the police had left, until any furious family had stopped looking for her, until the last of the uproar had died down, "I hid there. I stayed there for three days." Finally, she felt safe enough to emerge.

As soon as she was able to sneak back to her own neighborhood unmolested, Rossina determined to find new employment. Before long, she secured a position at a doctor's practice. Never certain what treatment she would get as a Black person, Rossina was relieved to find they appreciated her work. "Here, these White people loved me so much, and I enjoyed working with them."

She excelled in this job and eventually was able to travel to different parts of South Africa for work. "That was where I worked for a very, very long time." In fact, she was so good at her job and so loved that one day her employer came to her with a startling proposition that would ensure Rossina would be part of their family forever. "They said they wanted to buy me."

Rossina grows somber in her reflection. "Life under apartheid was bitter for a Black person. Generally speaking, we Black people were living under tough times." She had come of age under apartheid, and she had no hopes that the situation for Black people in South Africa would improve; the choice was tortuous. She had truly come to love this family; in "buying" Rossina, they were more or less asking to adopt her into their family and vouchsafe her care and safety for the rest of her life. Though accepting the proposition would have meant a secured income and stability of employment among people she greatly cared for, it was not an offer Rossina felt free to accept. "I refused."

Attending church services had been her solace and guide since she'd been a child. And now, at twenty-one years of age, as the difficulties of adulthood were beginning to weigh ever heavier, it was there she found her peace.

Unbeknownst to pretty, upright Rossina, she'd caught the eye of a fellow parishioner who imagined an attractive future together—but perhaps found her a bit intimidating. He asked for some help from a relative, the church's pastor. "This man told our priest that he loved me," Rossina recollects. "He'd been afraid to come to me personally, because I think he could sense that I was a no-nonsense lady." Here she bursts into laughter. "The reverend's family called on me and nicely and humbly requested me to be a wife to that man."

Rossina, in turn, brought the proposal to her own family. "I remember when I told my dad for the first time that somebody wanted to marry me, he asked, 'My girl, do you even know those people who want to marry you?'" The young man's immediate family lived a good forty kilometers away, so she couldn't say she did. But she respected the reverend's family, and so she felt comfortable agreeing to the marriage. She accepted the young man's proposal.

As was custom, Rossina moved into her husband's home after their wedding ceremony and lived with her in-laws. This arrangement brought its own set of problems for the young woman, who discovered that her new family looked down on her humbler rural origins. "His family members were just troublesome people. My husband's elders did not want a woman like me who was from a *township*."

After a time, she and her husband were able to move into their own home, and the relationship prospered; they went on to have six children. "It's a good family," she says. "It is not a rich family. I can say it is a poor family *and* a good family." She raised her children as she had been raised, to walk in righteousness. "I was a no-nonsense mother, so quick to give a child a hiding if they did not do things the right way, *heeee!*"

Though a strict mother, Rossina adored her children. So when her one-year-old daughter died, she was disconsolate. "I am the kind of a person who keeps quiet and doesn't ask people anything when something keeps my soul restless. I normally do this temporarily until I will be ready to talk. I feel good when I don't rush to say anything." For two months after the death of her child, Rossina mourned deeply, falling into illness, her body expressing the anguish of her spirit. "It was as if she had died in my arms."

Then, in 2015, Rossina buried another child—this death even less expected and more excruciating. Her firstborn son was living in another town, where he was a schoolteacher. One day, he called and asked his mother to come over. "When I got there, he asked me not to go back home but to stay and help him with some chores around the house, and so I did." But she could tell that something was wrong with him; an illness was sapping his energy. "I must say that he was not okay. He was not fine." Rossina does not name the disease, but she never left his side through his illness, caring for him as he grew weaker, tending his household for him.

One day, he died. "*Haai!* His death was too hard to accept."

Once again, Rossina turned to the church. She relied on the parish elders to talk and pray with her and consulted with a psychologist to cope with her enormous grief. "Nonetheless, there were times I would just break and feel the pain again."

In the intervening years, Rossina has found joy and healing in her family. "*Heee!*" she laughs, "I have *ten* grandchildren." Two of them—the children of her firstborn son—she's reared from childhood up until they graduated from university. She also raised one granddaughter until the parents could reassume her care themselves. Rossina is justifiably proud that all her grandchildren are either working or still in school.

Today she lives with one granddaughter in the township of Nkowankowa, about a hundred miles from where she grew up. Over the years, as her family has grown, she's softened. "The grandchildren love one another so much. You would be surprised at how we interact as grandchildren and grandma. We love each other so much. I do not even know how to put it in words."

The church remains her anchor. She is a faithful attendee at the Hope of Christ Church in Nkowankowa. "Praying is so good. *Eish!*" The message she receives there is her direction and hope. "You need to understand the sermon at the time the preacher preaches and welcome it. You could be hungry now, but if you believe in the word of God, you could be lucky to chance upon someone giving you twenty rand to buy something to eat. That is the blessing from God. Whenever you hear the word of God, you must take it with you and use it."

Rossina's train of thought is interrupted as her cell phone rings. She struggles to fish it out of her skirt pocket and pokes at the buttons to dismiss the call. "There is a lot I am doing in a day," she says, smiling. Maybe she'll start the day planning to focus on her sewing pile, but before long, the tasks will pile up, one atop the other. "Even today, I had been plowing." But she makes sure to carve out space in her busy week for practice with her beloved Vakhegula Vakhegula. She first heard Mama Beka on the radio and soon after joined the soccer squad. There she has found community, friendship, and an outlet for her competitive streak.

"Remember this!" she says, raising a fist, a callback to the schoolyard scrapper who proved her mettle as a fighter. That spirit thrives too.

8

Five Is a Lot

Now that I'm with Vakhegula Vakhegula, I'm happy. I'm no longer alone. I'm among friends, talking and laughing, finally unburdened from all my troubles.—Nkhensani Nyavani Florah Baloyi, Soccer Granny[1]

COACHES DAVID AND ROMEO PACED BACK AND FORTH ON THE SIDE-lines, knit scarves the colors of the South African flag draped around their shoulders despite the waves of sauna-like air radiating off the artificial turf in the midafternoon sun. (The recycled rubber tire crumbs *had* to be generating more heat than their clay practice fields back home.)

From the start of the Grannies' first tournament match, play on their side of the field had been chaotic as they clustered around the ball in a frantic effort to assist. I knew the feeling from my early soccer days, but I had since learned it's best to trust your teammate closest to the ball and get open to receive a pass. Maybe the Grannies were suffering from early game jitters?

One thing was for certain: Twenty hours of travel, jet lag, and relative humidity well into the nineties were doing them no favors. Team captain Granny Reineth was managing the field as best she could, and Romeo and David were yelling themselves hoarse from the sidelines. But Vakhegula Vakhegula were down by three points, and their opponents didn't show any signs of letting up.

However this game ended—in an embarrassing shutout or something a little more fairy tale—it was going to be well covered. Tessa wasn't our only coverage on the field this day; a camera operator from local TV station LexMedia was crouched atop his van, filming gameplay, and a sportscaster from ABC had just stuck a microphone in front of me. *What's the score?*

"Uh, our Grannies haven't made a goal yet," I stuttered, my breath strangely hard to regulate with that camera trained on me. "But not everyone could make the trip to America," I added, maybe a bit defensively. "Their best goalie is back in Limpopo." It was hard to tell if the sweat trickling down my temple was solely from the heat. "They're tough, though." I wanted to end on an upbeat note. "They'll score. I'm sure of it."

I was *not*, in point of fact, sure of it, but I hated to think of the Grannies' US television debut showing them in anything but the most flattering light.

A collective groan rose from the sideline, and I turned to see the Grannies' keeper once again retrieving the ball from the net. I wished the Bay State Breakers would exert some self-control and let up a bit. *I'm sure they respect the Grannies*, the reporter suggested of the opposition, *but they want to win games too?*

"Yeah, but there's no need to crush them," Catherine bit in from beside me. "Excuse me—I'm going to have a word with their coach."

While the ball was brought to the centerline, the Breakers took the opportunity to substitute a few players on the field. Lois, team captain and Breakers' defense, hadn't seen much play all game and was moved upfield. Meanwhile, Anne, cocaptain and one of their strongest players, was called off the field and made a beeline for her coach, just as Catherine descended. "Hey, can you ask the team to mellow out?" Anne pleaded. "We don't need to massacre them."

"Seriously. Let's see some good sportsmanship," Catherine said, glaring.

"Kick it out!" Allison yelled, pulling my attention back to the game. "Come on, ladies!" Play was again centered in front of the Grannies' goal. Lois received the ball, giving it only the gentlest tap, probably assuming the goalie would scoop it up. Instead, it rolled between the keeper's legs, into the net. Five-nothing. Lois's shoulders sagged and her head drooped. Raising her arm, she shouted, "Take me out, coach."

As the game clock ticked along, our crowd of spectators was growing. Players from other teams who'd wandered over to watch the game invariably began cheering for the Grannies. Several even came by with bags of lapel pins with their team, state, or country logos, gifts for the Grannies—a tradition established at the Olympics and carried over to other athletic events. This was my first Veterans Cup, but I already felt the spirit of hospitality and encouragement was pervasive.

Do any of our visitors speak English? the ABC reporter asked, interrupting my thoughts. I pointed out Beka and Beatrice, and he headed in their direction, other media outlets close behind. "My name is Beatrice Tshabalala," our youngest Granny said, taking the attention in stride. "And my football name—they call me Messi!" Like Lionel Messi, one of the all-time high scorers in professional soccer. "I am a striker," she continued, all confidence, "and I score a lot of goals—when I don't have a broken toe." Those of us standing nearby laughed appreciatively. "In South Africa, fields like this," she said with a broad sweep of the arm, "are reserved for the men's national team. We are very much happy to be here in America. The spirit is so nice. Thank you very much, people of America."[2]

Just six hours earlier, I'd awoken with a start, hearing the sound of Grannies' voices in the hotel hallway. My room clock read 4:45 a.m. The early morning sun bathed my room in a tangerine glow. By the time I'd scrambled out of bed, pulled on my hot pink Lexpressas shirt and opened the door to peer out, all was quiet again. Two or three bags had been placed outside of each Granny room, I saw, ready to be taken to the tournament. We had more than two hours until the bus would even arrive to take us to the soccer fields, but the Grannies clearly raring to go.

I tiptoed up the hallway and listened at each of their doors to the chattering inside. Beatrice popped her head out of one, and I gave her a little wave and a small smile. "Did you manage to get some sleep?" I asked, my voice low.

"We did," she whispered back, "but everyone is excited. Excited Grannies sing and dance, and it's hard to sleep when you're dancing," she laughed. "And with the time change, we woke up early."

"Oh, well, some good exercise today, and you'll sleep better tonight." They were going to be dragging by afternoon.

By a few minutes to six, the women had already formed a line just outside the doorway to the designated breakfast room, looking sharp in their white jerseys, black shorts, and white calf socks. Matching yellow bandanas were tied around every head, covering most of the hair. Given it was already lunchtime in South Africa, they had to be starving, I realized, motioning for them to come on in and start filling their plates. But they just smiled at me and stayed put.

At six on the nose, the four men arrived and went straight to the table, piling their plates with moist, cakey muffins, crusted bagels, and ripe berries and pouring glasses of juices and mugs of fresh-brewed coffee. Then, hands full, all four headed back to their room, presumably to breakfast in private. Only then did the women venture to the table to make their selections, pull over one of the hotel's padded ballroom chairs, or sink onto the floor to break their fast.

It was a simple spread, and we had no idea if the menu would be recognizable to our guests, but it was nourishing.

The Granny next to me forked a few fresh blueberries into her mouth. "Good," she said, pointing at her plate.

"Have you ever had them before?" I asked. She just shrugged, puzzlement showing on her cheerful face. Changing tack, I tried a simple "Good!" with a nod and was rewarded with a big grin.

"What are they called?" asked Beatrice, who was taking a seat on my other side.

"*Blueberries*—blue berries. Not a very creative name ..." I thought out loud.

A group of Grannies sitting nearby burst into laughter at something Beka had said in Xitsonga. "She's making fun of your A-*mayyyyyrrrrr*-ican accent," Beatrice confided with a grin. I flushed and smiled; I didn't mind that they were amused at my expense. Mostly, I was just happy to hear them laugh.

82

Breakfasted and refreshed, the Grannies carried their bags down to the lobby to meet the buses that would take us to the tournament. This team of Black women of all shapes and sizes drew stares and smiles from other hotel guests. One Granny, nicknamed "Bull," had caught my attention at the airport; her uniquely expressive eyes were hard to look away from. Now she stood next to me, meeting my gaze with a smile and wiggling her eyebrows playfully. I couldn't help but smile back. "Ready for soccer fun?" I asked. Bull nodded, took my hand, and walked with me toward the yellow school bus that had just pulled up under the hotel awning.

Holding hands with another adult felt odd; it wasn't something I'd regularly done since elementary school, I was sure. But more than any awkwardness, I felt a wash of gratitude and affection for this lady with the sprite's eyes, my new friend from halfway around the world.

The men were the first to push through the glass hotel doors and board the bus, taking their seats at the very back. Then the Grannies filed out, lugging bags of shin guards and soccer balls and boxes of sweatshirts and water bottles provided by generous donors. Many Grannies propped gear on their heads, wiggled their necks back and forth to adjust the balance, and strolled off, their hands free to carry smaller items. Allison, who could balance well enough to ride a unicycle, picked up a small backpack and tried to carry it on her head; each time it crashed to the ground. The Grannies laughed and tried to help her, but clearly this skill would take some practice.

Once aboard, I performed my head count, and some of the Grannies counted along with me in English, to my delight. I signaled to the driver that we were ready to go, and the engines revved. Seemingly on cue, the Grannies bowed their heads, murmuring quietly as one led them in prayer.

At the "Amen," Granny Josephine stood up, bracing herself on the seat in front of her, and began singing. It was obviously a song well-known to all of them, because at the chorus everyone joined in. I wished I could understand the words, but the melody would have to suffice; it was a cheery and catchy tune. One by one, more Grannies stood, clutching the seat backs and shimmying into the aisle, where they'd gently sway back and forth in dance. Before long, more were standing than seated.

They danced with foot taps and rolling hips—a great soccer warm-up, now that I thought about it. It brought to mind ski weekend bus trips of decades past, friends partying in the aisles—except we'd been a good fifty years younger than these women here. As the bus did its own shimmy, I was afraid someone might fall, but most of them were holding on with at least one hand. I let myself relax.

The moment felt magical. *They will touch your lives with an unforgettable experience . . .*

I pulled out my phone and dialed my favorite Granny donor from Canada. "Good morning, Isabelle." I said, my voice both cheerful and laden with emotion. "This is Jean Duffy. I'm with the Grannies on the bus headed to their first game. They're singing." I held the phone up for her to listen to a full chorus. "Could you hear them?"

"Indeed." Her voice cracked. "Tears of joy are streaming down my face. You've made me very happy. Now go, enjoy your experience."

When the referee blew two long whistles, indicating halftime, the Bay State Breakers ran to their sideline and the Grannies slowly shuffled to theirs, where they plopped onto the ground, legs straight out, and stared into the middle distance, clearly exhausted. Coach Romeo dragged the cooler over and passed out the bottles of water Heather had hauled in that morning, as Coach David consoled the team and offered guidance for the second half.

"They have to be *sweltering* in those," Allison murmured to me, nodding at the Grannies' modest black leggings under their shorts. Indeed, it wasn't ideal kit for our hot, humid weather.

The leggings, Beka had told me, evolved as part of the Grannies' uniform after they'd decided that playing in skirts was too cumbersome. "When they first put on shorts . . ." she delicately paused. "We respect our culture so much," she said, starting again. "So when they put on shorts, it was not okay with them. It did not suit them. So I suggested, *No, no, you put a tight inside. And* then *you put the shorts*. They were still complaining, but after a while they said it's better."[3]

As for the bandanas: "If you look at them, all of them, they are putting something on their head. When you are woman, you have to wear something. They believe in that. They are superstitious about gray hair too. Best to wear something on their heads to look good."

Refreshed as they possibly could be after a mere fifteen minutes' respite sprawled under a series of sun umbrellas offering a modicum of shade—also thanks to Heather—Vakhegula Vakhegula grimly hauled themselves to their feet and silently made their way back to the pitch, determined.

The Breakers had not yet scored in this half, thank goodness. But by this time, both teams were now walking more than running, no doubt the relentless sun having taken its toll. Granny Maradona showed nice foot control, but the Breakers intercepted a pass and lobbed the ball toward the Grannies' goal.

The referee pointed his flag into the field of play, signaling an offsides offense against the Breakers; this meant the Grannies would now be given possession of the ball. I observed that this was the second time Lois had been caught offsides. Was she *intentionally* going offsides to turn the ball over to the Grannies? Ah, Lois. Ever gracious, ever sportswomanlike.

Despite her generous attempts, one of the Breakers stole the ball from the Grannies, dribbled up the field, shot on goal, and scored. "Oh, give me a break," Heather cried with annoyance. I groaned.

Rather than doling out the usual congratulations and high-fives, Anne and Lois descended on their teammate. "What are you doing?"

The offending player stared down Lois. "*You* scored a goal."

"Yeah, and it was the worst moment of my soccer career," she bit back. "I feel awful about it; it was the last thing I'd wanted to do."

For once I was grateful that most of the Grannies did not have a strong command of English; they seemed oblivious to the drama underway, taking the pause in play to catch their breath.

I glanced at my watch; there couldn't be more than three or four minutes left in the game. It was to be a 6–0 shutout—not unlike the Lexpressas' first game.

That morning, despite having the best cheering section in the tourney—one shout of "Go, Pinkies!" making me huff-laugh particularly hard as I'd run by in my pink jersey—my own team had lost, 4–0. When we'd circled up after the game, Coach Catherine had been particularly encouraging: "You did well. They just put the ball in the net a few times. You win tomorrow." A win is always preferable, of course, but we'd nonetheless felt good about our effort: It had been a clean game, played to the best of our abilities on the day, and that was what mattered.

Hmm, I now thought wryly, *maybe the Grannies should play us* next.

Just then, Granny Lizzy—a wiry, sixty-three-year-old center forward who couldn't have weighed eighty pounds even after eating *all* the blueberry muffins in the land—sprinted off the field, tears running down her hollowed cheeks. She sat heavily at Beka's feet and plopped her head in her lap, her slender shoulders heaving as she wept. Beka stroked the top of Lizzy's head and spoke in low, comforting tones.

Coach David glanced at Lizzy, shook his head, and shrugged his shoulders, sending another player in to finish out the game.

I sidled over to Beatrice, who was icing her injured foot. "Is Lizzy okay?" I asked quietly; maybe she'd been hurt . . .

"Oh, she's okay," Beatrice reassured me. "She's crying with joy at the opportunity to be here, to travel to America to play soccer. It means so much to her." All the players felt indebted to Beka for providing them the opportunity to play soccer, Beatrice explained, and it was an emotional time.

"Lizzy lost five children to AIDS, you know," Beatrice continued. "Five is a lot."

My eyes shot to Lizzy, unable to imagine the grief she'd had to endure again and again. I raised my hand to partially cover my crumpled face, not wanting to make a scene.

"I lost friends, families, and neighbors to this epidemic," Beatrice continued in a soft voice. "My sister was unfortunate and contracted HIV, but because of the early detection she was able to take medication and is now living a healthy life. I try my best to teach the youth," she finished with a shrug and a sigh.[4]

In the earliest days of the epidemic, the South African government had downplayed the severity of the situation. Though AIDS was a devastating reality, affecting many, many South Africans, social stigma meant people hesitated to discuss it openly. But this was a time that called for more lifesaving communication, not less. An eighteen-year-old woman named Prudence Mabele bravely broke the silence, speaking publicly about her HIV-positive status at a time when medical treatments were only just emerging and few women if any were willing to discuss their diagnoses. Prudence dedicated the remaining thirty years of her life to HIV/AIDS activism. Undoubtedly her bravery saved many lives.

As the government response finally ground into action, prenatal clinics began screening expectant mothers and targeting care; at the peak of the epidemic, in 2007, almost one-third of women tested in these clinics were found to be HIV-positive. But with the introduction of antiretroviral therapy, mother-to-child transmissions decreased, and in time, deaths began to plateau.

Even so, now, as the Grannies were standing on the sidelines of a soccer field in Lancaster, Massachusetts, an ocean away AIDS was still accounting for a full half of all deaths across South Africa. Rural areas with limited access to health care and treatment sites—like Lizzy's hometown—were bearing the brunt of the devastation.

And here she was, bowed by the deaths of five children, an impossible burden of grief, even as the epidemic was only barely contained. Yet she kept going, putting one foot in front of the other.

"You know, she runs ten kilometers every morning," Beka said quietly, gently stroking Lizzy's hair. She'd trained for and run multiple marathons—those endorphins no doubt carrying her through some rough days. "Running is like soccer," Beka mused. "It's so good for you."

Now I better understood why Beka had fought so hard to make this trip happen for these women who'd suffered so much yet responded with dignity and perseverance and heart.

Beka's vision had brought each Granny to the game of soccer and now to this tournament on this pitch in a small town outside Boston. It was *my* responsibility to make sure their time here met all their expectations. I was not going to let the heat, the fatigue, and one team's misguided resolve to drive up the score ruin it for them.

The ref blew three long whistles. The game was over.

If the Grannies were dismayed by the lopsided final score, they showed no sign of it. Like an oversized game of bumper pool, they ricocheted around the postgame field, greeting one player after the next with wide smiles and all-encompassing hugs. They ran to embrace other Grannies and Breakers alike; they even hugged the referees. Vakhegula Vakhegula's two coaches added to the merry mayhem, giving high-fives to players all and sundry. I laughed as I saw one of the Grannies plant a kiss on Lois's cheek. Clearly for our friends from South Africa, playing soccer for fun was more important than a high score.

"Line up, Breakers, line up!" their coach bellowed. Both teams queued behind their respective goalie for handshakes and hugs, and as they passed one another, each Breaker presented a Granny with a pink gift bag.

Vakhegula Vakhegula's gift to the Breakers was song, led by Josephine, her fellow teammates echoing in a catchy hallelujah refrain. The two teams linked arms with one another, swaying to the music, joining in for the hallelujahs each time the chorus came around.

Black arms around White shoulders and White arms around Black shoulders—Tessa caught it all on camera. As the last lines of the song faded away, Josephine launched into another, and then another. Ear-to-ear smiles on their faces, the Grannies sang and stomped their feet in jubilant dance.

The Breakers may have been stingy with the ball during game play, but off the pitch their generosity was expansive as they unpacked a huge picnic lunch to share. We sat on blankets spread across the ground and feasted on an array of colorful homemade salads, half sandwiches stuffed full with meats and crisp lettuces and juicy tomatoes, dripping slices of watermelon, and bittersweet fudgy brownies. And water. *So* much water.

"How was it playing against the Grannies?" I asked Lois, who was tucking into a plate piled high.

"They're a bunch of women running about and having fun," she said around a bite of sandwich. "That's what it's all about. They're strong, plucky, feisty women to be celebrated."

Twice she'd been called offsides, I casually mentioned. A slow, mischievous grin spread across her face as she shrugged one shoulder, innocently.

Lois. Generous Lois.

Our stomachs full, the Grannies and the Breakers creakily stood and then clustered together for a joint team photo, players with younger knees down in front. The Grannies clapped and ululated—their exultant tongue trilling carrying across the pitch. As games concluded on nearby fields, the spontaneous singing and dancing attracted a crowd of players and referees. Dozens of cameras of all sizes pointed toward us, like paparazzi clamoring to capture the moment. Lizzy was smiling broadly. No tears now.

Granny Khune
We Danced Like Crazy

Granny Mamaila Chauke Novela is Vakhegula Vakhegula's goalkeeper. When the time came for fourteen of her fellow teammates to make the trip from Limpopo to Massachusetts, Granny Khune, as she is known by her friends, knew that her absence would cost the team some wins.

"When I am not available at the time of playing—perhaps I will be in Johannesburg for a visit—they call me and beg me to come back in fear that our team will be defeated. When this team started, I used to cry tears if we could be beaten. Each time I was scored a goal against, I would cry. I prayed to God-Jehovah in my heart, asking why he couldn't help me to catch it."[1]

Khune is happiest when she meets the other women on the pitch to play soccer. They've woven a sort of support system on the field and off, where friends call and check in on friends who haven't shown up to practice.

She knows it's something of a feat to be playing soccer at her age and is proud of it.

"Oh, my years? Now you have raised a heavy issue. I'm a pensioner, and I don't know my age. I have been receiving the government pension money for a long time." Given that

Mamaila "Khune" Chauke Novela. Nkowankowa, Limpopo, September 2021. *Photo by Dineo Raolane*

in South Africa old-age grants start at sixty, Granny Khune must be well along in her years.

Khune smooths the traditional Tsonga *nceka* she wears, a cloth of pale blues and greens, tied over one shoulder. To purchase a *nceka*, Khune first had to plow the land, grow and then gather maize grains, and finally take them to the shop. "With the grains we collect, we are also able to buy beads like these." She gestures to her necklace—a colorful grid of pink, lime, yellow, navy, turquoise, and orange. If the grains don't weigh enough for what she wants to purchase, she gathers more maize from the field and returns to the shop.

Khune learned her farming skills as a young girl, when her daily help was important in maintaining the family plantings and livestock. The Tsonga have long raised cattle, and the size of a man's herd is a measure of his wealth. A fenced *kraal* to corral the livestock would be encircled by cylindrical earthen *rondavel* huts, each capped by a thatched roof. Traditions have been passed down, from one generation to the next.

"My first work in the morning was to sweep the yard," Khune recounts. "Then I would go to the *kraal* and release the goats to graze. I herded my family's cattle—a boy's task—because we were all girls at home. I would even harness the cattle and plow. After finishing my other chores, we would go out to the field to catch locusts and mopane worms. We would cook them for dinner. My family ate porridge and wild spinach."

Farming is heavy work, and despite the family's best efforts, sometimes the harvest was insufficient to feed all five of them. Eventually Khune's father, like so many other South African fathers of the day, left his family to seek paid work in Johannesburg. "Sometimes he would come back home to stay for a long time without working," Khune recalls. "It was too heavy for us. It was very hard indeed, and there was nothing one could enjoy. We were living in hunger." She pauses and then repeats with emphasis, "*We. Lived. In. Hunger.* When there was not enough food for us, my granny taught my mother that sorghum for making traditional beer could also be ground to make us something to eat." At times the family would slaughter a goat or a cow and feast for a time on the meat.

Khune began attending school, but her studies were interrupted daily when she had to run home to tend the goats.

"My parents kept on asking me who would take care of their animals if I was going to school. So I had to leave school. My father had two wives. With the other woman he had three girls and one boy. All those girls did not attend school, just like me."

The pressure on Khune was too great, and the family's needs won out: After only two years of schooling, she was forced to drop out. Today it upsets her greatly that she is unable even to write her name. She feels education was a missed opportunity that would have substantially lightened her load if she'd only had her family's support.

"We have lived through suffering because of having been denied the opportunity to study. That suffering has haunted us until today. The only child who attended school amongst my siblings was the last-born child, but he ended up not attending because he did not like it. He cried every time he had to go to school."

Boys, the young Khune felt, only meant trouble, and she hoped for a house full of daughters when she grew up and became a mother. She even carved a special doll out of wood and dressed it in its own *nceka*.

But before she could marry, Khune had to attend *khomba*, the training every Tsonga girl completes as an initiation into womanhood. Conducted by the elder women of the community, Khune's *khomba* lasted three months, during which she never went home, learning everything crucial for her passage from childhood into adulthood. The girls were taught the roles of women in the community, how to be a good wife, what it means to be a mother, how to keep house, and how to tend crops. They also learned special ritual dances, which quickly became one of Khune's greatest pleasures. "We danced like crazy to the music, shaking and swinging our hips."

Upon emerging from *khomba* as a full Tsonga woman, Khune was expected to adhere to certain expectations: Cousins did not marry, for example, and there were no child brides. According to tradition, a man would send a grass ring to the woman he wished to marry. If the feeling was mutual, she would send a grass ring in return. The fathers would then grant approval for the marriage and negotiate how many cattle would transfer from the groom's family to the bride's.

"I don't remember when exactly I got married," Khune says, but other details are etched in her memory. "His sister was sent to propose to me on his behalf. She came to my home and chose me from all the girls at home; she preferred me, the darker one. And the sister took out a picture of this man and showed it to me and said, 'This is the man I am requesting your love for.' This man had not seen me before; he was just looking for a woman. Whether that picture was really him or not, I did not know. It could have been a picture of his son, and I would only find later that my husband-to-be was an old man, born a donkey's age ago! How would I have even known the truth in those days?" She bursts out laughing at the thought.

The man's sister told Khune she would be the second wife—a practice many first wives advocated, hoping to increase their stature within the household and spread work among more hands. Khune needed some time to think about the offer and asked the sister to return on the morrow.

The following afternoon, studying the portrait again, Khune made her decision. "It's fine," she said, "I love him." With that, her family sent the man's sister home with a necklace, and Khune's family received a cash bride prize. "Do you know five rand?" Khune asks with a laugh. "Can it buy *anything*? How many sweets can it buy?"

Khune's wedding would have been structured on the traditional Tsonga two-part wedding ceremony—including a formal departure from the bride's family and a celebratory welcoming into the groom's household. The bride wears a cheerful, brightly colored dress, the layered skirt ruffles sewn to quiver as her hips shimmy to the lively Tsonga music, blended from string instruments, antelope trumpet, drums, and tambourines.

As tradition dictated, Khune moved in with her in-laws, where she swept the home, helped with the cooking, collected firewood, and learned the routines and customs of her new family. She would rest after supper and chat with her husband's first wife, who had her own adjacent home facing the *kraal*, where she would have moved after the birth of the first child. As a Tsonga family grows, the mother and older sisters care for the youngest, sons help herd goats and cattle, and daughters gather firewood and fetch water—just as a young Khune had. Over time, sons marry and expand the clan settlement with the next generation, and the cycle starts anew.

Within the traditional Tsonga family, the father has the ultimate authority and is to be treated with respect. So when Khune's husband decided to move to Johannesburg for work, she was resigned to single parenthood and the increased burden it would bring. She visited her husband in the city when she could. In the meantime, back at home, she busied herself with raising their three sons and, finally, the daughter she'd always wished for.

Years later, after her husband had passed away, Khune missed having someone with whom she could share her problems. "The hardship in my life worsened. I did not only raise my children after the death of my husband; I also had to raise the children of my husband's first wife." In order to feed the many mouths, Khune now had to call upon everything her grandmother and her mother had taught her about making do and turning scarcity into enough.

When Khune's children grew to be adults, they started their own families, and she worked hard for their sake and her grandchildren's sake. "People hired me for cleaning their yards, and others hired me for plowing their lands and paid me. I am so proud that I am so good in plowing. Even at times of no rains, I can plow and plant whatever I feel like, and it grows well under my care. My hard work has also benefited others who were poor like me, because when I had enough food to share, I would share with them to feed their kids."

Khune had managed to nurture her growing family into stability. But even now tragedy managed to find her. In 2002, one of her sons died.

"I still remember this day vividly, and I won't forget it. He left three kids. I kept on asking myself who would raise those kids. Every time when the sun set, I cried. After the death of my second-born son, my first and third sons took the responsibility of taking care of their brother's kids.

"While my third son was raising them, he suddenly fell ill. His illness lasted not even two months, and he died. You know, if your relatives keep on dying one by one in a short space of time in front of you, you end up not being well. I had a terrible headache that persecuted me for so long."

The trauma of losing adult children cuts deep, and Khune cannot even name aloud what ailment took the lives of her sons. Access to health care can be irregular in parts of Limpopo, and many find themselves well into an illness before they even realize they've been sick. Further complicating an already fraught situation, stigma often prevents open acknowledgment of certain diseases, which means the necessary prevention and treatment education often are unavailable until it's too late. In the early aughts, for example, when the AIDS epidemic was ravaging the South African population, the associated cultural taboo and shame silenced families, making the deaths of their loved ones even harder to endure.

It was during this darkest period of her life that Khune found the faith that helped restore her hope for the future. She was baptized in the Zion Christian Church as an adult.

"Those days, if someone was a believer but had tough problems like mine, people had a funny saying. They used to say that such a person must 'tell her knees.' By this they meant go down on their knees and pray.

"After starting to attend the church I started having hope that these kids would be under God's care and that God would have mercy on them and myself. I also believed that God would heal my soul. My soul has settled since I became a believer."

Today Khune now lives with her daughter and her grandson. She cleans their home and prepares meals for her grandchild. Prayer marks the passage of the day. "When I am done, at around ten o'clock I pray. At twelve o'clock again I pray. The same thing will happen again at three o'clock. I feel so good by praying because it puts my soul in a comfortable state. I pray to God to have mercy on me and to make me be able to take care of my grandchildren. I pray also for my relatives and all people of the world who are like me for God to take care and have mercy on them."

Deftly weaving together all that her heritage has taught her and the realities and opportunities found in twenty-first-century South Africa, Khune is a modern Tsonga woman, leaning on her faith but using her own resourcefulness. "I relied on God that he would take care of me. I also realized that working hard was the only thing through which I was going to survive my situation," she muses. "I am proud that my kids are adults now and that heavenly God has spared my life that I am even today a recipient of government money because of my old age."

And finally, after years of labor, Khune has also found time for some much-deserved recreation. "In my life right now, I am so proud of playing football and that I while my time away by playing it." She smiles. "I am the one driving Vakhegula Vakhegula."

As the team's keeper, she knows much depends on her skill. "Everything I am doing in the play field during playtime comes from my heart," she says, pointing to her heart, "and from my head. Playing football has changed my life to be good."

9

R-E-S-P-E-C-T

We compose our own songs. When we come together, we sing. Before we play, we sing. Before we go home, we sing, we dance. In our tradition, we dance using our waist. It makes us exercise for the second time. That's what I believe in. So we play soccer, we sing, we dance.—Rebecca "Beka" Ntsanwisi, founder of the Soccer Grannies[1]

BY 9 A.M. THE HEAT WAS ALREADY UNMERCIFUL; IT WAS SHAPING UP TO be a beastly hot second day of tournament play for the Grannies.

As soon as they stepped off the bus, they were swarmed by soccer players, as if they were touring rock stars. "Welcome!" "We're *so* excited you're here." "Vakhegula Vakhegulaaaa!" As quickly as players could hand out pins fashioned with team logos, the Grannies would secure them to their yellow-and-lime-green shirts.

"Good crowd to cheer them on today," Lois said as off-duty refs, players from other teams, and their fans and family members took to the sidelines to watch the game.

"I know," I said. "Allison's made a list of names and jersey numbers so we can cheer for them by name."

The Grannies' competition for today, the San Diego team, arrived at the field looking super fit, with taut muscles and a healthy glow (must be all that California sunshine and avocado toast). "We're thrilled to play with you," one of them said, hooking Grannies Ennie and Mercy in an exuberant bear hug.

The Grannies burst into song. I was starting to recognize their repertoire by this point. At the chorus—*Sha-way! Sha-way!*—the Grannies put their hands on their hips. The San Diego players did the same. The Grannies raised a knee and stomped a foot down. San Diego followed suit. They'd come together to play soccer, but instead a dance party was underway.

The head ref glanced at his watch and whistled the players onto the field; today dancing would have to suffice for the warm-up.

"Good luck, Beatrice!" Allison shouted as Vakhegula Vakhegula's keeper gingerly tested weight on her sore foot.

The game ball was positioned at the centerline, in front of Maradona. The ref checked that both goalies were ready and then whistled. The Grannies' second game was underway.

"Go, Maradona!" "That one's number 8—Rossina." "Go, Rossina!" "*Nice*, Rossina." "Looking good!" "*Yes*, Flora." "You got this, Beatrice!" "Good pressure, Gayisa." The Lexpressas on the sideline were making full use of our Vakhegula Vakhegula cheat sheet.

They were playing well today. (I *knew* they'd just needed a good night's sleep.) "Knots of players dance up and down the field, waltzing around the ball, nudging one another aside," the *Los Angeles Times* had written of the Grannies' playing style. "It scuttles between their boots like a frightened animal looking for a hole to hide in."[2]

Just then, San Diego's right wing crossed the ball to their center forward. Beatrice dove . . . but San Diego scored.

"That's all right." "Good try, Beatrice!" "Shake it off, ladies."

As play resumed, San Diego appeared to throttle back and give Vakhegula Vakhegula extra space to handle the ball. Beka, Lexpressas, now San Diego—the list of folks who instinctively responded to the Grannies with empathy and even affection seemed to be growing.

Just before half, a press team from the *Boston Globe* arrived. While the paper's photographer captured the on-field action, Heather, Lois, and I descended on the reporter.

"They're still jet-lagged from their long trip, yet they have energy to end the game with song and dance!"

"We didn't even know for sure they were coming 'til just a few days ago."

"We're still catching our breath, and it's been a challenge, but when we watch them play, we know it's the right thing."

"Soccer's a universal language. It brings everyone together."

We were veterans of media spin at this point.

San Diego scored early in the second half, making it 2–0, and again the level of play mellowed.

I know what it is to be gifted space to handle the ball. I play a weekly pickup game that started as all women, but over time more and more fast, skilled men joined us. Sometimes players give me space with the ball even though they could easily steal it; it's my weekly dose of humility, but it pushes me to up my game, too.

San Diego passed to players behind them, moving the ball toward the Grannies' goal. San Diego made a bad pass—on purpose?—and my new BFF chased the ball. "Go, Bull!" I screamed. The defenders hung back a little as she dribbled toward their net. With thirty seconds remaining in the game, Bull passed to number 10.

"Nice pass, Bull—GoGoGoGoGoGoGo!" screamed Allison, jumping up and down as team captain Reineth stopped the ball with the side of her foot. Turning toward the San Diego goal, she slammed it into the net—their first goal of the tournament!

My hands flew into the air. "Vakhegula Vakhegula!" The Grannies ran to the nearest player of whatever team and hugged them. Vuvuzelas brayed. The crowd resounded. A whistle blew, three times. Game over.

The San Diego team lined up in two facing rows and created a tunnel with their arms. The Grannies paraded through and then, gathering at the edge of the field in a half circle, broke out in song (of course). San Diego clapped to the beat as Josephine sang each short verse, and the rest of the Grannies joined in with every chorus. At one point in the refrain, they each raised a knee, stomped their foot down, and swung an arm over their shoulder. The only word I understood of the catchy tune was "A-may-ree-kah" as it came through the chorus each time.

I turned to Beka. "What's this song about?"

"The Grannies are carrying their bags, and they're going to America."
Ahhh—the arm swing was the women throwing their bags over their
shoulder. *Song-as-narrative*. I'd have to add that to my list of Reasons
Why the Grannies Break Out into Song, adding it to *Because they're on
a bus*, *because a new team arrived at the field*, and *because they've just lost a
game*. Everything they did seemed to be accented with song and dance.

Their next number had a word that sounded like *amour* in it. Beka
translated it for me. Roughly it went something like this:

> We are the Grannies.
> We have no enemies;
> We fight only disease.
> We play football and shoot to score,
> And now we run with ease!

Feeling my throat tighten, I reached for the stockpile of tissues in
my pocket.

The San Diego women circled up. "What can we sing?" They con-
ferred among themselves before launching into the Beach Boys' classic
"California Girls." Then it was hugs, hugs, hugs, all around.

"I want to say how happy we are to welcome you to the United
States," said one of the California players, her hair in a high ponytail.
"We're thrilled to have the opportunity to meet you and join in a game
of friendship." Upon Beatrice's translation, the Grannies cheered. "I hope
that this game will only be the beginning of a friendship that will one day
carry our San Diego team to South Africa." More cheers.

"*Inkomu* means 'thank you' in Xitsonga, our language," Beatrice said
in return. "Thank you for the nice time and for the way you play with
us here." She motioned to the field behind her. "We noticed that if you
wanted to score more goals, you could score a lot of goals. But you are
just giving us a chance so that we can play. You see, we are just Grannies,
just happy to play. We would like very much for you to come to South
Africa."

"Sounds like we're going to have a tournament in South Africa,"
Allison whispered to me as my hand clutched my heart.

"Yeah—Beka's already said something about it. It would be amazing if somehow we could get a few teams from the States to go over." Here we were, not even halfway through the Grannies' time in "A-may-ree-kah," and I was already getting excited about our next adventure together. If I'd only known, those months ago, when first watching those Granny videos . . .

Hands clapping, vuvuzelas droning, tongues trilling—Vakhegula Vakhegula celebrated the day, the game, the burgeoning friendship. The San Diego women couldn't figure out how to ululate, but one of the players showed the others that you could make a similar noise by stretching your thumb and index finger across your mouth and repeatedly whacking your cheeks. Soon all their players were doing it, sending the rest of us into belly laughter.

After the requisite joint team photo, Lois turned to me, beaming. "One of the San Diego players said this was her best soccer moment ever, seeing the Grannies dance like they'd won the World Cup." (*Dancing in appreciation of a trophy not actually won, but well deserved*, I noted.) Lois sighed a happy sigh. "Now *this* was a respectful game—you could feel the love. And was just so fun to see the Grannies score!"

"R-E-S-P-E-C-T, find out what it means to me . . ." I whisper-sang under my breath. And for the next couple of hours Aretha was on repeat in my brain.

I heard hooting and looked up to see the Grannies pointing and laughing: Tim-the-tournament-chair was riding in a golf cart, and at the wheel was Granny Beauty, steering in tight circles on the centerline of the field.

Soon after, when the Pinkies took to the field, the South African contingent mostly napped in the meager shade, awakening only to noisy cheers when we made a goal. A low-scoring game was just what they needed to rest, and we graciously delivered: Our game ended in a 1–2 loss for the Lexpressas.

For today's lunch, the Massachusetts Adult State Soccer Association introduced Vakhegula Vakhegula to the American hamburger—beefy, juicy, with all toppings, and, naturally, potato chips on the side. Chatter and giggling filled the shade tent as we ate. On the ground by Coach

Romeo's feet lay a discarded vuvuzela. One of the Grannies picked it up and blew into it heartily. To her surprise, a piece of ground beef shot through the horn and across the tent, sending the Grannies into fits.

Laughing, I turned to Beatrice, who, I noticed, was wiping away tears. "You don't understand," she said, voice breaking. "I've known these women forever. I've *never* seen them laugh so hard." I handed her a tissue from my stash.

Promptly at 6 p.m., the elevator door in the hotel lobby pinged open and a bevy of Grannies paraded out. My eyes widened: This was the first time I'd seen them in traditional Tsonga attire. The bright, saturated colors stood out against the subdued beige of the lobby. Turquoise, crimson, and royal blue knee-length skirts with yards of fabric in layers of tight pleats swished when they walked. Gold, emerald green, and pinky-orange hues accented equally colorful blouses, each with a black sash that knotted above one shoulder and extended down to the far knee. Rainbows of patterned ribbon flittered off the garments. Some of the women wore headscarves reminiscent of the colors of the South African flag. They were all adorned with beaded headbands, necklaces, and bracelets.

"Oh, *wow*," I enthused, "you all look so great." Beatrice's hair was now in shoulder-length beaded braids. Another elevator full of Grannies arrived, adding to the kaleidoscope.

We shuffled over to a corner of the lobby, where the TV was set up, and settled in to watch the evening news. "And next," the local ABC anchor teased, "a South Africa soccer team of grandmothers takes to the field in Lancaster today." Chirps of delight rose from our semicircle of couches and chairs.

When the camera panned across several soccer fields, settling on the Grannies' game, already underway, cheers erupted in the lobby. The reporter introduced the tournament and the team as Grannies dribbled and passed and challenged the opposition whenever they had the ball. Watching footage of themselves, the Grannies all wore broad smiles and murmured appreciatively. The reporter showed restraint, respectfully not mentioning the final score, while the camera now focused on the postgame singing and dancing. I glanced around the hotel lobby and wondered if the Grannies realized that most American teams don't celebrate with song and dance at game's end. Onscreen, Beatrice was ready for her close-up, telling the reporter how excited they all were to be in America.

As other tournament attendees passed through the lobby, they gathered behind us to catch the coverage. The Grannies always seemed to attract admirers, I noticed; appreciation and joy seemed to follow wherever they went. "There are very few times in life that you can be part of such a wonderful thing and have such fun doing it," Lois was saying on screen.

Applause, cheers, and whistles split the air as coverage switched to the latest scoop on the Red Sox.

But Vakhegula Vakhegula's limelight wasn't yet to fade. We ushered everyone to the parking lot to drive to the annual Veterans Cup celebration banquet, where I knew they'd be the belles of the ball. Once again, Bull and I held hands.

"You look just *lovely,*" I said, motioning to her outfit with my free hand. Her eyes laughed and her eyebrows wiggled.

On the grounds of a fancy hotel, some miles away from where we were staying, a ginormous white tent had been erected under which maybe six hundred tournament players, organizers, refs, and coaches were already mingling. (Seriously, we could have placed goals on either end and played a game under it.) The evening's festivities were to include a Yankee-style barbeque dinner, a live band, dancing, and, undoubtedly, plenty of speechifying. As we paraded toward our assigned tables, the Grannies garnered appreciative *oohs* and *aahs*. They were the best-dressed team by far.

I stood back until our guests had taken seats. My buddy Bull's table was already full, so I slipped into an empty chair next to young Coach David. He'd just taken a big bite out of his hot dog when I asked, "So, what's it like to coach the Grannies?"

He covered his mouth with one hand and held up a finger with the other, nodding a quick acknowledgment-cum-apology while he finished chewing. "It's not always easy," he said, placing his napkin on the table. "My friends tease me. *Why are you hanging out with those old women?*" he mimicked in a high-pitched, singsongy voice. "*Why don't you get a real job?*" (It would seem teenagers are the same the world over.) "But they were jealous when they heard I was going to America."

"Ha—I bet they were," I laughed. "But you should be proud of what you're doing. Someday you too will be old, and hopefully there'll be a soccer team for *you*." By now I well understood what a stress reliever practice was for the members of Vakhegula Vakhegula; players may arrive at practice full of worry, they all said, but after running, kicking, and laughing, it was all smiles by the time they left. And if a Granny didn't show up to practice, the coaches would go to her house in person to make sure everything was okay. They'd created a real community for each other. It was beautiful to see.

Thunder rolled in the distance, and the twilight sky began to darken just a little bit faster. The band began its first song of the evening—"I'm your Venus/I'm your fire/At your desire"—and the Grannies perked up. They began to push back from their tables and drift toward the center of the dance floor, moving to the music. I thought about how I'd seen them break into dance a half dozen times; this was the *first* time it was on an actual dance floor.

Several men from the Japanese team, wearing white headbands with a red sun, glided over toward the gently swaying women. But a Lexpressas player moved in front of them, arms crossed, quelling them with a stern look. From a nearby perch, she chaperoned for the rest of the night. I'd increasingly noticed our protective instincts perk up around them. Initially we'd been moved by the video, and then we'd felt an obligation for their safe travel as their hosts. This afternoon, we'd all been transformed into crazed soccer parents, screaming ourselves hoarse on the sidelines. With every passing day, their heartbreaking mix of toughness and vulnerability was bewitching us.

"And now," the bandleader called out, "a special treat from our visitors!" Granny Josephine, who'd evidently made her way onto the stage while I'd been lost in thought, graciously took the microphone with a smile (unlike me, she seemed to have no qualms about having twelve hundred eyes trained on her) and began singing the "Amour" song.

The other Grannies chimed in, and the rest of us all clapped to the beat. More cameras flashed.

"Vakhegula Vakhegula!" one of the Japanese men wailed.

Next thing I knew, Lois was prodding me toward the microphone. "Go ahead and say something."

I blinked.

"Maybe thank everyone for their support?" She urged, gently pushing me.

I ascended the stage in a semi-dazed state, trying to focus on a few familiar faces beaming up at me from the throng.

I'm pretty sure I acknowledged the hard work of the folks who'd made the evening possible—the tournament sponsors and players for the kindness and generosity they'd shown—and I talked about how great it was that the Grannies had managed to come all this way to play. I translated the song they'd just sung—how the Grannies were here to play, have fun, and be healthy.

I must have done okay, because the crowd of my fellow soccer players cheered. I paused and used the moment to take another deep breath. Putting my hands to my heart, feeling a bit wobbly, I concluded simply, "We love you, Grannies."

Wild applause and hollers sounded in agreement. Two thumbs up from Lois, standing in the front row.

I rather numbly made my way off the stage, back to my teammates. Well? It hadn't killed me. When it came to the Grannies, I guess I cared so much that I just *went* for it.

A soccer player approached Lois, waving something in his hand. "Still collecting donations for the South Africans?" he asked, handing her the hundred-dollar bill. "They just *made* the tournament for me."

From my comfortable wallflower position at the side of the tent, I watched dancers bobbing in the glow of the colored lights to a Beatles medley. "Jean," said Allison, leaning next to me. "Beka says she's tired and wants to go back to the hotel. We should gather up the drivers." Just then, a bolt of lightning lit up the tent and the sky released sheets of rain. "Well," she hedged, "let's give it fifteen minutes until this storm passes."

The wind picked up, blowing the rain sideways and driving diners near the tent's edges toward the center for greatest cover. Another streak of lightning lit up the surroundings—not a good time to be near twenty-foot-tall metal tent poles. We hustled the Grannies into the safety of the nearby hotel's lobby.

As Grannies flapped water off their skirts and Lexpressas pulled damp hair off their faces and necks, Beka took me aside and asked if this was an appropriate moment to present us with a gift they'd brought. "Sure," I said, uncertain what this would entail. We guided our group toward a quiet corner.

Heather, Anne, Lois, Tim-the-tournament-chair, and I were invited to stand together. Before us, two Grannies spread a cloth on the ground and motioned for us to kneel on top of it. One by one, the Grannies came forward, dressing us in a hand-embroidered shirt or tying a wrap across one shoulder. They brought forward beaded headbands and bracelets and tiny beaded bags to hang around our necks.

The Lexpressas clapped, Tessa snapping photos all the while. My face flushed with embarrassment, but they were clearly expressing their thanks, so I accepted with humility and enjoyed the moment.

Sniffling (of course), I rose to my feet, and we all made our way to a cluster of couches to wait out the worst of the storm. Beatrice had begun chatting with a young couple milling nearby; when she learned they were about to be married, she excitedly summoned the Grannies to circle around, and they started singing, to the amazement of the young betrothed. Two or three Grannies at a time would step forward to the middle of the circle, turn their backs to the couple, and shake their hips, sending their skirt ruffles into frenzied vibrations. A crowd gathered in the lobby to watch the traditional Tsonga wedding dance, as the couple's nervous grins softened and warmed. At the close of their song of celebration and blessing, the Grannies knelt in front of the happy couple, clapped, and blew whistles.

10

Ukuleles and Vuvuzelas

Eh, for the communication? Thank God that there is what is called
body language. You know, body language speaks fast. I am busy learn-
ing the language because I want to have a very nice relationship with
them.—Abraham Sevor Kwabena, Soccer Grannies coach[1]

"Bull!" I called, motioning her over. "Bull, this is my daughter."

"I'm so happy to meet you," Karen said with a smile.

Bull told me I have a beautiful daughter. When a couple of Grannies began stroking her blonde ponytail, Karen flashed me a look of amused surprise. But she seemed to take it all in stride.

For this game, their final match of the tournament, the Grannies were wearing white jerseys. Lime green kerchiefs with a band of pink flowers capped their heads.

One Granny, bending over to lace her cleats, struggled to reach her feet. "May I?" Karen asked, quickly kneeling to tie the shoelaces.

Nearby, Beka sat in a collapsible camp chair, thumbing through a newspaper. I put my hand on her shoulder in greeting; she looked tired.

She'd slept much better last night, she assured me—"Thank you for asking." But "we're glad today's is the last game." No surprise there.

I saw she was reading the *Boston Globe* article from that morning.

A fantastic photo of the Grannies celebrating with the San Diego team spanned the front page of the sports section, but I'd been less enamored of the reporter's choice of words: "Long before Reineth did the chicken waddle windup and kicked the ball that scored her South African team's first goal at a soccer tournament here yesterday . . ."[2]

The casual snark felt disrespectful! That reporter should try playing three days' worth of soccer, back-to-back, in ninety degrees' relative humidity *at the age of eighty*. Some people.

The Grannies' soccer skills were described as "more pluck than prowess." Fair enough. But "when they finally left the field, some of the South Africans sought help from ambulance workers nearby, as others walked off their pain." Oh, please. I hadn't heard of any Grannies requiring medical attention, and I'd been there the whole time.

I was disappointed that my hometown paper had missed so much of the heart of the story, the larger issues that the *New York Times* and *Los Angeles Times* had captured. But I knew how much Beka valued publicity for the team, so I had to be happy the *Globe* had covered their visit at all.

Now Beka was translating the article for the Grannies gathered around her. (I briefly considered suggesting that she translate "chicken waddle" as "the glide of a graceful crane.")

"May I keep this copy?" she asked, looking up at me. I guess she hadn't been upset by the reporter's tone.

"Oh, sure," I said, kneeling beside her chair. We were at the halfway point of their visit, the tournament was wrapping up, and, crazy as it was to think of it, it was already time to talk departure logistics. "Hey, Beka, do you think the Grannies can maneuver through the airport with two roller bags each? Heather's collected some secondhand suitcases, and we asked around and a bunch of people are ready to donate whatever stuff would be most useful to you all back home."

"Clothes for children would be wonderful," Beka said without hesitation.

"Underwear!" yelled a nearby Granny, with possibly even less hesitation.

Not so different from my own grandmother, then. She could never have too many flannel pajamas and high-waisted briefs in her bureau.

The competitors from Hawai'i arrived, decked out in pale blue jerseys punctuated with a single red hibiscus. They greeted the Grannies warmly and expressed their delight to be playing soccer with them. (Vakhegula Vakhegula were celebrities by now, after all.)

For most of the first half, Hawai'i controlled the play, connecting on passes and carrying the ball toward the Grannies' goal, which Beatrice—once again in goal—kept stopping, hopping on her good foot to regain her balance.

"Nice save, Beatrice!"

Allison turned to me. "Did you know Beatrice is a reserve police officer?"

"*What?*" So many talents. I already knew she had worked for the Department of Justice and been a senior administrator at a hospital *and* held a degree in theology. She'd told me of her love of preaching and her dream of one day opening her own church. And here she was, bouncing along the pitch, playing keeper *with a broken foot*. I needed a nap.

"Good defense, Flora," shouted Heather, as a Hawai'i player made a weak shot on goal—intentional?—which Beatrice easily scooped up.

"Jean?" I turned to see a white-haired gentleman wearing a broad-brimmed hat and carrying a folding chair that doubled as his cane.

I smiled at him expectantly, blankly.

"E. B. Swain. Pleased to meet you," he said, offering his hand. "I had to see the Grannies in action."

E. B. Swain . . . E. B.—then it clicked: He was a doctor from Connecticut who'd read about the Grannies in the *New York Times* and sent us a contribution. He'd even called me a few times during fundraising to check on our progress.

I was so touched he'd come to see us in person. Ignoring his offered hand, I instead gave him a quick embrace. "Thank you so much for making the trip!"

E. B., yet another Granny admirer, unfolded the three legs of his cane-slash-seat and perched next to me.

A cheer from the crowd drew my attention back to the pitch. Beatrice was on the ground, emerging from the net with the ball in her arms and a wide smile on her face. She'd held the score to nil-nil and was well on her way to winning most valuable player.

But even Beatrice's athleticism had its limits, and soon after Hawai'i managed to score, twice in quick succession.

The coaches ran up the sidelines, shouting advice. The midfield Grannies connected on a nice string of passes approaching the Hawai'i goal. The defense appeared to be giving them space to handle the ball. I explained to Karen and the doctor that each team was taking a little while to figure out how to play the Grannies in a respectful way.

"*Good* shot, Lizzy. Next time a goal."

"Yes, Beauty. Awesome pass."

"Nice *de*-fense, Norah; keep up the *de*-fense."

"Way to run it, Mercy."

"*Great* throw-in, Josephina."

"Vakhegula Vakhegulaaaaaa!"

We were referring less and less often to the team roster cheat sheet, I realized.

Reineth demonstrated her ball-handling skills as the Grannies charged up the field in support.

"Four on three," Allison bellowed. "Go, Grannies!" More Granny players were attacking the net than there were Hawaiian players defending.

Another shot on goal missed by a few feet. That's the worst; I hate when I visualize the perfect goal but my skills just can't get me there. If the other team were to stop me with a great defensive move, that'd be one thing; but when it's my own failure to execute . . . *ugh!* I hate it.

The Grannies remained on the attack, with only measured resistance from Hawai'i. Maradona and Lizzy carried the ball up the field, displaying a perfect series of give-and-go passes, allowing Maradona to cross the ball in front of the net to Lizzy, who tapped it into the goal.

Mayhem broke out on the field.

Lizzy, Maradona, and even the Hawaiian keeper celebrated with a six-armed hug. On the sidelines, we were crazed. Karen was screaming. Coaches Romeo and David had launched into a vuvuzela duet. I clasped my hands in delight.

The head ref glanced at his watch, patiently waiting for the celebration to wane, and then whistled to signal the end of the game.

The teams lined up behind their goalies. As they passed by each other, the Hawaiian players hung a lei of green leaves around the neck of each Granny. Karen handed water bottles to jubilant Grannies as they paraded off the field.

While they had outspirited their opposition during the previous days' postgame festivities, today the Grannies faced their fiercest competitors yet. Hawaii celebrated with strumming ukuleles and sang, "Tiny bubbles/ pearly shells." The landlocked Grannies countered Don Ho with a song about carrying your babies while working in the field (translation per Beatrice). Then Hawai'i sang about the sea, replete with hula sways.

"Hey, T," I called to the little boy on the bike, "where's the cookout?" Not slowing as he raced by, Heather's son, Tamerat, pointed ahead to a cluster of townhouses surrounded by trees. (This was not, as we'd had to explain to the Grannies, "Jean's village"—just a run-of-the-mill American neighborhood.) Mark carried the beer and Karen the fruit salad, complete with fresh blueberries. We made our way past a few condos with swaying balloons at the doorways—marking where the Grannies were now staying.

Several of Heather's neighbors had generously offered to open their houses to us so the Grannies could enjoy a bit of American home comfort once tournament play had wrapped up. Heather had chosen hosts who lived close together and could take two or three Grannies so they'd each have a buddy.

At a grassy area encircled by the townhouses, some fifty people were milling about half-laden tables, a few smoking grills, and dozens of lawn chairs. They were neighbors, Lexpressas, their families, and, of course, our South African visitors.

Tonight I was wearing the traditional Tsonga attire I'd been ceremonially gifted the night before: a yellow beaded choker-style necklace with stripes of green, pink, and blue, and a maroon wrap, tied over one shoulder, just as I'd seen them do. Printed at the center of my wrap was the larger-than-life full-color face of a Black man identified as Mswati III—crowned king of Swaziland—as he'd looked at the age of eighteen, the youngest ruler in the world in his day. He had enjoyed the ministrations of fifteen wives and a famously lavish lifestyle. Nelson Mandela he was not, I concluded, but I was still so grateful for my Granny gift.

"Our cultural exchange is proving memorable for both my neighbors and our visitors," Heather said to me in a low voice, eyes wide with meaning. Evidently, one hostess had given her own bedroom over to the Grannies and opted to sleep on the sofa. Her guests were flabbergasted, unable to comprehend that a White person would give up her bed. Another Granny had remarked at breakfast that prior to this trip she hadn't ever eaten with a White person before. Not once. I took a sharp inhale, my chest suddenly tight. Heather's eyes still wide, she slowly nodded in exaggerated significance. I wondered—had any of Heather's neighbors ever hosted a Black houseguest before?

Apparently the size of the modest townhouses was considered palatial to some of our guests. I was grateful we hadn't put them up in McMansions. It felt peculiarly important to me that we provide a more modest view of America.

Other feedback was more amusing. "One of my neighbors ran over to my condo in a panic," Heather said, her voice colored with a laugh. "She was in a total tizzy, yelling, 'Heeeeeeeelp—they don't speak English! *They're in the bathtub.*'" Heather had rushed to her neighbor's house in alarm, sprinting up the stairs to the bath, where she'd found two Rubenesque Grannies, standing in the tub, in all their God-given glory and nothing else, struggling with myriad silver knobs on the tiled wall, clucking in frustration. Oh, I knew this unique torture full well—foreign plumbing is *the worst*. I remember tentatively approaching my first-ever squat toilet, panicking over which direction to face, praying that I did not slip into the murk. "The Grannies shrieked when we got the warm water started," Heather said. "I think it was a good shriek."

Beka and Mark were in conversation, chatting about the team. "How old are your players?" he asked.

"The oldest is eighty-four years," Beka replied. "She didn't travel to America, but she plays every week." Mark's mother is an avid tennis player in her eighties; he knows the type.

"But you have to understand," Beka continued. "American women can play soccer. In our culture, it's taboo. Before I started this team, these women could not even think to play. Many of them never even had a chance to go to school."[3]

"Beka," said Allison, walking up to our group, "I was just talking to Beatrice, and she told me your games in South Africa are only thirty minutes. The Grannies never played a ninety-minute game before?" Beka shook her head no. "Oh, my god! What kind of hosts are we?" Allison cried. "We made them play jetlagged, in sweltering heat, ninety-minute games, three days in a row! Oh, Beka. Your women are so tough."

More Lexpressas were arriving, carrying cling-wrap-covered bowls of salads and sides and trays of desserts. At the grill, Heather's husband was tending a variety of sizzling meats. "How are our gogos this evening," asked Tessa, her huge camera bag slung over one shoulder.

"Gogos?" I echoed, 97 percent certain she was not inquiring about nightclub dancers.

"*Gogos* is the Zulu word for 'grandmothers,'" she explained. "It's a term of endearment." *Gogos* are respected elders in the community who help raise the grandchildren with love and discipline. Traditionally their approval is sought for prospective marriages, and they run the home if the grandfather dies or is away, holding everything together and making the family's day-to-day decisions.

"Ooh, excuse me," Tessa said quickly, "I see a photo opportunity." And with that she hurried away to train her camera on a circle of Grannies, Lexpressas, and kids. Bull grabbed my hand and pulled me into the circle too; Karen joined us. Granny Josephine led us in song, as usual taking each short verse for herself, the rest of us meeting her with the chorus—*Sha-way! Sha-way!* More or less in unison we raised our knees and then stomped our feet, smiles contagious. I met Karen's eye with a big grin.

More women and children joined us, our circle growing. The Grannies sang their "America" story-song about leaving their fields and taking a big trip. I did my best to follow the dance moves; the footwork was straightforward enough, but you had to catch the right spot in the song to extend one arm high in the sky and then back down and across to the far hip. The Americans sang a few folk songs, and the Grannies whistled in appreciation. My *gogos* finished with what I thought of as the "Amour" song—the one about the Grannies fighting only disease. Lizzy and Allison took hands to twirl in the middle of the circle, finishing the song with a laughing embrace.

"Meat's ready!" Heather's husband called from a cloud of smoke. Reineth gathered Vakhegula Vakhegula into a tight circle. Each woman closed her eyes and began reciting her own prayer aloud, creating a murmur of blended voices. I bowed my head. The benedictions concluded, Heather announced, "*Dinner* is *served*," and motioned us over to the tables, now completely covered in dishes heaped high. As usual, our male South African guests availed themselves of the buffet first. (Perhaps chivalry in the case of fast-acting poisons?)

I claimed a lawn chair between Bull and Beatrice and balanced my full plate on my lap. "That's the pap I made," said Beatrice, pointing with a smile to the golden mush I'd zeroed in on while making my own way through the line. One of Heather's neighbors had taken Beatrice to the store to buy white cornmeal so she could prepare the pap, a staple of their diet. "It's not quite the same as home. I couldn't find all the ingredients."

I took a bite and found it had a texture like polenta or grits and a mild, sweet, nutty flavor. "I like it," I said.

We sat in the twilight, fireflies dotting the air. Bull and I chatted the evening away between mouthfuls, and I remember thinking the communication was a fun challenge. We stuck to simple topics like that morning's soccer game and the weather. I probably asked her about her kids. At one point, Karen crouched before us and snapped what would become my favorite picture of our time that summer—Bull and me, eating dinner together. I lean toward her with a grin as she looks wide-eyed with surprise, her hand covering her mouth, like we're in cahoots. I'm in the traditional attire, and Bull's in her T-shirt and blue track pants—a literal cultural clothing exchange.

Upon arrival to the United States, members of Vakhegula Vakhegula kneel, prostrate themselves, clap, and ululate—a traditional greeting of the Venda ethnic group and ceremonial expression of respect and gratitude. Boston Logan International Airport, Massachusetts, July 14, 2010. *Photo by Tessa Frootko Gordon*

Granny Florah Maceve arrived prepared to share with her American hosts everything worth knowing about her country. Boston Logan International Airport, Massachusetts, July 14, 2010. *Photo by Tessa Frootko Gordon*

(L–R) Grannies Josephine Nkuna, Ennie Moyo, and Annah "Bull" Masesa Vuma flabbergast the Americans with their talent for carrying bulky items, hands-free. Veterans Cup, Lancaster, Massachusetts, July 15, 2010. *Photo by Tessa Frootko Gordon*

Anne Strong defends the Massachusetts Bay State Breakers against Norah Mtileni's attack on behalf of Vakhegula Vakhegula at the twelfth annual Veterans Cup. Recently rechristened "Soccer Fest," the annual tournament, run by the US Adult Soccer Association, features women's and men's divisions for players ranging from forty-plus to over seventy-five years of age. Lancaster, Massachusetts, July 15, 2010. *Photo by Tessa Frootko Gordon*

Josephina Baloyi and Josephine Nkuna (brandishing vuvuzela) rally their fellow Grannies. Lancaster, Massachusetts, July 15, 2010. *Photo by Tessa Frootko Gordon*

(L–R) Pat O'Conor, Kate Benson, Heather Broglio, Joy McCallum, Stacey Hamilton, Saie Sabet (partially obscured), and Catherine Steiner of the Lexpressas cheer on their favorite South African team. Lancaster, Massachusetts, July 15, 2010. *Photo by Tessa Frootko Gordon*

Lizzy Mongwe, veteran marathoner, is one of fourteen footballers who traveled from Limpopo to compete in the Veterans Cup. Lancaster, Massachusetts, July 15, 2010. *Photo by Tessa Frootko Gordon*

An impromptu dance party breaks out following tournament play, attracting media attention. Lancaster, Massachusetts, July 15, 2010. *Photo by Tessa Frootko Gordon*

(L–R) Power brokers Catherine Steiner, Heather Broglio, and Beka Ntsanwisi plot greatness from the sidelines. Lancaster, Massachusetts, July 15, 2010. *Photo by Tessa Frootko Gordon*

Hands on hearts, the Grannies sing the South African national anthem: (L–R) Beauty Kgatle, Rossina Mathe, Josephine Nkuna, Josephina Baloyi, Gayisa Modjadji (Vakhegula Vakhegula), Lois Kessin (Bay State Breakers), and Catherine Steiner (Lexpressas). Lancaster, Massachusetts, July 15, 2010. *Photo by Tessa Frootko Gordon*

Accompanied by a delighted Jean Duffy (upper left, chin on hand, Kleenex in pocket), Vakhegula Vakhegula gather in traditional Tsonga dress to watch their gameplay featured on the ABC evening news. Lancaster, Massachusetts, July 16, 2010. *Photo by Tessa Frootko Gordon*

Heather Broglio and Lois Kessin (foreground) enjoy Jean Duffy's (flustered) reaction to being adorned in traditional Tsonga attire by Josephine Nkuna (L) and BFF Annah "Bull" Vuma. Lancaster, Massachusetts, July 16, 2010. *Photo by Tessa Frootko Gordon*

Beatrice "Messi" Tshabalala receives a well-deserved high five for defending goal against Hawaii's Holomua. Lancaster, Massachusetts, July 17, 2010. *Photo by Tessa Frootko Gordon*

Between matches, the Grannies consider the competition. These athletes remind us that sport does not belong to the young alone; bodies of all ages, sizes, and abilities benefit from playing the beautiful game. Lancaster, Massachusetts, July 17, 2010. *Photo by Tessa Frootko Gordon*

(L–R) Beka Ntsanwisi, Beatrice "Messi" Tshabalala, and Norah Mtileni proudly accept Vakhegula Vakhegula's Veterans Cup championship trophy for the over-sixty division. Boston, Massachusetts, July 18, 2010. *Photo by Tessa Frootko Gordon*

(L–R) Chrestina "Maradona" Machebe, Dineo Raolane (referee), Sam Broglio, Allison LaClaire, and Ella LaClaire scrimmage in the Grannies' hometown of Nkowankowa. Limpopo, August 8, 2011. *Photo by Lafe LaClaire*

(L–R) Tamerat, Heather, and Sam Broglio evince attitude even after a long, event-filled day in Nkowankowa. Limpopo, August 8, 2011. Photo by Catherine Steiner.

Ennie Moyo begins her twilight walk home. Nkowankowa, Limpopo, August 8, 2011. *Photo by Catherine Steiner*

The chief arrives to observe National Women's Day festivities, escorted by a coterie of obeisant village women and his council of elders. Limpopo, August 9, 2011. *Photo by Catherine Steiner*

A traditional Venda dance is performed in commemoration of National Women's Day. Limpopo, August 9, 2011. *Photo by Catherine Steiner*

A parade of local delicacies is laid out for the visiting guests—including this bowl of mopane worms. Limpopo, August 9, 2011. *Photo by Lafe LaClaire*

Sam Broglio is greeted like a rock star by the village children. Limpopo, August 9, 2011. *Photo by Mike Broglio*

Granny Bull
The Fierce Fighter

"I was an intelligent girl," Annah Masesa Vuma says, repeatedly tapping her finger on her forehead.[1] "I schooled until standard five." But by the time she was nine or ten, her formal education was over. "It's just unfortunate that I never had money when I was young to school further. Perhaps if I'd had that chance, I could have been a doctor."

Known as "Bull" by her soccer buddies, she was born in the small village of Burgersdorp in the province of Limpopo on January 10, 1943, the first of six children. Like many of the Soccer Grannies, as a small girl Bull liked jumping rope and was fond of playing *diketo*—a game played with stones, where the object is to move a set number of them on the ground in or out of a hole during the toss of one stone into the air, much like jacks. She and her friends spent most of their free time playing outside. "We went swimming at the river, and that made us *so* happy."

Bull was happy to enjoy the pleasures of childhood and avoid all things objectionable—like *boys*.

"One thing that disgusted me was when I noticed that there were some girls who were doing some naughty things with boys. My grandmother used to tell us that a girl should

Annah "Bull" Masesa Vuma. Nkowankowa, Limpopo, September 2021. *Photo by Dineo Raolane* first grow, get married, and go to join her in-laws while she was still good. I am proud that I did not want to hear anything from anyone wearing trousers."

But even while quite young, Bull shouldered her share of responsibility to assist the family. "We collected wood. We fetched water from the river." One of her favorite chores was periodically resurfacing the home's floor with a homemade plaster made of cattle dung. "We would take the *vulongo* and mix it with sand to make a good mortar. Then we would take a flat, smooth stone." Bull demonstrates how she carefully leveled the mortar by moving her hand back and forth. "Then we would take only *vulongo* and apply it nicely to the already smoothened floor. It looked beautiful."

She was also expected to help her mother tend the homestead.

"My mother's work was to plow. Me, as the first child, I was to hold a hoe during plowing to help plant the seed. My father had donkeys. To get the plow started, we called them by names—Jessey and Japez.

"We harvested. We did everything. We were eating wild spinach, homegrown chickens, and pork. If it was a season for other fruit to be harvested, we would rise early, take a basket, and walk to a certain mountain that produced so many lychees. You wouldn't eat without working first."

Bull's father was a cook at the JCI Mine, where he worked "until he became a pensioner. Job opportunities were there, and we were not suffering."

For the few years Bull attended school, she quite enjoyed her studies and made many friends. Every afternoon they would walk home, chatting and laughing together. But they didn't *only* play at *diketo*.

"At the point roads diverged to take different directions toward our homes, one of us who was the strongest would suddenly block us and draw a line on the ground, and then say to all of us, 'Any one of you who feels that she can fight, I dare her to skip over this line.'"

It was a ritual challenge Bull loved—and was quite prepared to take on. "I dared to skip over the line myself. Then the fight would start. We would fight each other with all our strength."

She and her friends enjoyed the sporting competitions so much that they soon established their own *musangwe* fight club. "We formed ourselves into a group of girls who were coming from Burgersdorp, and we would go challenge another group of girls at another village." Everyone standing in a circle, one by one, pairs from the rival groups would walk to the center and spar, until everyone had had a chance. Teammates would yell encouragement as the girls proved their toughness. "We would really fight during those days."

As an older girl, after she stopped schooling, Bull labored in the fields alongside her mother to help feed the family. It was grueling work, and she loved dancing as a welcome break. "A tycoon family owned a brass band. We would go there every Saturday in the afternoon to dance. And before it became late, we would go home to sleep." Sometimes Bull would visit a newly married friend, usually living at the in-laws' place, where she would help with the chores. "We would grind the maize, collect wood, wash the family's laundry, and clean their house. We enjoyed it so much when we were treating one of our own with such kindness."

Eventually the time came for Bull to start her own family. She was married in 1960. "Yes," She looks down to count on her fingers. "I was seventeen."

It wasn't a match Bull had chosen for herself, but rather one that had been arranged for her by family members.

"My husband and I, we did not meet. There was no such a thing as a guy meeting a girl and telling her that he loved her. No! A gentleman would go to his aunt to tell her that he saw a beautiful girl to whom he got attracted. His aunt would go tell the lady that her relative named So-and-So loved her."

Sometimes women would run to their grandmothers for advice. "So, Granny," these girls would say, "I am scared; you are the only one who can tell me what to do," and tell her of the proposed match. "If the granny approved, she would answer that it was time for her to get married, as she was a grown-up girl now. Then the granny would go see the gentleman's aunt and tell her that the gentleman might visit. After a few weeks, the gentleman would visit the lady's home."

Once in a while, a woman would reject a man's courtship if she thought he was unattractive; the grannies would again advise. "Those men who are ugly are the ones who will take care of you," they would say. "Handsome ones will easily be taken by other women."

When Bull officially accepted her future husband's proposal, the marriage settlement was negotiated. "In my case, he paid 115-rand bride prize"—approximately $130 of today's US dollars. The contract paid, it was time for Bull to begin married life. "They came to marry me, though my heart was not absolutely settled." Even so, she went through with the ceremony. "We celebrated in dance." When the festivities were over, she was welcomed into her in-laws' household, where she was to help run the home.

Her husband had employment in Johannesburg and so returned there immediately after the wedding. But work was not steady for the Black men of South Africa at that time. "Jobs where people worked for White people, those kinds of jobs were scarce." Unemployment was a constant threat. "We were suffering because my husband came home and stayed for years, not working." But mouths still had to be fed, so Bull turned to the skills she had learned from her mother.

"We depended on farming and grinding maize to survive. We had to plow and harvest a lot of maize. We cooked and ate *moroho*, wild spinach. Working for a White man was not common. What was common was to work for ourselves to survive, and it was through farming and plowing for life to go on."

In addition, resourceful Bull would continually turn to entrepreneurship to make ends meet. "In my life I have been blessed with a business mind. I started my first business when I was living in Meadowlands, zone 8, number 556." Meadowlands was an area outside of Johannesburg established as part of the Natives Resettlement Act of 1954. Black families had been forced by police to gather their belongings. They were transported in trucks from the designated White areas of Johannesburg to be zoned by ethnic group in flimsy housing with no toilets, running water, or electricity.

"Life was too tough. We were suffering, so I ended up making a business to survive. My late grandma used to visit me through dreams. Let me tell you that you must never let anyone lie to you that there are no spirits at cemeteries. Those people are our ancestors, and one day they will give you luck. So I dreamed my late granny saying that I must go to a certain dumping place."

Bull asked her other grandmother, who was still living, to accompany her to the dump, as it was then 3 a.m., and she was scared to go out alone.

"Shortly after we had walked past a clinic, I saw my late granny, but she quickly disappeared. We knelt and prayed, and then I continued to walk, following my late granny's shadow. Suddenly her shadow disappeared. I stood still a bit. Then I saw my late granny pointing me at something to take. I found that it was a five-hundred-gram Lactogen tin."

Inside the battered tin of Nestlé infant milk formula, Bull found a roll of one-rand notes and five shillings. Amazed, she tucked the windfall in her clothes and went home, puzzling over what it could mean. The next evening, "I dreamed my late granny telling me to open a tobacco business." A neighbor loaned Bull a board to grind tobacco and a sieve to sift the snuff, and with that her first business was launched.

She was simultaneously tending the land, running her shop, keeping house, and raising a family. "I was still breastfeeding my firstborn child when I started that business," Bull recalls, remembering how thrilled she'd been, even before the baby had been born, to become a mother and start raising a child. "I kept on asking myself if it was indeed *me* having a baby." Over the years, she and her husband would have three daughters. "We were a good family."

But the peace was not to last.

"Things went wrong only when my husband started to tumble. By the word *tumble* I mean when a man leaves his home to attend to his cheating business. He was not coming home, and whenever he *did* come, he would tell me that he had been working overtime."

But Bull was wise to his deceptions, and they troubled her greatly. Soon, she was once again visited by her late grandmother in a dream. "She showed me this man with another woman, embracing each other."

It was 1977; Bull was only thirty-four, the mother of three, putting her everything into keeping her family safe and healthy. But tensions had grown unbearable with her husband, and eventually they erupted into open animosity.

"One day he came home and found me wearing my Swiss Mission church attire, ready to go to the church service. He ordered me to disrobe. He took that church attire of mine and a box of matches and set it alight. That was the beginning of the fierce fight between us. We lived the life of fighting from that time until 1979."

During these two years, Bull's husband, determined to maintain absolute supremacy under his own roof, did not allow his wife to attend her family events. This pained her greatly. "During my uncle's death, he refused me to go to attend his funeral. Most heartbreaking was the departure of my dad. I couldn't go, and that ate me up. It pained my heart."

Soon, the fighting turned physical. "My husband beat me. Too much. Too much. He hit me every night." Bull raises her eyebrows, eyes wide. "I used to have teeth," she says, stopping to remove a dental bridge, revealing a gap of four front teeth. The abuse only grew worse.

One day, Bull decided she'd had enough.

"My husband arrived home from Johannesburg late at night. He knocked on the door. No one immediately heard the knock, because my children and I were fast asleep. Finally I heard the knock. As soon as he entered the house, he wanted to know why I had taken such a long time to open the door for him. He started beating me, but that night I fought back.

"At one stage during our fight, I fell, and he was beating me while I was seated. I asked him to let me stand but not beat me while I was seated. I told him then that he was ill-treating me and enough was enough. I further told him that he was to make sure to beat me to death that night, because if he wouldn't, I was going to pack and go home after the fight. He asked me where I would go, as I was just a bloody dog."

With this recollection, Bull pauses, checking her emotions. "I replied to him that I was *not* a dog."

The situation untenable, Bull knew what she must do. "I had to get out. No good. I get a divorce."

Any fear she may have had that things would only grow harder without a husband to help carry the load almost immediately dissipated; life improved dramatically after the divorce was finalized. "I have experienced joy I had never thought I would ever experience in my life since we parted. I think God knew that my children wouldn't have a good future if I were raising them with that man." The ever-resourceful Bull began to flourish once she'd left the abusive relationship. "After we were divorced, I did everything and completely relied on myself for the future of my children. I had cattle. I had goats." Bull soon started a new venture, selling homemade sweets to pay for her children's schooling. She knew how hard life could be for a woman without an education, and she wanted something better for her girls.

All three daughters are now grown, with families of their own. "They are now well settled at their homes with their husbands. One is working in Ireland, and she made me board a fly machine. Yes, a lot of people haven't even boarded a fly machine. I am proud of that, but I don't brag about it," Bull says with a laugh.

Today she has seven grandchildren and three great-grandchildren. One granddaughter is a lawyer and one a doctor, career opportunities Bull never had. She is elated to see her family thrive.

She now lives alone in a small cottage, a lifestyle she finds she quite enjoys after such an eventful life. "I don't feel lonely! I stay with God."

Her routine is much less frenetic now that she has only herself to care for. "My house and its surrounding, it is very clean. I get up in the morning and clean my house. In the afternoon before the sun sets, I clean my kitchen with a mop and check everywhere dirt might have accumulated and clean it. I check all the rooms."

Ever the entrepreneur, Bull cuts down and hems sackcloth to sell as small rugs. "Let me just say that I am a seamstress. I learned how to sew back when I was living in Johannesburg. I used to look at other women wearing beautiful and fashionable dresses, and I would just look at them and then go to sew them and sell."

The living keeps her comfortably occupied, but she always makes sure to leave time in the day for exercise. "Some days at 5 a.m. I walk with others to the Letaba Hospital and then walk back"—a good five kilometers from the village. "It's a very long distance for someone my age!"

Though she was already leading a very active life by most standards, as she grew older, Bull could still feel her health going downhill. "I used to feel like blood had concentrated here," she says, touching the back of her shoulders and neck. "It felt like I could burst at times—horrible."

Then, one day in 2007, shortly after she'd turned sixty-four, she received an invitation that was to prove a major turning point in her life. "I was at a church service when a certain woman called some of us to come to the play field." It was Vakhegula Vakhegula. "That was how we started playing soccer! We were younger then; we were playing like nobody else, and no team could beat us."

In short order, Bull's health improved; she felt stronger, and the aches in her shoulders and neck disappeared entirely. "Football has really helped me a lot. I don't feel anything wrong with my body. I am not even under administration of any pills."

Now entering her eighties, Bull has grown to rely on the community she's formed with her fellow Soccer Grannies. It provides a sort of rhythm to her week, along with her devoted membership to the Zion Christian Church, which she has maintained all these years. "If my faith was just a stupid and useless faith, I would have drunk alcohol," she says with a laugh. "I would have also long *loved* to tumble."

Rather, her relationship with God fills her life with a deep sense of meaning. "I don't believe in things that are just nothing; I believe in Jehovah, the God of Christ. I taught my children love according to the book of Corinthians—that a person is a person *because* of other people." It is a life shaped of mutual caring, respect, and leaning on community.

"My life goes well because of this faith," she says simply. "What I will never forget is to thank God for having grown me up to this age."

Rain Falling on Parched Land

What the elders see while sitting, the young ones standing on their toes won't see.—African proverb[1]

THE GRANNIES PEERED OUT THE SMUDGED BUS WINDOWS AT THE upscale shops along Charles Street. Shiny panes of glass showed the wares; taut awnings shaded the cool, welcoming doorways, propped open in the summer's warmth. The bus stopped at a light and turned, grinding up a steep incline. Off to the right, urbanites walked their dogs through city parks. To our left were rows of stately brick townhouses laced with climbing ivy, their windows framed with glossy black shutters, planters sturdy atop front stoops, overflowing with riotous blooms.

We were passing through the posh Beacon Hill neighborhood of Boston, some of the most expensive real estate in the entire city. With a wash of shame and relief, I realized the Grannies couldn't be aware that these homes had the multimillion-dollar price tags while a few miles away, exorbitant rents meant a single apartment might house multiple families pooling their money, each household getting a single bedroom.

Now that the last Veterans Cup match had been played, we'd thought it might be nice for the Grannies to have a day to just relax and sightsee. All too soon they would board their plane home and I would return to the grind of the workweek.

An impatient driver honked as our bus pulled to the curb in front of the copper-domed Massachusetts State House. The Grannies gingerly stepped off the idling bus, dressed in matching white shirts and smart gray caps. Through the wrought iron gates, flung open in welcome, and up the wide granite stairs we made our way, together. With a start, I realized that these were the very steps where Tessa had stood, sixteen years before, waving the flag of South Africa in celebration of Mandela's election.

We toured the opulent House and Senate chambers—leather, mahogany, crystal. State Representative Byron Rushing, member of the Black Caucus, led us out onto a wide columned porch overlooking the Boston Common, a green expanse of lush, neatly trimmed lawns criss-crossed with pedestrian pathways. From our shaded perch, he pointed to a bronze relief statue of a colonel on horseback with volunteer infantry marching alongside. "This statue honors the Black men who fought in the Civil War," he told us. "Take a close look as you depart. The artist brought Black men into his studio as models."

Diligent staff passed out pins in the shape of Massachusetts, which the Grannies secured to their shirtfronts, heavy at this point with tokens from well-wishers and friends. For Beka, there was a framed proclamation: *In recognition of your extraordinary dedication and resilience to improving health and lives through your courageous tenacity*. A flurry of photos captured the Grannies expressing their thanks in a song that echoed through marble hallways.

Back on the street, I squinted in the bright sunshine as our group climbed slowly onto the bus again for a twenty-minute drive to Castle Island, where the view spans Boston Harbor to the Atlantic Ocean beyond. There were finer beaches outside the city, I told Beka, but this time of year they were plagued with biting dark green flies. "No, this is perfect," Beka reassured me. "Most of the Grannies have never seen the ocean before."

Some of the women splashed shin-deep into the ice-cold water, and others scoured the beach for shells and colorful rocks. One asked if we had containers to take seawater home in memory of this extraordinary day.

On blankets we set out a picnic of spicy rotisserie chicken and seasoned rice. I sat next to Beka with my plate on my lap, wiggled my toes in the sand, and felt the warmth of the July sun on my skin.

"For us, it was a roller coaster ride," I said weaving my hand up and down and almost knocking my sunhat off my head in the process. "We were thrilled when you got visas but then devastated when we thought we couldn't find flights for a reasonable price. But in the end, it all worked out. I can't believe the total cost was almost exactly the amount of money our sponsor gave us," I said, my eyes widening, shaking my head. "It was miracle after miracle, right?" I looked to Beka.

"Oh, yes," she said. "When it is hard, you need to hold onto your dream. Your perseverance is tested." This made her thoughtful. "You know, when we go back home, they want to greet us. They're planning a dinner, but I won't attend that function. The Grannies may attend, but I will not attend." Bitterness tinged her voice. "They failed me." *They* must be the government officials who'd reneged on their promise to pay for the flights. "After all I suffered for this country. After I won so many awards."

My heart went out to Beka. To give and give as she did and then to feel as if it were taken for granted . . .

"I do my best," she said with a weary sigh. "But in the end of the day, the president was supposed to be proud of us, but let me down. I am angry. I am *very* angry."

I wasn't sure what to say to this. I absolutely understood her indignation, though, and why she really wanted a trophy to take back to South Africa—a symbol of everything they'd accomplished *without any help from the government.*

"Now my struggle is, when we go back home, we are happy, yes, but we still have to repay the person who helped with visas. I have to pay for transport from the airport to the villages." It would be late night when they arrived, which would bring its own set of problems. "Crime is bad there," Beka said, her face grim. "If they know you're coming from America, they'll think you have valuable things in your bags." She sighed. "I must protect them. I must deliver each Granny to her home. I want them safe."

My shoulders drooped. "Yes, we want them to be safe."

The women chatted and ate around us; one group was laughing uproariously over something or other. How little I knew of the challenges Beka was facing down. I'd become so attached to these women, and it alarmed me to think of them in peril. By now, everyone in their hometowns would have heard that Vakhegula Vakhegula had visited the United States. My stomach churned.

"Okay, Beka," I said, resolved. "What do you need to get everyone home safely? Taxis? How much would taxis cost?" Together we brainstormed. Could she put one of the male escorts in each taxi and have the men dropped off last? I knew we couldn't settle all the travel expenses before the Grannies departed, but when South Africa Partners had agreed to collect donations for us, this was just the sort of conundrum they prepared to take on. Maybe they had the means to give Beka an advance to cover this last leg of their journey home. I also knew I could call upon a few folks who'd made larger donations and see if they could give a little more.

We'd pool our resources to get that little bit of extra money that would make all the difference to the Grannies' safety.

High levels of crime and poverty often coexist, but it is rampant income inequality that drives lawlessness. Lawlessness increases as social norms are eroded by external pressures—such as limited opportunities for employment, a lack of education, and fractured family structures. The province of Limpopo, I had come to understand, was struggling with all three.

Just like Bull, who'd sold sweets to make extra money after her divorce, the resourceful could often stave off the worst of poverty through a little creativity and hustle. But even with supplemental income, these families were often facing tough choices when the bills came due; many were only one illness away from destitution. And when you can't afford a prescription, you use whatever you have on hand—even if the medication was prescribed for someone else or for a different ailment.

In impoverished households in Limpopo, school fees and uniforms are often the first expenditures to be dropped when money is tight.

I thought again of how young Beka had pleaded with her parents to pay for uniforms for classmates who'd been going without. Education, she'd understood even as a child, is a vital prerequisite to finding stable employment; students who complete a secondary education in South Africa greatly improve their prospects for finding work.

But even understanding this, sometimes longer-term aspirations are derailed by the immediacy of poverty; many leave school for a work opportunity that will pay the bills *now*, despite the implications it will have for their future ability to earn.

And so it is community, and often a group of neighborhood women, that steps in to try to fill the gaps for the poor of South Africa. Prayer groups originally organized by missionaries for the women in their congregations have evolved into *manyanos*, support groups where the economic insecurity and political strife facing each woman can be shared by the group. Here they affirm that God alone has the power to save and provide for their families. Not long ago it was also here that they once beseeched God to bring an end to brutal apartheid. The *manyano* women gather under the trees to pray, do crafts, and eat together. If one member of the group grieves, they might devote the entire meeting to prayer and song. Getting advice from one another and knowing that they are not alone is a comfort. They take on projects like planting a community garden or stepping in to provide childcare during a family crisis. Together the women find empowerment and hope through positive change.

Another coping strategy are women's savings groups, called *stokvels*, where money is pooled for the benefit of the group. Participants invest when they have extra money and then together determine how to allocate the funds when unexpected expenses arise. Like an insurance policy, the *stokvel* is a creative, resourceful survival strategy for coping with poverty, offering these women a bit of control.

Similar but more focused shared aid is found in burial societies, to which each member contributes monthly and then withdraws when a need arises to cover family funeral expenses. *Stokvels* and burial societies also protect money from potential family disputes—grannies squirreling away funds to help other grannies. But even this community-based aid comes with its risks: Members may disappear or renege on their commitments.

To battle steadily rising unemployment and the broadening income gap between its richest and poorest citizens, in the mid-1990s the postapartheid government finally extended full old-age pensions to Black residents aged sixty and older. These grants exceeded the national average income, so many elders were now making more money than they ever had during their entire working lives, often making them the primary earners for their entire extended family.

The relief funds have been like rain falling on parched land—desperately needed but not nearly enough. Many pensioners share the monthly payout with their children and grandchildren, stretching it well beyond its intended beneficiaries. The state also gives supplemental grants to mothers to cover childcare costs, but sometimes the money doesn't reach the grandmother bearing the actual childcare expense.

As such, the old-age pensions and childcare grants have often become the source of nasty family fights. Even worse, in some cases adult children and teenage grandchildren have stolen the pension money, sometimes resorting to violence to do so. My shock and disgust that a grandmother, working so hard to keep the family afloat, would ever be targeted by her own family doesn't make the violence any less likely.

I looked at my friends—one dozing in the sun, a gentle smile on her relaxed face; one by the surf's edge, yipping at the cold bite of the water lapping at her bare ankles, her companion laughing and pointing; one sitting with her arms around her knees, gently swaying side-to-side, humming a tune to herself. To make sure the Grannies got home safely, I'd ask and ask and ask, until we'd found enough.

Granny Norah
The Hard Way

"I am so proud of being involved in football,"[1] says Norah Mtileni, sixty-seven, resident of Nkowankowa. She's a wife, mother, grandmother, entrepreneur, and athlete. "I started with Vakhegula Vakhegula right when they first formed," she says, with obvious relish. "It changed my life. I used to get tired easily, but since I have been playing football, my body is so strong, and a lot of aches have gone. I have been a happy woman since I have been playing football. My fellow sisters—we take care of one another. I am living so well. My soul has settled."

Norah has seen her share of adversity throughout her life. She grew up in a poor family, and her father died while she was very young; she doesn't remember him at all. "To be honest, life was too hard because my dad was no more. It was a mammoth task for our mother to raise us single-handedly. All in all, we were five children. My mother plowed and ground maize so that we could eat."

Maize—a central part of the South African diet—would have been supplemented by produce from the family garden. And when that wasn't enough, the family might ask for food donations from relatives, neighbors, or friends.

Norah Mtileni. Nkowankowa, Limpopo, September 2021. *Photo by Dineo Raolane*

Life became harder as Norah's mother struggled with single parenthood. "All the partners my mum had afterwards, to help her to raise us, did not make life any better. There was abuse. Sometimes she would be beaten in front of us, and that experience left my heart in tatters. My mother really raised us the hard way."

Like most girls of her age who grew up on cattle *kraals* in that era, Norah helped herd and plow, collected wood for the fire, fetched water, did laundry, and ground maize down to a fine flour for cooking. But she hoped for something more for herself. Just as she reached school age, however, "someone said school was for boys and we girls needed the time to do our chores," so she was not permitted an education. "That is very painful," she recollects, her brow furrowed, "because sometimes one thinks that perhaps she could have been something big if her parents had allowed her to go to school." She shakes her head. "Truly, by refusing us to go to school, we were sinned against."

As an older girl, Norah and some of her friends sought work at nearby farms to help their families make ends meet. "Life then was too hard. We could see how our families suffering." The income she brought in, however meager, would have been critical to her family's well-being.

She looked forward to Saturdays when she and other girls dressed in traditional attire and went to dance to the percussive *xigubu* music. "Life was going on just like that."

Soon after Norah came of age, she began drawing the attention of boys. "I was married a long time ago." She laughs. "I cannot tell when exactly I was married—likely because I'm not educated?" Even so, she remembers clearly what happened. "One day when I was out relaxing with my friends, I came across this man who told me that he loved me. He kept on telling me this for a year, and I was still refusing. I told him that I wouldn't love him because he was a local guy; I wanted to marry someone from beyond our village."

Her suitor moved to Johannesburg to work but continued to write Norah letters declaring his love, vowing to never stop pursuing her. Finally Norah wrote back, agreeing to his courtship. Soon after, his elders came to her house to negotiate with her mother in the traditional way; it wouldn't do to overtly acknowledge that the couple had already met, corresponded, and decided on a future together. His parents showed her a photograph of her husband-to-be. "Without delay, I told them that I loved him."

Life was hard for the young couple. Her husband's elder brother advised him to come home from Johannesburg to be with his growing family, but there were stretches when her husband had no work. They would ultimately have seven children—two girls and five boys. "*Heei!*" Norah exclaims "Life was too heavy for us. So often we did not have food and our kids were starving."

South Africans use the expression *eating from one pot* to describe how community helps meet basic needs. "We shared our problems with some of our relatives," Norah recalls, "but still life was hard." Asking for help is never easy. "We really have raised them the hard way," she repeats.

Her husband managed to find temporary work, and to help support her large family Norah started a business selling secondhand clothes while also working at a local factory. The beaded purse she now wears around her neck was sewn by a grandmother also looking to make ends meet.

Life was already stressful, and when one of her children began suffering from mental illness, Norah soon grew overwhelmed. "I got depressed," she says. "I didn't know what to do." She knew he would become a target in the community, and it weighed heavily on her. "Many Africans, we believe that when one's mind is ill that it's a result of witchcraft. My blood pressure was always high because I would worry."

She began to lean heavily on her faith. "Whenever I have difficulties in my life, I end up kneeling down and praying. I report all my problems to God. I am just happy for the love of God. My faith is in my heart, and I find my life goes well when I live it according to the way God wants."

Today several of Norah's children have moved away for work—to Johannesburg (250-plus miles away) and Cape Town (more than 1,000 miles away). As for her grown children who cannot find work, sharing housing across multiple generations helps stretch the family's income further. In a home shared with these adult children, her husband, and four of the grandchildren, Norah is kept busy.

"I wake up early and do exercises. I stretch and I also jog about five kilometers. I take care of my grandchildren. I bathe them, cook for them, and feed them. I take my grandchildren to school. When I feel like praying, I pray. I also sweep and wash laundry. Just like that, life goes on."

She teaches her grandchildren to respect their elders, for *a house without a grandmother is like a road that goes nowhere.*

"I am so proud that I have grown up to this age and that I am a pensioner," Norah says. "With the government money I receive every month, I can buy for my kids everything that makes them happy."

By pooling resources, relying on community, and working well into old age, Norah has found a hard-won stability for her family.

"I have since become aware that everything that happens to one in life must just be accepted regardless of how hard it is," Norah says. "This was hard for me, but I told my God that I was going to accept it because it was meant for me."

In wisdom, acceptance, and perseverance, for Norah life goes on—just like that.

May You Score Many Goals

Doesn't life go on? Yes, it goes on.—Mamaila Chauke Novela, Soccer Granny[1]

MY BUDDY BULL WAS MOTIONING FOR ME TO SIT NEXT TO HER. IT WAS our last bus ride together before she flew home.

"Seventeen, eighteen, nineteen," Allison counted out. "No one lost!" A playful cheer rose along with a few hands in the air. The bus's angry diesel engine revved, we lurched forward, and off we went, headed for Harvard Stadium to attend a professional soccer game.

In point of fact, we were off to a *women's* professional soccer game. Boston's squad had helped found the Women's Professional Soccer league three years earlier and was supported by a fervent if smallish fan base, despite the constant naysaying that women's sports would never bring in enough people or money to sustain meaningful sponsorships. The thing of it is, if you don't give a team sufficient exposure, it's hard to reach enough fans and generate ticket sales, and then the naysaying becomes a self-fulfilling prophecy. It's the age-old battle for parity that women's sports have waged. But our group would holler our support and cheer on the Boston team to victory.

As we pulled up to the stadium, we were met by staff who led the Grannies to VIP seats right at the edge of the field—thanks to Lois and her connections. Allison and I joined a group of Lexpressas in humbler seating and lent our whistles and fist pumps as the home team took to the field in blue and white.

I watched the players sprint back and forth in precision-passing drills and then hammer shots on goal, wowed by their power and agility. One of the Lexpressas tapped me on the shoulder and pointed to the mammoth stadium screen: "Welcome to the South African women's soccer team, Vakhegula Vakhegula!" it read, and then switched to the camera feed, which was panning down the row of field-side seats. One by one, the Grannies' faces lit up as they saw their images on the big screen.

Allison and I were on our feet, hollering ourselves hoarse, when her cell phone rang. "It's Heather," she said. One of the Grannies had been stung by a bee, and the bite was reddening and swelling; Heather was hoping one of us had a Benadryl. "I'd love to avoid a hospital visit, if we can." We rummaged through our bags and pockets, and one of the Lexpressas struck gold. She handed the packet of antihistamines to Allison, who ran superhero-style through the stands. Fifteen minutes or so later, she shuffled down our row again ("Excuse me. Excuse me. Sorry! Excuse me. Thanks."), back to her seat, with good news: The Granny had responded to the medication, and the swelling and excitement both had subsided.

At halftime, we stood to stretch our cramped legs, and Lois marched onto the field, all business, placing herself before a microphone that had been positioned right in front of where Beka was seated. She set a giant canvas sack at her side and did one of those piercing two-finger whistles. (*Jealous.* Try as I might, I've never been able to master that whistle.) "Ladies and gentlemen," she addressed the crowd, "your attention, please." Eventually, the chatter hushed. "Tonight, we are fortunate to have some special guests in attendance, the Vakhegula Vakhegula women's soccer team, here all the way from South Africa."

A cheer rose from the stands.

"This week," she continued, "these women participated in the Veterans Cup, the largest annual adult soccer tournament in the United States. And so it is with great pride that I present this . . ."—here she paused as she bent down and futzed with the canvas bag. Her movements were like a slow-motion replay. She stood up, her arms slipping out of the bag—"... to the winners ..."—to reveal a gleaming two-foot-tall golden trophy cup! Raising it over her head, she finished in a booming voice—"... to the winners of the 2010 Veterans Cup Women's Over-Sixty Division."

I couldn't believe my eyes. A red, white, and blue ribbon attached to the cup's handle fluttered in the breeze. Ladies and gentlemen, I thought to myself, here are your 2010 champions. It was perfect—absolutely perfect—exactly what Beka had wanted to take back to South Africa.

Pandemonium broke out as the Grannies pulled themselves to their feet. No translation needed here!

Lois was extending the cup to Beka, which she took to cradle in her arms, wearing the biggest smile I'd seen on her face since she'd arrived.

The Grannies cheered, ululated, and blew their vuvuzelas. Tessa clicked away, capturing the joyous moment. The Grannies filed out of their seats and ran onto the field, surrounding Beka and the trophy, reaching out to touch it, turning to Tessa with wide smiles as she snapped pictures of each of them. For her part, Bull posed while planting a kiss on the golden cup.

By this time, I'd sidled my way over to their side of the field. "Lois!" I called out. "Lois, the trophy is fabulous. Tell me, tell me—how did you pull it off?"

As soon as she'd heard about Beka's desire to go home with a trophy, Lois told me, she'd gone straight to the favorites of the over-sixty division. "At first they suggested the Grannies borrow the trophy and take a picture with it." Lois wrinkled her face in disgust and annoyance before her eye took on a mischievous gleam. "You can imagine how thrilled I was when they didn't take the division." She talked to the *actual* winning team's captains, and they were all more than delighted to bestow the trophy on the Grannies. They told Lois, "The Grannies won this competition hands down with their spirit and enthusiasm"—a popular sentiment among Veterans Cup players.

"Oh, this is fabulous. Knowing how much it means to Beka to bring home a trophy after all they've gone through? How proud will they be to show this off to their families!" I could already see the golden cup on display in Beka's living room—excellent company for her dozens of other awards.

This was the perfect finale for their visit.

"Lois," I said, my voice full of emotion, "you have my vote for Most Valuable Player."

The next morning, a towering pile of donations sat on Heather's driveway, listing ominously to the right. She'd really rallied the Lexpressas, her neighbors, and a bunch of other generous souls to gather suitcases, clothes, soccer gear, underwear (*never* forget the underwear), and even a pair of small soccer goals for the Grannies to take home with them. Beka had said the children's clothes would go to orphans whose parents had died of AIDS and also to some of the many grandchildren being raised by our own Grannies. We'd initially investigated shipping the donations to South Africa so they wouldn't have to haul everything with them, but the cost was prohibitive. Whatever they couldn't carry off with them to the airport, we'd donate to a local charity.

Heather's bathroom scale stood in the driveway, in front of which the Grannies queued, one by one hoisting their new luggage, stuffed with donations, onto the scale. If the bag weighed fifty pounds or less, Allison slapped a piece of green tape on it; if it was too heavy, Lois and Anne removed some donations or exchanged heavier items for lighter ones before weighing it again.

Once everything we could fit had been distributed, Heather had us circle up. It was time to exchange our parting gifts.

Beatrice was the first to step forward. She presented the Lexpressas with soccer balls on which had been scrawled, *May you score many goals.*

"Oh, this is too precious to kick," I objected, turning mine in my hands to see the signature of every Granny who'd made the trip.

Some of Heather's neighbors gave Beka a photo album filled with pictures taken over the past week.

There was a moment of quiet, and I felt that familiar flutter in my stomach. Stepping forward, I thought about how we'd found each other, across an ocean, through a shared love of soccer. These women we'd come to know had fought against social pressures to play the game, and in doing so built strength—inner and outer—to stand tall and face difficult challenges. Witnessing this had changed me.

"I can't tell you what a delight it's been to have you here," I started out, my voice a bit quiet. "You've inspired us with your zest for life." I cleared my throat and started again, my voice stronger. "We've loved kicking the soccer ball around with you, and we hate to say goodbye. But we'll see you again, soon, in South Africa—because we are sisters in soccer."

Moments later, as Beatrice finished her translation, the Grannies took up a cheer. But I wasn't done.

"When you arrived at the airport, some Grannies laid down on the ground to show respect and express thanks. Now we want to show our respect and to thank *you*." I kneeled down and bent my head low, until it touched the ground. As if we'd rehearsed it, Lois, Anne, Heather, and Allison joined me. I looked up again a second later, and several Grannies were getting on their knees too, while the rest clapped. My eyes welled, but I could still see clearly enough to make out Lois wiping her eyes too. Getting to my feet, I had to move off to the side for a moment to regain my composure.

I felt a hand on my shoulder, and I turned to see Beka. It was time.

"Beka," I said. "Thank you. *Thank you* for bringing the Grannies to America."

She held me firmly at the elbows and looked straight into my eyes. "You must come to South Africa next year." Her voice was strong and steady. "Yes, next year you have to come." She smiled, pulling back. "That's my dream. It will make us so happy."

We turned, our arms around each other's waist, and walked back toward the group.

"When you come there," she said—always planning ahead, never stopping to rest—"you will find us prepared with the Grannies. We will do something great. So just come to South Africa next year."

She stopped and once again turned to me. "Jean, I wish to thank you for the support. You are the first people from another part of the world to believe in us." (I kind of laugh-sobbed and wiped at my eyes.) "The Grannies have flown for the very, very first time in their lives . . . the very first time. And they are so excited and happy to be in America." She smiled again. "Thanks. So much."[2]

She turned to the rest of the Lexpressas and fans. "We'll be in touch, my sisters," she said in a strong voice, nodding firmly—almost a dismissal. I sensed her exhaustion and anxiety to start the journey. This goal had been met; on to the next one—getting the Grannies home safely.

I made my rounds, saying final goodbyes, shaking hands with the men and hugging each of the Grannies, before Heather accompanied them to the airport.

I saved my friend Bull for last. I squeezed her hand and told her I would miss her. She smiled, her eyebrows going up and down, which I interpreted as waves of happiness and sadness; I felt the same way.

"Thank you for the way you take care of us in America," she said. "So happy to be a guest. The buses. Playing soccer. Laughing. America is so beautiful. I don't forget it."[3]

I headed for my car without looking back. It was a while before I could start the engine; I didn't want to drive home until I could see clearly.

That night, Heather called me. My family was out for an evening ice cream cone, and I had to balance my cell phone with my dripping double-scoop. She was calling to fill me in on the Grannies' departure.

They'd circled for a prayer before boarding the yellow school bus for the ride to the airport, she said. "Coach Romeo was in tears saying goodbye to Dan"—her neighbor who'd hosted the men. "Then Dan put his arm around his shoulder and walked him to the bus."

As usual, the men had boarded first, taking the back seats. (I don't know if I would ever get used to that.) Heather was left to help the Grannies lug their fifty-pound bags up the narrow stairs of the bus. It was so full; luggage was on the seats, wedged at their feet, and in the aisles.

"Oh!" she said. "You know all the pins the Grannies collected from the various teams? One Granny had every pin on her shirt. When she was going through security, she set off the metal detector and had to remove every last one of them and go back through!"

"That's hilarious!" We both laughed at the image. "But, Heather, was it *so* hard to say goodbye?"

"Yeah, it was sad, but it was a bit of a relief too, I have to say." I completely understood. It had been an intense week, and we were all sort of in shock that we'd managed to pull it off without any real problems.

"Heather, so much of the trip's success is thanks to you—how you coordinated every last detail of their visit."

"You know," she said, "I've always told people I play soccer with a great group of women. But it really wasn't 'til we took this whole thing on that I understood just how great. Every time I'd ask for help, I'd get at least three offers, minimum."

"Sisters helping sisters," I said.

"Yeah," she said. "Sisters helping sisters."

A week later found Catherine, Allison, and me at Heather's dining room table, armed with ballpoint pens, a stack of stamp sheets, and a bottle of wine. It was time for thank-you notes for all the Bring-the-Soccer-Grannies-to-America boosters.

"Did you see the *Lexington Minuteman*?" I asked, pulling the local paper out of my purse and plunking it next to a pile of cards. A full-color photo captured me—vuvuzela clutched in hand—grinning and hugging a Granny.

"Yes!" said Heather. "I saw it!"

Allison picked up the newspaper. "Love this quote from Beka: 'I knew something big would come my way. I still believe something bigger is coming.'"[4]

"That's how she does it," said Catherine, uncorking the bottle. "To the Grannies," she toasted, raising her glass. "And to us, for helping pull it off. *À votre santé* . . . to your health."

Beka had emailed me—we were back to only written communication—that the Grannies had made it safely home and everyone had been so impressed by the trophy. She was already busy distributing the clothes, and she'd started building another house for a family in need. She repeated her desire that we visit South Africa next year so she could show us all she's done.

"I'm in for it," said Heather, to enthusiastic nods around the table.

But first things first: We turned to the stack of a hundred thank-you notes waiting to be addressed and signed. On the front of each card was a photo of the Grannies playing soccer at the Veterans Cup, and inside was a quotation from Carl Sandburg: *Nothing happens unless first we dream.* We set to work circulating the cards, signing them round-robin style.

"How insane was it to think we could bring nineteen people over from South Africa," Heather marveled. "What on earth made us think we could pull it off?"

"I kept coming back to the feeling that we couldn't give up," I said. "Every time we hit a problem, I just knew we couldn't let the Grannies down."

"Ladies," said Allison, "we're a good team."

"Hey," said Heather. "How 'bout we invite a soccer team from Antarctica next year? Whatcha think?"

Part III

The Goal

If there is one thing in this planet that has the power to bind people, it is soccer.—*Nelson Mandela*[1]

13

Mopane Worms and Sequined Gowns

Nkowankowa is a vibrant town—a small town. It's full of friendly people. Although it's a small town, there is still a lot of inequality among the people, where you can find your neighbor living in a shack while you live in a big house. You can find different people from different cultural backgrounds.—Beatrice Nyeleti Tshabalala, Soccer Granny[1]

ONE THOUSAND NINE HUNDRED AND FIVE KILOMETERS NORTHEAST OF where the southern tip of the continent of Africa juts into the South Atlantic and Indian oceans, bracketed between dense woodlands and game preserves watered by the drowsy Limpopo River, sits the township of Nkowankowa, population 22,484. The streets, laid out more or less in a grid pattern, are lined by mostly single-story buildings—convenience stores, a post office, a grocery—painted in bold reds, yellows, and blues, their windows covered by metal grills. About a five-minute walk from the restaurant Chicken Miami—a squat concrete block with a couple of picnic benches shielded by a metal awning, everything painted in red and green—is the stadium, where the green grass accommodates the local preoccupation with the national pastime.

It was here on a cloudless August morning, thirteen months after the Grannies' visit to the United States, that Catherine pulled our rental sedan into the parking lot, careful not to hit any of the hundred or so

145

women assembled. The blur of striped skirts, wraps, and headscarves in every color of the rainbow descended on us in a swirling horde.

"It's a sea of Grannies!" I squeaked.

Joining Catherine and me in our expedition from the States were Heather and family, Allison and family, and Karen, the older of my two daughters. We submitted to the frenzy of embraces, mostly from women we'd never met, but occasionally we'd see a face that provided a jolt of affection and familiarity. "Oh, Lizzy," I said, wrapping my arms around my friend's tiny frame.

It was a welcome like none I had ever experienced.

Grannies who'd assembled from nearby communities blew vuvuzelas and ululated. They shimmied their hips and clapped their hands. Amid the bustle stood a beaming Mama Beka, orchestrator of our grand welcome. Cameras snapped photos of the joyous reunion. Heather's son, six-year-old Tamerat, cowered shyly in the car until Heather scooped him up and carried him into the fray, where Grannies fussed over him and cooed before turning to her seven-year-old daughter, Sam, asking for their picture to be taken as they posed with the little strawberry blonde.

I made my way through the throng to Beka, who took both my hands and squeezed them between her own. "I'm so glad to see you, my sister," she said.

I looked into her eyes, searching for reassurances that she was still healthy and strong, that her resilience was besting her never-ending battle with cancer. She looked good—radiating that calm and power—and I allowed myself to feel relief. I'd so looked forward to seeing her.

She leaned in toward me. "You were careful driving? No incidents?" Our after-dark arrival in Johannesburg had concerned her, and even before we boarded the plane in Boston, she'd made us "promise you won't stop at any traffic lights. Don't stop at the side of the road in the country either, because someone may come out of the bushes."

Carjackings, she'd told us, are epidemic in South Africa. Sometimes the attacker bumps your car from behind; you get out to examine the damage, and he jumps behind the wheel and takes off. Or the attacker stages what looks like an accident and waves you, the good Samaritan, over to help. I could very easily fall for either of those tricks. But Beka had told us to keep the car doors locked and the windows up in the cities. We'd heeded her guidance, I assured her, and eased our way through traffic lights that first night in Johannesburg.

A young woman stepped forward, holding a toddler. Beka introduced me to her twenty-four-year-old daughter, Nkhensani. "Her name means 'grateful' in Xitsonga," Beka said, beaming with obvious pride. I located Karen nearby in the crowd and pulled her in for introductions.

"And who's this?" Karen asked, taking the outstretched hand of the child in Nkhensani's arms.

"This is my little sister, Reneilwe," Nkhensani said. "It means 'given.' She just had her second birthday." And gently bouncing the child, "We have a wonderful mama, no?" I was not going to argue that point.

The meanings of names in South Africa carry great significance. Nelson Mandela was born Rolihlahla Mandela. His first name means "to pull a branch off a tree" or "to stir up trouble," which fits the active resistance of White domination and apartheid that consumed his life's work. Throughout Africa as a whole, names have long been sacred in traditional cultures. The soul and spirit are named, not just the physical being. Sometimes a name might be based on an event around the time of the birth. Perhaps a child born following a family death or tragedy will be called "comfort." How fitting that a baby girl appearing after a long line of boys might be known as "we have waited."

I had no idea what Karen's name meant; I'd just liked that it sounded like "caring."

Just then, I spotted Bull, looking radiant as ever. "My friend!" I exclaimed, reaching for her. "How are you?"

"Happy, happy to see you," she said as we embraced in a bear hug. (I had forgotten how strong she was.) "Come, come," she said, taking my hand and Karen's too.

We walked with the Grannies past the stadium to an open field beyond it. I recognized the dry and dusty field from the videos of their practices I'd watched so many times. Rolling brown hills were visible in the distance; a couple of trees shaded some tables. Bull motioned to a row of chairs, but I opted for a blanket spread on the ground, happy to leave the seats for others.

The unreality of actually being here kept pushing in. We'd been planning this trip for a year, practically from the moment the Grannies' plane had left the tarmac last summer. I knew we were lucky to be embraced by these women; ours wouldn't be a sterile tourist experience lifted from a guidebook's pages. That said, we *had* opened our trip with a three-day safari before meeting up with the Grannies; seeing animals roaming in the wild proved a delightful introduction to the beauty of South Africa. But still, as memorable as the sight of giraffes grazing the treetops had been, it was Beka and the Grannies we were here for.

Beka had been eager for us to visit, repeating her invitation month after month. Even as we'd assured her our plans were well underway, she began dropping hints that something special was in store for us but remained mum on the details. When we'd asked if we needed to pack any special clothes, it was, "No, no! Just come, just come." Type-A planner that I am, I forced myself to roll with the adventure and let the ambiguity add to the unreality and excitement of the moment. After all, Beka and the Grannies had graciously gone with whatever we'd planned the previous summer; now it was our turn.

"We welcome our guests from America," Beka said, her strong voice quieting the chatter. "We want to show you a special time in South Africa." She then nodded to a line of women in matching skirts, adorned with beaded headbands, necklaces, and armbands. Two carried drums and set a rhythm as they paraded past us before sitting on the ground. Meanwhile, the other women formed a circle around them and began singing and dancing. The drummers' beat quickened, and the dancers matched the pace. The wash of colors swirled faster and faster. I was dizzy with their magical performance and squeezed Karen's hand as an anchor.

The hip-shaking *xibelani* invites the dancer to literally "hit the rhythm" and is performed while wearing a skirt with colorful ruffles around the top, designed to accentuate the vibrating movements. Long performed by Tsonga women, these steps have been taught by one generation to the next, and the next, and the next.

All of Tsonga traditional dance follows a musical calendar. In parallel with the planting season, there are hoeing, weeding, and then reaping songs. Once the garden is harvested, herding songs are sung as the cattle return to graze and fertilize the garden plots. During the long winter months, traditional children's story-songs are shared before the fire. Other dances are tied to important life events—like circumcision, puberty, and, of course, weddings. Thus music establishes a rhythm for the passing seasons and accentuates life's milestones.

Before us, the dancers stilled and the drummers quieted; we applauded and whistled, our hosts eagerly peering at us to see our reaction. (They couldn't have been disappointed.) Beka invited us to a lunch the women had prepared, which was laid out on the folding tables set up under the trees' canopy. I saw platters of grains adorned with fresh tomatoes, mangos, and avocados. There were bowls of the cornmeal pap Beatrice had made for us in America.

Beatrice, I thought. *Why wasn't she here . . . ?*

Bull took my hand and pulled me over to the buffet, where I picked up a plate and slowly made my way behind Allison and Catherine ahead of me, sampling from an array of beautiful-looking offerings . . . until I stopped before what looked like a bowl of dried caterpillars.

"Are you getting one?" Catherine asked, a devilish smile on her face, holding up her plate where a single blackened wooly larva curled in rigor mortis.

"N-no," I began. "Am I . . . missing something good?"

"They're mopane worms," Allison said brightly. "You've *got* to try one." Karen and I watched in dread as one by one our travel companions plucked the rigid caterpillars from their plates and gamely popped them in their mouths. (Is this how our Grannies had felt when we'd fed them hot dogs and mayonnaise-laden salads?)

Even though I felt . . . hesitant, I also wanted to be open and respectful of their culture and generosity. And besides—I'd promised myself to say yes to as many new experiences on this trip as possible. Mustering my courage, I turned to the serving bowl and gingerly selected two of the more salubrious-looking specimens, giving one to Karen.

"Here goes," I said. With an open can of soda on standby, I popped the worm in my mouth. Karen did the same. I did my best to keep a slight, curious smile on my face as I crunched into the charred exterior before the leathery skin momentarily streeeeeeetched and then suddenly gave with a *pop*. A grassy, moist burst hit my palate. I'm afraid I didn't do a good job hiding my reaction. I chewed and swallowed as fast as I could, washing it down with the bubbly soft drink.

Bull was looking at me, her eyes sparkling.

"It . . . was good . . ." I said weakly.

She laughed outright. "It's *good*," she repeated with emphasis, eating two more—*pop*, *pop*.

My unsophisticated palate aside, the mopane worm is actually a caterpillar, identified in nature by its white and yellow stripes and short black spines. It feeds on the leaves of the mopane tree, hence its name. If not harvested at the larval stage, they grow into emperor moths, with orange, brown, and white markings and four eyespots. Wherever the mopane tree grows, women and children pluck the caterpillars from the branches, squeeze and discard a green goo from the insects' insides, and then dry them in the sun. The worms are a great source of protein and iron—a nutritional powerhouse—and can be stored for months.

As I enjoyed the rest of my (worm-free) lunch—which I really did enjoy—two teams of Grannies scrimmaged for our entertainment, one kitted in red, one in white. They opened the match with a few songs and sang in celebration of goals too. They appeared to be having as much fun singing and dancing as they had chasing the soccer ball. This was the lighthearted play I'd loved best when I saw them take to the field in Massachusetts.

When the game finished, Beka asked the American contingent to sing a song for everyone.

We exchanged blank looks. After a brief conference, we settled on an oldie we all knew:

> Make new friends
> But keep the old.
> One is silver and
> The other's gold.

The second time through, I cued Karen to join a couple beats later, and we sang the simple tune a few more times as a round. We should have practiced—or maybe stuck to one key—but the Grannies cheered us with enthusiasm regardless.

"Now it's time for the surprise," Beka announced with a wide grin. "It's just a short drive away."

At her direction, we piled back into our cars and made a curious little caravan through Nkowankowa. We pulled up to a church building and parked in the lot behind, where a white tent loomed, large as the church itself. What could this be?

Stepping inside I discovered a festive scene of a hundred people in suits and fancy dresses. A portable hard floor had been laid down in the center of the tent, where partygoers danced to live music from a three-piece band. Ringing the space were large round tables, decorated in white tablecloths and colorful floral centerpieces, where people happily chatted and ate. (A brief scan revealed no mopane worms.)

"Oh my gosh, look!" said Heather in an excited whisper. "It's Beatrice!" I turned where she was pointing, and, sure enough, there was our youngest Granny, seated at a long table at the front of the tent, dressed in a lacy, fitted gown, sparkling with peach-colored sequins.

Wait.

"Is this . . . a wedding?" I asked, confused. "*Beatrice's* wedding?"

Beka clapped her hands into a clasp under her chin and nodded with glee.

From our spot lurking at the tent's entrance, we caught Beatrice's eye. She looked astonished, then so happy. Beka, I gathered, hadn't told Beatrice what the surprise was either.

Our scheming Mama ushered us to an empty row of folding chairs on one side of the tent, where we each took a seat, trying to look cool and sophisticated and like we totally weren't sauntering into the reception wearing sneakers and baseball caps. I leaned in toward Beka and whispered, "Is this okay, ten of us crashing Beatrice's big day?" She would be thrilled, Beka assured me, that we had stopped by, and, besides, we wouldn't stay long.

The keyboard, electric guitar, and drums played lively music. Four women held microphones and sang and swayed to the music. "I hope Beka doesn't want us to sing for this group," Allison deadpanned.

As if reading our thoughts, Beka then stood and asked us to address the group with a few words. My travel companions all turned to me, smiling sweetly.

Fine.

I was led to one of the microphones on the edge of the dance floor and felt in my stomach only a faint fluttering (of emperor moth wings?) as the master of ceremonies introduced me in Xitsonga. I heard "Vakhegula Vakhegula" and "America," and then he handed me the microphone.

What an honor it had been to have Beatrice, Beka, and the Grannies visit the United States, I told the sea of faces looking at me. Beatrice had defended the goal with diving saves, I recounted, despite playing on an injured foot. As I focused on my friend, I slowly warmed to my subject. "In fact, the team returned to South Africa with the trophy," I bragged, as Beatrice nodded with a smile. I paused to wait for the emcee's translation. Beatrice, I continued, had been central to connecting our two groups, serving as translator, her personality shining through with animated gestures no matter the language she was speaking. "May Beatrice and her husband have many happy years together," I wished in closing, to a warm round of applause.

I turned to the group and suppressed a relieved sigh. Beka smiled; I sensed she was proud to be hosting her friends from America.

Then we were invited to greet Beatrice and her husband. When I got my chance to hug her, I congratulated her again and thanked her for being so gracious about our wandering in off the street into her wedding reception.

She laughed at me. "I'm delighted you could stop by, my friend! I was afraid I wouldn't get to see you at all." Beatrice turned to her husband and introduced us. He was the Grannies' team doctor, she explained.

I looked at him again and this time recognized him from a video about the Grannies' improved health after joining the squad. "Another benefit to playing soccer!" I declared, and then shrugged. "Sometimes you find love."

After we'd all greeted Beatrice and wished her happiness, Beka shepherded us out of the tent and back to our cars.

I squinted at the sun, still high in the sky. I was surprised—perhaps because I associate wedding receptions with evenings, probably because I was still a little jet lagged.

Hey—if the Grannies could play tournament-level soccer three days in a row with a seven-hour time difference, then I would certainly embrace whatever it was Beka had in store for us next. I was just super grateful that it *wouldn't* be tournament-level soccer three days in a row. And probably not more mopane worms.

Probably.

Granny Omo
Like Two Hands That Wash Each Other

Uyazi Asnath Shiviti, known to her friends as "Omo," is seventy years old and remembers a time before the modern dwellings of Nkowankowa existed. Today tidy, one-story brick and cement-plastered houses with orange and maroon roof tiles bake in the subtropical sun. Waist-high cinderblock walls border each home, encircling small, well-swept yards where a lovingly tended tree or two may grow, mostly surrounded by bare ground.

"Our houses were mostly *rondavels*,"[1] she recalls—round huts capped with cones of thatched grasses, often hand-hewn by village girls, like Omo and her friends. "[Some] days we would take our laundry and wash it at the river, and when it was time for ironing we collected wood and made a fire. We heated the iron on fiery embers."

Unlike many other girls of her era, Omo was able to complete primary school. "*Heee!*" she exclaims, recalling the five-kilometer walk each way, taken in the morning at a fast clip to avoid punishments for tardiness, perhaps even faster in the afternoons to rush to her beloved church youth choir rehearsals. The ensemble visited sick and elderly parishioners and competed in—and often won—singing competitions.

Uyazi "Omo" Asnath Shiviti. Nkowankowa, Limpopo, September 2021. *Photo by Dineo Raolane*

Omo's father worked in Johannesburg as a wine steward. "It was tough because he came home only during December holidays," she says. "That was hard for me, but I must say that it was always such a joy when he visited. He'd bring us delicacies like bread, jam, butter, fish oil, and *biltong*," a preserved beef.

White business owners relied upon dedicated Black staff, like Omo's father, but this interdependence did not align with the long-term goals of the separatist regime. To keep the Tsonga in their designated and under-developed homeland of Gazankulu, the apartheid government had tried to engineer local work opportunities. Toward that end, Nkowankowa was founded in 1962. Wider, modern roads were paved for trucks to transport goods manufactured in its local factories to buyers across South Africa. Soon neighborhoods of four-room homes sprouted up to house laborers and their families.

Ten years after the government's attempt to invent Nkowankowa as an industrial center, half of South Africa's 750,000 Tsonga still lived outside of the homeland designated to them by the apartheid regime, instead clustered in urban areas because there was no work back home. The situation worsened in the mid-1970s with the worldwide recession, which spiked already high unemployment throughout South Africa. Now even the larger, wealthy White cities suffered, and more Blacks were sent back to their enervated lands. Rural areas like Nkowankowa were hit hardest.

It was right around this time that Omo married. Her husband was fortunate to have steady employment with a railroad company in Johannesburg, but this left Omo to raise their six children by herself. When the railroad redeployed her husband even farther away, to Cape Town—more than a thousand miles from home—he made the difficult decision to give up the paying work and return to his family instead. But work in Nkowankowa was scarce. "For us to survive, my husband ended up opening a *spaza* shop," selling the townsfolk their daily conveniences—like a cool drink, a pack of cigarettes, or a loaf of bread. "That made our life better."

With a little left over after bills had been paid, Omo and her husband would sometimes venture into town for a night out. These were vividly happy times for her, full of gifts and embraces and shared laughter. Then one day, with no explanation, he was gone. "He just left us here and went away. *Eish!* Our last-born child was in grade one." Suddenly Omo was the sole provider for herself and six children.

About this time, Nkowankowa was again receiving attention from the all-White government. Still determined to block the flood of unemployed Black men into White cities, the government extended the town's railroad and piped in water, offering lucrative incentives to lure industrialists to the area. The large available labor pool, a railway serving nearby citrus-packing plants, and natural resources for timber and furniture businesses made Nkowankowa an attractive investment opportunity. Almost one hundred firms constructed plants in the township between 1983 and 1985. Omo was able to find steady employment in town.

But the initial boom of commercial success was soon a bust, with some seventy of the new businesses closing or relocating, Omo's company among them. The shuttering of each sent ripples across the community, impacting the livelihood of its workers. Reasons for business failures varied: Periodic droughts had hurt fruit and vegetable yields, impacting the downstream packaging and processing. Factories struggled with an unreliable water supply due to faulty pipes. Most companies were profitable only with government incentives, which owners knew were temporary.

While Nkowankowa had undoubtedly benefited from the government's interest, fleeting as it was, no investments had been made in schools, medical care, or other social services critical to the town's long-term economic stability. Short-term employment hadn't been enough to lift the town out of poverty or relieve the unemployment and related social crises. Omo prayed, set her shoulders, and persevered, determined to do right by her children—her "gifts from God." She qualified for a loan, which she used to open a business that she operated out of her home, raising her family's standard of living. Finally she could begin to ensure the future well-being of her children. "I am proud that I was able to pay all the school fees," she says. "My youngest daughter even went to tertiary school."

By 1994, the Rainbow Nation was filling with hope: Apartheid had crumbled, and President Mandela and the African National Congress ascended. But confronting the legacy of racial segregation and its resultant economic inequality would prove a herculean task.

The ANC set goals to improve quality of life for all its people—Black, White, and every color in between—by bringing electricity to hundreds of thousands of additional homes each year. Electrification has changed the lives of South Africans; with this new power—both literal and figurative—a woman with a sewing machine or a hair dryer might work from home and generate income to support her family. The government program was a qualified success: By 2011, almost everyone in the province of Limpopo had electric lighting, although only half had electricity for cooking and heating; others still relied on burning wood. More than half of homes enjoyed the modern conveniences of television, a refrigerator, and a cell phone.

The ANC's larger economic plan to revive the country relied heavily on foreign investment. But when that largely failed to materialize, the government, in a bind, opened the economy to cheap, foreign-produced consumer goods. But this devastated those same industries at home. Once again, factories closed and workers were let go.

Omo's children, now grown, began their job searches in a devastated economy. "*Eish!*" she exclaims, "it is tough." One son won a coveted full-time position teaching at the school. Others haven't been so lucky and are piecing together work in part-time gigs or temporary contract labor as they are able. Her youngest has a degree in management science but has yet to find a job. "And what's worse, she has kids." Despite Omo's sacrifice and labor and hopes for a better future, she is seeing the next generation bowed under the stresses of unemployment and income instability.

Omo worries about the quality of life her children will enjoy. She understands why today's disaffected youth might be tempted to make choices that feel good in the short term, but she really cannot understand the lack of foresight.

"One day in 2011, my fifth-born child went to church. After the church service, instead of coming home, he went to drink alcohol. When he was coming back home in the evening, some bad boys stabbed him in the head with a knife." His friends rushed their bloody, unconscious friend to the hospital. When he had stabilized and was able to make his way home, the sight of his bandaged head shocked Omo. How could those town boys have attacked her son?

Morning broke after a fitful night of sleep, and Omo found that his condition had worsened. Back to the hospital. When at last he was discharged and fully recovered, she thought surely he would never drink again. Soon her hope soured into disappointment. Her son seemed blind to the mercy God had shown saving him from death.

She still encourages him to stop drinking, but she can't seem to get through to him. "He tells me he has problems that make him drink. I always ask him if those problems go away when he's drunk or after drinking. He keeps quiet. That disappoints me." A mother cannot live her adult son's life for him, so instead she prays—and frets.

But this son's troubles cannot be Omo's only concern. Today her household includes two grown daughters, their children, and the children of a daughter who has passed away. "I am personally fine," she says, "but the only thing that bothers me is my house is so small for us. I don't like being in my bedroom because it's so overcrowded. I would love to extend the house by another two rooms for my kids' use."

Though it is cramped, the togetherness suits Omo. She considers her children and grandchildren to be blessings. "God did not bring us into this world to live as islands. We are born to help one another."

She chuckles. "I tell them, as siblings they must always stick together. Just like two hands that wash each other, so must they be."

Omo finds respite in Vakhegula Vakhegula, where she can move her body, be with friends, and even travel sometimes. "Soccer has really changed our lives, because we visit different places we had never thought that we could ever visit. We sleep in hotels and lodges, and it's really nice."

The regular practices get her out of the house and onto the pitch, where she's grown stronger and solidified friendships.

But the end of the day finds her back home, where she cooks and cleans, tends and fusses. In this way life continues for Omo and her household, in their single-story cottage in Nkowankowa with its small yard and well-swept stoop.

14

Thunder

Some people think football is a matter of life and death. I assure you, it's much more serious than that.—Bill Shankly, Scottish football player and manager[1]

AFTER DAYS OF SEDENTARY BUTT-IN-SEAT TRAVEL—INTERNATIONAL flights, drives across the South African countryside, an extended safari from our perch in a bouncing Land Rover—I was delighted when Beka announced we were to play a friendly soccer match with the Grannies. My legs were desperate to stretch and run.

As always when we met Vakhegula Vakhegula on the soccer field, a festive, carnivalesque atmosphere took over. It didn't matter that we didn't all speak the same language; we would whistle, hoot, wildly gesture—anything to make ourselves understood to one another.

Thirteen months before, back in Massachusetts on one of the last days of their visit to the States, the Grannies had scrimmaged with us one morning. We were joined by various Lexpressas family members and a few tournament fans. Heather's neighbor Dan—who'd been housing the four South African men and had his own regular soccer game on Sundays—had opted to join us instead, saying, "I can play with my team any week."

We'd gathered that day on the synthetic turf fields of Lexington—constructed over what had once been a landfill—chattering and laughing. Allison's daughter was riding a five-foot-high unicycle, balancing with tiny front-and-back motions as Grannies gathered around her to pose for photos snapped by Heather's husband, a part-time sports photographer.

Some forty of us took to the pitches that morning as a sort of end-of-trip soccer free-for-all before our friends were to fly back to South Africa. That day the soccer fields of Lexington saw unusual diversity: Grannies, Lexpressas, husbands, and kids dashed over the turf outfitted in ad hoc team uniforms. Coach David, I noticed, had chosen to play barefoot. That morning Vakhegula Vakhegula had shown up in bright yellow jerseys and matching bandanas, but as we took to the fields, some Grannies were elbowing their way into old forest green Lexpressas jerseys. Our team was retiring them now that we had our new hot pink kit, and we'd decided to gift the old uniforms to the Grannies as a memento of our time together. Bull had clutched hers to her chest in delight.

"I've never had more fun," Allison had called to me as we ran and passed, whiffed and collided on that July day. It had been beautiful chaos.

On the opposing team, Coach Romeo had been weaving nimbly around the other players, showing off his talented moves. As he maneuvered past one of the Grannies, she lost her balance in her haste to get out of his way and fell, her leg splayed at an alarming angle. Play stopped as Romeo knelt to help her and two Lexpressas each took a hand to hoist her up; the resilient Granny just laughed. Heather's son, Tamerat, was on my team, and on his tiptoes the five-year-old couldn't have reached past the waist of most players. But everyone made sure to keep an eye on the little guy, controlling their speed to keep from running into him and making sure to frequently send the ball his way.

When two Grannies collided and fell, teammates circled around, clucking and offering an arm up. But without hesitation, the players were back on their feet and running toward the goal. Moments later, one of them kicked a shot on goal. The ball missed, but her soccer cleat flew off, flying into the net. "That counts as a goal," I argued, as laughter rang out on both sides of the field. "I'd says it's worth *two* points."

In another critical moment of gameplay, the ball had ricocheted off someone's back into the goal. *Still counts.*

Bull, I noticed, was always on attack as she played, challenging whoever had the ball when they came near her. She was tough—the kind of player you wanted playing with you, not against you.

Beatrice's foot was feeling better, and so she was back on the field. At one point a teammate threw a ball from the sidelines, and Beatrice capitalized on its momentum to score. She broke into a victory dance with fast footsteps and fists pumping in the air.

"*Laduma! Laduma!*"

"Goal! Goal!"

Now, on the field in South Africa, our equally friendly, equally chaotic match a year later saw the American contingent doing its part to bring a little diversity to Nkowankowa Stadium. (No dusty field for our humble scrimmage; Beka had reserved the town's soccer arena for us!)

On the well-maintained pitch, a mix of South African Grannies, middle-aged American women, and children passed the ball up the field, control ricocheting between the two teams. No one cared about the score—we played for simple love of the game.

I covered the sides, running up and down the pitch, passing to Grannies on my team whenever I could. Nimble Lizzy was in a forward position for our team, and Bull was always open in just the right spot. Together the three of us set up a few plays that threatened the goal, but Allison—destroyer of fun, annihilator of joy—was just too talented and kept spoiling our attacks. This called for a change in strategy.

"Allison," I suggested sweetly, "don't you want to take a break and get some water, maybe? Just for a few minutes. I bet you're thirsty . . ."

The ref blew the game-ending whistle. (In addition to making calls on the field, she attended college with Beka's financial assistance. "She's very smart," Beka had told me as the young woman had beamed with pride.) Soggy and heaving, we gathered for a photo that captured the moment: smiles galore, arms draped around each other's shoulders, all of us elated to be together again, playing the game that connects us.

Football has been long loved in South Africa. Much more than a pastime, it has been inextricably woven into the history of the country.

Black South Africans had readily adopted the game upon its import by British colonialists in the second half of the nineteenth century, stamping it with a distinctive cultural brand of play. Diviners used magic and herbal potions to improve the performance of players, protect them from injury, and scare the opposition. From Indigenous stick fighting they brought the tradition of praise names; one player was called "Scotch Whiskey" because his play was so smooth that even a little made spectators forget their worries.

But in the early twentieth century, as a White mania for racial separation began to rend all aspects of South African life, not even the pitch remained an apolitical field. As apartheid began suffocating the Black population, soccer became critical for coping with the mounting hardships. Despite enduring long working hours for meager wages, fans would make lengthy trips across cities to play in and watch matches. Lively discussions about goals saved and scored and dubious referee calls distracted from weightier troubles. The pitch became the one place in apartheid South Africa where Black men were still free to exercise their strength and power.

Understanding this well, White authorities made it increasingly difficult for Black soccer organizers to gain access to fields. The situation worsened in 1956, when laws were passed mandating racially separated sporting activities. Interracial competitions were now forbidden within the nation's borders. Only Whites would be allowed to represent South Africa in international competition, even though at the time they comprised less than 20 percent of the country's population.

Black South Africans demanded that the world witness their oppression; athletes called on the International Federation of Association Football to take a stand, and in 1961, FIFA suspended South Africa.

This marked one of the first international condemnations of apartheid, signaling a critical shift in how the world would contend with the lawful cruelties in South Africa. Soon the International Olympic Committee took similar damning action. Though apartheid wouldn't be dismantled for another three decades, pressure from the international community would ultimately prove devastating as cultural and economic sanctions levied by governments, businesses, and religious organizations followed the athletic federations' lead. Indeed, the long-standing sports boycotts arguably impacted the morale of White South Africans more than diplomatic isolation and financial sanctions ever did.

In response to the revolutionary work done by the ANC to defend the rights and freedoms of Black South Africans, that party was outlawed in 1960, and soon its most influential members were incarcerated on Robben Island—a grim prison on a desolate isle about four miles off the shore of Cape Town, on the southeastern-most point of the country. Conditions at Robben were abominable—dank cells, inadequate protection from the elements, beatings and even torture by guards, vermin-infested food, forced labor in the island's limestone quarry—and prison authorities made sure to forbid the playing of soccer, understanding how meaningful the game was to the incarcerated.

After years of inmate petitioning and under pressure from the International Red Cross, conditions began to incrementally improve on Robben Island, and in 1967, formation of a soccer league was finally permitted. Those precious minutes of game play, spent kicking around a ball that was initially fashioned of rags, became critical to the men's sense of dignity; on the prison yard pitch, they "felt free"—if only for a few minutes.[2] Nelson Mandela, one of Robben's highest-profile inmates, was barred from taking part in the matches, but he watched the games from the window of his cramped cell—until prison authorities built a wall with the express purpose of blocking his view.

As meticulously as prison conditions would allow, the imprisoned men followed FIFA regulation play, to train for life, they later said, to prove to anyone watching that they were capable of hard work, organization, administration, and teamwork. On that Robben Island squad played Thabo Mbeki, Kgalema Motlanthe, and Jacob Zuma—the three men who would go on to be elected the Republic of South Africa's second, third, and fourth presidents.

Back on the mainland, activists across the nation were using soccer to their advantage. Operating in secret, leaders of the ANC capitalized on travel across international borders to attend matches, where they would meet with revolutionaries in exile, able to advance critical discussion and strategizing in person. Proceeds from tickets sales for these games were funneled to finance antiapartheid activities.

By 1992, the grip of apartheid was weakening—not from a disavowal of racist notions among power holders but from decades of targeted struggle for Black liberation within South Africa and decades of ongoing pressure from international sanctions. South Africa began to repeal some of its worst race laws: Blacks were finally allowed to own property, homelands were declared nation-states, passbooks were abolished, and Black people could live in urban centers. This progress was sufficient to convince FIFA that South Africa should be welcomed back to competition. Bafana Bafana—South Africa's racially integrated soccer team— was formed, and they played the nation's first international match in three decades.

"*Laduma! Laduma!*" the fans had cheered upon every goal. *It thunders.*

Outside Nkowankowa Stadium, the sun was hanging low in the sky, a gorgeous mango glow. The Grannies decorated us in multicolored lilac and turquoise wraps and rose and lime beaded headbands. I was given a handmade basket woven through with tangerine diamonds and aqua stripes. In turn, we presented gifts carried from the States: yellow kerchiefs printed with the South African and American flags, *Soccer Sisters* in flowing script between them. Beaming, our Grannies tied them on their heads atop the headscarves they already wore.

Night was about to fall, and Beka was anxious for the Grannies to start making their way home. Some had trekked several miles from nearby towns to join us. Earlier in the day, as we drove into town, we'd seen signs posted by the police department that read, "Lonely walk at night can be dangerous." The warning now took on more meaning to us.

But before Beka could coax them on their way, the Grannies drew into a circle to make a final prayer to close the day, as I had seen them do so often Stateside. They had gathered together just so before every meal, during each bus ride, and after each soccer practice and game—to give thanks, to ask for blessing, to feel God's presence. Some heads would bow low, but more often faces would raise upward. Sometimes one Granny would lead the prayer, the others interjecting invocations. Other times, they would pray aloud together, many voices merging into one choir of petition and thanks.

This night, at the amen, heads were raised and smiles stretched across faces and a low chatter began as each Granny who lived nearby balanced a chair or a folding table on her head and began the walk homeward.

In the parking lot, I caught up with Bull, smoothly making her way, delicately crowned with a large basket brimming with picnic supplies. "Oh, Bull," I said, taking her hand, "it's been so wonderful to see you again." She grinned and nodded, bobbing her head in agreement. It was a marvel that the heavy burden she carried didn't topple.

Granny Gayisa
God Is My Protector

Modjadji Mdaka Gayisa sits serenely in the shade, near the Nkowankowa Stadium. She is crowned in a turquoise head wrap with *Vakhegula Vakhegula* printed on it, itself haloed by a braided ring of brightly colored cloth. Her eyes reflect a knowing acceptance.

"I taught my kids prayer and worshipping the Lord," Gayisa says, "and I like it because they have followed me to be worshippers. I have taught my children to fear God. I taught them how to pray and that God is there."[1] Prayer has threaded her entire life. "Sometimes my children call me from wherever they will be and request for me to pray for them on the phone. That makes me feel happy."

Like the vast majority of South Africans, Gayisa is Christian and frames her week around religious services. Her life is rooted in her faith, and her faith is rooted in her country's history, born of work that began in the eighteenth century. With the arrival of other foreign expeditions, European missionaries began travelling by ox-drawn cart into the interior of present-day South Africa, seeking converts among the Indigenous population. Soon European and American mission stations dotted the landscape, drawn as much by

Modjadji Mdaka Gayisa. Nkowankowa, Limpopo, September 2021. *Photo by Dineo Raolane*

the favorable climate and low risk of malaria and other diseases as by the souls to be saved.

The adoption of Christianity was slow, however, because its teachings clashed with dearly held aspects of Indigenous beliefs: Early converts were ostracized for abandoning their ancestors, and evangelists condemned traditional practices of polygamy, instead holding up marriage as a sacred institution between one man and one woman.

But the missions made critical inroads in establishing schools where new converts were taught to read the Bible, thus providing the first formal education for Black children in present-day South Africa. Mission trade schools taught stonecutting, masonry, and carpentry.

More impactful than any educational opportunities, Christian belief offered a connection to God, an all-powerful helper and life companion. A divine aid and source of internal strength was certainly welcome in an increasingly brutal regime of Black oppression. During the most painful moments of her life, Gayisa has found herself drawing on God's support.

"I lost my firstborn child. He had just become a policeman. When he arrived at work, the new police graduates had to travel somewhere by bus for further training. On the way, the bus had a terrible accident that robbed the life of my son." Gayisa takes a deep breath and clasps her hands together. She speaks slowly, her eyes looking down as if she were reading poetry from the ground. "I learned that the life of a human being is like a flower: it withers. But the love of God will always be there. It is just that when we are hurt, we forget that God is there. He is there all the time. During that time of my life, I felt like dying, but God helped me to persevere."

The colonial government inflicted abysmal and prolonged mistreatment on the native population, and many—the contemporaries of Gayisa's parents and grandparents—turned to spiritual bolstering. Some White activist priests understood the pain of their congregants and chose to fight the injustices, using the church to organize the community to rally against the colonialists. In these instances, the church became an even more meaningful refuge for Black South Africans.

Many early African church leaders and ANC nationalist leaders traveled abroad and took inspiration from African American leaders and churches and from historically Black colleges and universities. Once back in South Africa, they found themselves discriminated against by the White leadership within their home churches. In response, a number of African-initiated churches were formed, run by Blacks, reshaping Christianity to accommodate African views.

Here Christian belief was interwoven with traditional spiritual practices, most notably respect for ancestors and physical and spiritual healing practices. "We Africans cannot ignore the dead," Desmond Tutu once wrote. "A Christianity that has no place for them speaks in alien tones."[2] The Zion Christian Church, founded in 1910 in Limpopo, remains one of the largest of these new churches assembled to celebrate a uniquely African Christianity.

By the mid-twentieth century, the overwhelming majority of Black South Africans identified as Christian—including Gayisa and many of the other Grannies. Throughout the devastating apartheid years, the church remained a vital spiritual resource.

The separatist regime dealt another blow to Blacks in South Africa by shutting down most Christian mission schools in 1953 with passage of the Bantu Education Act. Government subsidies to these institutions were withdrawn, and Black children were only permitted to attend the segregated federally funded schools, reducing opportunities for many to receive any education at all.

Gayisa's brothers enrolled in the state-sponsored school when she was a child, but she was denied an education altogether; her father believed a girl did not need schooling. "He was more interested in the money he would be paid when it was time for me to be married than he was in my education. I do not know how old I am because I have never gone to school."

Yet her father chose other meaningful ways to show Gayisa his love and affection. "As a first child, I was my dad's darling. My father was regarded as a tycoon by people in the village because he had a good job in the Hillbrow area of Johannesburg as a restaurant waiter." When he visited home, he brought gifts from his work in the wealthy Whites-only neighborhood. "I received more things and nicer clothes than my brothers and sisters," she recalls mischievously.

While her brothers were at their lessons, Gayisa would stay close by her mother's side. "She would take me along with her when she went to plow. We would work together, and whenever I got tired, my mother would allow me to rest and give me the baby from her back to take care of while mother was busy continuing to till the soil. After work, when we'd arrive home in the afternoon, I would start preparing dinner, as my mum would be exhausted from plowing."

Gayisa took well-deserved pride in her contribution at home. "If a girl plowed, collected firewood, and plastered the house floors and walls to make them look nice, people would approvingly say she was strong." She found the praise meaningful and satisfaction in using her strength.

Dance became a favorite pastime. Along with her sisters, she found a community of friends in a local dance troupe that would travel to other villages to compete. Practicing to the beats pounded out on the surfaces of collected tins, their little ensemble became a force to be reckoned with. "They never made the mistake of leaving me at home, because I was really good at dancing; I always won competitions for our group." Money would be collected from spectators as the dancers shook and twirled, and at the close you knew you'd won if a one-rand note made its way into your pocket.

Her husband-to-be first admired her while she was dancing at a friend's wedding. After seeing her on the dance floor, he frequently visited her village. "We eventually met one day," Gayisa recalls. "He proposed to me, but I refused and joked that my husband had yet to be born." Her suitor refused to be dissuaded. She laughs. "My friend stood a few meters away to make sure nothing unfortunate happened between us while we talked."

He persisted, and eventually Gayisa decided that he was the man for her and they were betrothed.

Once married, she moved into her husband's childhood home, where she began helping her mother-in-law with household chores. Her husband worked locally until their first child was born and he felt the pressures of family responsibility. He went to Johannesburg to seek a better job and visited home regularly.

In the following years, Gayisa gave birth to two more children.

Then her husband stopped coming home. Before long, he stopped sending money for support. Gayisa found herself with three children and no income. She mustered her creativity, physical strength, and trust in God to find ways to provide for her family. "I started selling bananas to school kids. I survived on selling. I also held a job at an orange farm as a fruit packer." She shrugs. What else was she supposed to do? "Life went on."

As she struggled through single motherhood, Gayisa found herself drawing from her deep well of faith. "I thank God for helping me live a good life," she reflects today. "I thank him for having helped me raise my children on my own during difficult times."

In the twenty years that followed her husband's abandonment, Gayisa only ever saw him on a few occasions—once at the funeral of his uncle and two years later when he returned to bury his own father. He chose to not attend the funeral of the son who was killed in the bus accident. "That nearly killed me," Gayisa says, hands over her head. Even today the emotions are raw. "It was shocking to me that the person with whom I had made my children did not want to be a part of the funeral. That hurt me so much that even when I am alone and the thought comes to me, I just break down in tears."

Gayisa never considered remarrying; that would have stood contrary to all her religious beliefs. "The Bible speaks clearly that two people, being husband and wife in marriage, are one flesh. I was fearful of God. One other thing was that I kept on believing that my husband would come back home one day." When she finally learned of her husband's death, Gayisa made the journey to Johannesburg to attend his funeral. There she learned he'd taken another wife and had started a second family in the city.

That he'd stopped coming home and stopped supporting the family finally began to make a bitter kind of sense.

Today Gayisa is the sole survivor of her family of five brothers and sisters. She now lives with her remaining son and a twenty-one-year-old grandson. Her daughter has two children of her own and lives and works in Pretoria—some 250 miles from Nkowankowa. Despite having never attended school herself, Gayisa has taught her grandchildren the importance of education. "I am happy that they have attended school all the way through university."

Every morning, Gayisa rises at 4 a.m. and begins her day with prayer. "I thank God for letting me live to see another day." Her soul having been fed, she then takes care of her body. "I do exercises; I jog on the road." With this, the day's labors begin. "I start cleaning my yard, and when I am done with that, I start cleaning the house. After that, I start cooking." She deep-fries savory stuffed dough called *vetkoek*, which she sells locally along with colorful beaded purses.

It's at her twice-weekly soccer practices that Gayisa can unwind from all her hard work. "I've had stress since my husband and child passed away. Exercising really helps me." After joining Vakhegula Vakhegula, Gayisa could once again find joy in the healthy movement of a strong body. "Football has brought me peace in my life," she says. "I go home tired and feeling refreshed." She takes her cues from some of her oldest teammates, Grannies well into their eighties who defy all convention and make their way to the soccer pitch. "I want to continue playing soccer, and I won't stop until I can't run or walk anymore. I find help and happiness from the team."

But even beyond their time spent on the pitch, Vakhegula Vakhegula is precious to Gayisa for the moments of shared prayer. "There is nothing in my life greater than God," she says with a smile. "I am myself because of God, who has protected and saved me until today. I trust so much in the Lord. This God is a protector day and night. God bless you."

You Strike a Woman, You Strike a Rock

If you want to go fast, go alone; if you want to go far, go together.
—African proverb[1]

"Is that the chief?" I asked, looking at the young man in a striped tunic and black slacks.

"*Head down*," Beka whispered with urgency. "Don't look him in the eye."

I quickly dipped my head in obedience but subtly angled my neck so I could observe the pageantry out of the corner of my eye. Women carrying baskets walked on either side of the chief. They approached with their heads lowered and shoulders hunched, eyes on the ground. As the chief strolled by the row of open tents, women dropped to their knees and bowed low, their heads touching the ground.

"May I photograph him?" Catherine asked Beka in a hushed voice. *Yes, but be discreet.*

From stolen peeks, I pegged the chief to be somewhere in his mid-thirties. "He looks younger than I would have expected."

"It's true," Beka said in a low voice. "See the older men following behind? They provide guidance to help him make wise decisions." In rural villages like the one Beka had taken us to visit on this day, the governing chief is still selected by the council of elders. Typically he is the oldest member of the longest-standing and strongest clan; his responsibilities include allocation of land and resources (like piped water), mediation of disputes, and blessing ceremonies.

My stomach rumbled. I hoped this chief would soon turn his attention to blessing lunch. Hours had passed since our hotel breakfast—a simple repast of coffee, fruit, and rusk, a crunchy twice-baked biscuit. We'd eaten quickly because Beka was meeting us at 7 a.m. to transport us a few hours north toward the border with Zimbabwe.

We'd first cut through a verdant strip of country, where the favorable climate supported the growth of the bananas, mangos, tomatoes, and avocados we'd seen in the pyramid displays of roadside vendors. We drove behind trundling pickups jenga-ed with furniture, boxes, and bags, covered with flapping tarps. I feared the precarious loads would topple should they hit a bump on the thankfully smooth highway. Other single-cab *bakkies* had some twenty men standing in the flatbed cargo area; we exchanged smiles and waves—probably, I figured, their regular morning commute to a commercial farm to pick some of that produce.

Then, cresting through gentle, rolling hills, the landscape turned slowly tan, then brown, and golden in the late-morning light. Finally we pulled off the highway onto a flat, straight, unpaved road, cinnamon puffs of dust trailing behind us. Now in every direction arid reds, ambers, and browns were accented with tussocks of low scrub grass. There were no buildings in sight.

Our progress was slow on this bush road. From the back seat I peered around the driver's headrest to check the fuel gauge—relieved to see it was still three-quarters full.

After the better part of an hour or more jostling through the savanna, we came upon a village of perhaps a hundred tiny one-room houses, fashioned of brick and sheet metal. The roofs were either thatched grass—holdovers from the once-ubiquitous *rondavels*—or yet more sheet metal, which I thought must be oven-like in the baking sun. Bright blue plastic drums next to each dwelling held the household's water supply, filled every few days when the delivery truck came through, Beka told me.

"Some villages don't have any water," she said, as our sedan pulled to a stop. "And this can be a huge problem. In this village I asked someone to help me to put in a borehole. But some villages—I'm telling you, some villages, they don't even have that; they simply don't *have* water. They drink water alongside the animals. It's not clean. Whenever I can find the money to drill boreholes for a community, they're much better off. Then they don't have to go to the river where it is not as safe." She added with a simple shrug, "Crocodiles may just come out."[2]

This village was mostly bare ground and sparse vegetation. And I noticed no wires carrying electricity to the homes; it seemed the government's electrification program had yet to reach these bushlands.

But they had a soccer field. As we piled out of our cars, we walked across the level expanse, gingerly stretching our limbs after the long car ride. A row of yellow tents bordered one side of the dusty field, their backs hung with colorful blankets. We were escorted to the centermost tent—the guests of honor today?—and offered chairs looking out onto the field.

Men and boys had gathered under the few trees on the far side of the pitch; women with babies and toddlers were joining us in the tents. I played peek-a-boo with a sweet tot peering over her mother's shoulder.

This village boasted a women's soccer team, but Beka's work here was so much more. Once a month she repeated this same journey by taxi to oversee education programs for the girls, teaching contraception and HIV/AIDS prevention, which would give them a better shot at long, healthy lives. In other similar communities, she worked with outside donors to provide building materials for local families, which they used to construct snug homes.

I could only imagine the numbers of villages that needed someone like Beka. What had brought her here, to this particular town? And what about that family she'd written me about all those many months ago—those orphaned children who'd gone to live with their ailing uncle and aunt, eleven squeezed into a hut built for less than half as many? Seeing this unassuming hamlet gave me more understanding of what Beka sees all around her.

Wherever she was drawn by need, Beka worked, building connections, earning trust. The natural reward for a successful intervention was only more requests for help. The need seemed never-ending. How did she face it with determination and not just crumble?

"After I got back from America, the powerful people in villages like this one showed me more respect," Beka said. "They were more eager to work with me, to help me get things done."

I began to see that everything Beka did was purposeful. When we were struggling to bring the Grannies to Massachusetts, we'd questioned spending such resources on a trip. But that brief impulse—thankfully overridden—had completely missed Beka's larger strategy: to leverage the trip to the United States into positive press for her work, which would then bolster her bona fides back home, thereby fostering local cooperation. Beka sets her sights on big dreams and talks boldly of her vision. In turn, the pieces of the puzzle come together and interconnect—she gains access and partnerships to do vital on-the-ground work that is too rarely prioritized.

In this remote village, I sensed they didn't host White American visitors often, if ever. It felt weird—uncomfortable, a little bit—to be honored as visiting dignitaries. Yet I was now coming to understand that our presence today, in the northern savannas of South Africa, wasn't about my embarrassment over whether or not I deserved distinction. Beka had worked hard to earn the respect of these people, so if my being here helped her out—if this sun-burned, pale lady with the funny, broad accent and weird hat coming all the way from America would help her build another house for the next family of orphan children—well, I would gladly put up with an exhibit-behind-glass feeling.

As the chief and his entourage took their seats in the shade tent behind us, my stomach had no compunction about regally announcing itself. I hunched over in my chair, hoping to muffle its rumblings.

A woman lugged a thirty-gallon steel drum to the center of the field. A girl in a pink shirt and skirt raised a stick over her head and brought it down, hard, onto the lid with an echoed resound. *Boom, boom!* Near her, two girls sat on the ground and played smaller drums, beating an ornate, textured rhythm around the repeated bass *thwoomp*. A line of some twenty young girls wearing fuchsia headbands and turquoise skirts sang and danced in snakelike formation. They circled around the drums, stomping their bare feet into the earth. Dried seedpods tied to their ankles rattled, *chaka-chaka*, with every intricate tread—intimating the voice of the gods and ancestor spirits.

Drawn into the dance, I almost forgot I was open to scrutiny in my front-row seat. The unhurried tempos and quieter beats subdued me, slowing the blood in my veins. At the faster, louder, brighter crescendos, my breath quickened.

Suddenly, quiet.

The drumming had stopped, and a man bellowed through a megaphone in Venda as the dancing girls ran off the field. Three women now approached the line of drums and began to play. A succession of more women, outfitted in aquamarine and ebony, danced into view. Shaking their hips with violent, precise juts, they whorled beaded belts into a quivering chatter. The young chief, I saw from stolen glances, was gabbing with men on either side of him, paying little attention to the spectacle before us. It was mundane for him.

When the performers finished, we Americans burst into applause as folk around us called out in approval. The women, broken from their whirling trance, smiled broadly and shuffled off the field, heads bowed and eyes averted as they passed the chieftain and his coterie of elders.

As it happened, our visit to that small town fell on National Women's Day, when all of South Africa celebrates the twenty thousand women who, in 1956, took to the streets in protest of new apartheid restrictions that jeopardized a woman's ability to care for her family. The passbook laws under protest that day had initially been used to control the movement of Black men only. When the travel restrictions were extended to Black women—threatening their ability to convene the family, to travel to places of work, and ultimately to feed their children—they would not accept it.

On August 9, 1956, when those women met on the streets of Pretoria, it was illegal to assemble in large groups. Nevertheless, a date for the protest was carefully scheduled to fall on a Thursday, when most Black women were given their one day off in a backbreaking workweek. Fearing a decisive and brutal police response, these women grouped inconspicuously in twos and threes, fully aware of the peril they faced. They'd seen their husbands beaten, their sons imprisoned at the hands of White police officers. The act of will on that day was deliberate defiance—a cry of piercing resistance that shook the nation.

The twenty thousand, many carrying babies on their backs, stood together, burning their passbooks in smoldering heaps, singing a warning. *Wathint' abafazi*, they droned, *wathint' imbokodo, uza kufa*.

> You strike a woman,
> You strike a rock.
> You will be crushed and die.[3]

Their resolve shouldn't have been startling. By this point, the women of South Africa had a decades-long history of pushing reform—especially where it meant organizing to protect vulnerable mothers and children. Historically treated as property with few rights, women were considered minors in the eyes of the law throughout their lives. They could not hold their own bank accounts. If their husband died, they might register the family home in their son's name, lest they risk being chased from their house as a squatter. So when apartheid began to codify the oppression of Black people in service of a White superstate, Black women bore the weight of a double oppression.

In response, women activists founded trade unions in the industries where they had long labored: laundry, clothing, furniture, and baking—the perfect training grounds for leadership as they asserted power and improved working conditions. The Federation of South African Women was formed to target political change: majority rule, an end to apartheid policy, and rights and freedoms for women.

Women organized to fight a proposed fare increase on the buses from townships to urban centers, some walking ten miles each way to work in support of the boycott. When a rally of five thousand women was met with armed police who beat the assembled and arrested thousands, and the government announced legislation that would have ended the bus service entirely, these women did not waver. Ultimately it was the government that caved, and the bus fare increase was rolled back.

In the 1950s, as male leaders of Black resistance increasingly faced prison, exile, or even death, South Africa looked to its women, seasoned fighters in the battle for civil rights. As her husband scratched twenty-seven years' worth of lines onto his prison walls, Winnie Madikizela-Mandela continued his work, chipping away at the control of the White power-holding minority—*chip, crack, splinter*—that would ultimately free her husband from his incarceration and bring apartheid to its knees.

"We are aware that the road before us is uphill," she said, "but we shall fight to the bitter end for justice."[4] And bitter it was. As the government saw the threat she represented, she was arrested, imprisoned, and tortured. But even from her own cell she would not be silenced.

Every August 9, South Africa honors these women. The observances vary from household to household, town to town. Maybe a housewife will take a break from her daily labors, put her feet up for a change, and rest. Maybe a group of girlfriends will head to a restaurant for a celebratory dinner in honor of their forebears. Maybe an office will have a moment of remembrance for the women who paved their way. Increasingly, walks are held to reenact the original protest of 1956.

Now, on National Women's Day 2011, in a small, dusty town in the north of Limpopo, a woman spoke to our crowd from the scratchy microphone inside the shade tent. Her speech was mostly in the Venda dialect, but I understood passages in English.

"We are grateful to the courageous women who protested against apartheid." The microphone in the tent screeched with feedback. "Without their actions, women would not have been granted the right to vote. Today we celebrate the powerful women in our lives: mothers, sisters, and friends who protect, nurture, and guide us through life's journey."

When the speech ended and the applause died away, half the women who had been gathered in the tent scattered, only to return a few minutes later carrying colorful pottery or woven bowls laden with food. They were serving us lunch.

Once the last of the dishes had been carefully placed along the tables, the chief rose from his seat in the tent and moved to fill his plate. As special guests, we were next invited to help ourselves. Behind us were all the village men, and then gaggles of children moved into the queue. Finally, once every other plate had been filled, the women took their portion.

Back when the Grannies had visited us in the States, the men in the South African contingent had always assumed for themselves pride of place. But it wasn't just that they ignored lines and headed straight to the food table or chose the best seats on the bus that rankled me. It was that they left the women to struggle with their own luggage. It was that the women made no fuss, seemingly comfortable with the arrangement. At the time, I had struggled with my discomfort every time this happened. I was genuinely trying to observe without judgment, to leave room for acknowledging how norms and etiquette differ across ethnic groups. But a lifetime of "women and children first" had left a mark on my psyche, and I was wrestling to make sense of this flip-flopped chivalry.

Now I was seeing the village women prostrate themselves on the ground as the male chieftain passed, not even deigning to look at them.

If I forced myself to think about it, was there really any *natural* order that said women should go first? Should be waited upon? Should be protected? I honestly didn't think so. But my emotions felt like a knotty, gnarled mess inside of me. I could not tease the strands apart, and there was no correct answer.

The feast looked plentiful enough to feed the entire village, but when filling my plate I was been mindful to not take too much. I couldn't recognize many of the dishes, but they appeared to be made from dried grains and legumes. Fresh fruits and vegetables would be scarce where water was a precious commodity, I figured. Laid out were several bowls of mopane worms, which I left for those coming after me. (No sense being greedy.)

Plate full, I returned to my seat next to Catherine and tucked into my lunch. Watching the village women slowly shuffle through the food line, I allowed myself a private, furtive smile as I contemplated a female chief taking command of this village. While it's true that chiefs are almost always men, on a few occasions women have been selected by the council of elders. Usually they are temporary leaders, perhaps a wife assuming the power of her late husband until her eldest son is old enough to step up. The wisdom and even-handedness of these women, I have to believe, is no different from the judgment of their male counterparts. But the power these women wield has to be precarious, conspicuous as they are. They are reportedly challenged—threatened, even—by male relatives queasy to see so much power commanded by a woman, or maybe just eyeing an opportunity to ascend the hierarchy. But the importance of women chieftains isn't about optics. Sometimes it takes a woman in charge before health-care education is prioritized, before other women and the community's children are given a critical voice.

During apartheid, South African women held barely 3 percent of all government seats. When Nelson Mandela and the ANC assumed power, that figure rose by tenfold, to almost 30 percent. Today almost half of all legislative positions in South Africa are held by women.

And yet my Grannies are still not safe walking alone at night. "I'm scared because I stay alone," Bull had said. "They rape and steal; they break the house. And sometimes they kill you."[5]

This is a great contradiction of South African history, where on the one hand, powerful women have shaped the nation's story from the precolonial period to the present, and on the other, women continue to endure high rates of gender-based violence, sexual violence, and intimate partner violence. I thought about Bull standing up to her abusive husband. *I am not a dog.*

Send one young woman to university. Build one house to shelter a woman and her grandchildren. Start one more women's soccer team. Beka fights these battles in her own way.

After lunch, the village women played a short soccer game. We clapped and cheered from the sidelines, and they acknowledged us with smiles.

By the time the game ended, the afternoon sun had traveled far across the azure skies, and it was time to begin our drive back home.

"The chief has gifts to present to you before we leave," Beka told us. I raised my eyebrows, surprised. The man himself stood next to a table with an array of handmade baskets. As we approached, he nodded and handed each of us our gift. I thanked him as I received mine—a basket of bright yellow, black, and green with a handled lid. Beautiful craftsmanship— excuse me, *craftswomanship*. Upon closer examination, I saw it had been woven from colored plastic bags. Mere trash, discarded, had been seen for the resource it was, lovingly braided into something beautiful and useful.

Later that night, at dinner, Beka told us that the chief had initially wanted to honor our group with a much larger gift—a cow. Luckily, he had heeded her wise and undoubtedly diplomatic counsel and refrained. I guess she figured it would have been too great a headache for us, trying to get a heifer through US customs.

So discreet, our Mama Beka.

The Baobab Tree

I want them to have a safe spot, where they can sit, sing, and feel love.—Rebecca "Beka" Ntsanwisi, founder of the Soccer Grannies[1]

I HAVE A FAIRLY REALISTIC VIEW OF MY STRENGTHS, AND I AM NOT myopic about my weaknesses. I'm very logical and organized and love my lists. I make a mean super-fudgy chocolate chip brownie. I'm easygoing and can get along with most anyone. On the flip side, I have a fear of heights that tethers me to the inside railing of lookout towers. I cannot (will not?) walk in heels. Not a social butterfly, I glue myself to my husband's side when forced to attend parties.

Without any doubt, I do not have the ease and quick thinking necessary to excel or even participate in the world of live radio. Which is why I was dumbfounded when the SABC radio announcer whom I *thought* I'd been watching host his live hour on the air as a silent *guest*, turned to me and introduced me to his listeners.

"Friends of Mama Beka are always welcome to the show," he said in a resonant, perfect-for-radio baritone.

I'd been set up.

It was our last full day in South Africa. The following afternoon we'd fly out of Johannesburg and arc our way back to Massachusetts.

For our final outing, Beka took us on a driving tour of Polokwane, the capital city of the province of Limpopo. It was nothing like observing gnus grazing on safari, the festive reunion in the Grannies' hometown, or the cultural immersion of the remote village where we'd celebrated National Women's Day. Rather, today we drove past tall, modern office buildings, interspersed with green, sloping park expanses.

South Africa has it all.

But the sight of most interest to us on this fine late winter day in Polokwane was built in time to host the nineteenth World Cup.

On May 15, 2004, President Nelson Mandela had been given a seat of honor in the front row of a lavish auditorium in Zurich. FIFA president Joseph "Sepp" Blatter walked to the podium, where he was handed a large, creamy white envelope. He was about to announce to the world which nation had won the bid to host the 2010 World Cup. Throughout South Africa, people were collectively holding their breath, their clasped hands and anxious toots on vuvuzelas captured on simulcasts across the nation.

"I discover it with you," Blatter said to the nervously chattering assemblage as he carefully ripped the envelope and slowly began to pull out the card. "The two thousand and ten FIFA World Cup ... will be organized—" Pandemonium. Shouts and crying broke out as "South Africa" appeared in large sans serif font above the torn envelope's edge.[2]

Tears of joy streaked down Mandela's face as well-wishers swarmed to embrace their beloved Tata.

The tournament would be staged in Africa for the very first time in its seventy-four-year history, and the young democracy of South Africa would host the world only twelve years after the sport's governing body had lifted sanctions that for so many years had barred it from play.

It was a time of great optimism and pride for the Rainbow Nation. In short order, nine cities were chosen to host the games, Polokwane one of them. Scaffolding sprouted along the horizon as beautification projects were undertaken and a brand-new soccer stadium was slowly erected—part of the more than $1 billion the government ended up spending on improvements in advance of the tournament.

The new Peter Mokaba Stadium is a modern structure, designed with the baobab in mind. The stadium's architect borrowed from the iconic tree's squat, sturdy trunk to create four towers grounding the four corners of the arena and supporting the roof, which was designed to flex with the seasonal wind and rains.

It is a sight to behold.

During the World Cup, it held some forty-one thousand fans, come together under the open sky of South Africa to cheer the sport they loved.

As she led us around Polokwane, Beka relayed how special hosting the World Cup was for her city and her country. The job creation, infrastructure expansion, and urban renewal provided a considerable boost to the economy and national pride. "It made clear the importance of sport and how it can bring everybody from all over the world together," Beatrice told me—a theme obviously dear to her heart.[3]

After our tour of the city, we got to see where Mama Beka had become a national icon. The state-owned South African Broadcasting Corporation has an enormous presence in Polokwane and hosts five television and nineteen radio stations nationwide, including the station that hosts Beka's weekly call-in show.

She led us up a wide hallway with giant windows on either side, granting views to a veritable light show of blinking electronics. Radio announcers wearing headphones were seated in front of display screens. Through the glass, I watched one host engaged in animated, hand-waving discussion. I looked for a flashing "On Air" sign, but evidently my expectation was out of date.

Beka opened one of the studio doors and motioned for us to enter. She whispered something to the lanky broadcaster, who smiled at her and nodded. I was busy gawking at the equipment and so missed when she backed out and closed the door behind her.

"Listeners," he said in a voice made of melting chocolate, "we have some special guests with us in the studio today. Your names?"

If I'd had a wearable fitness tracker in 2011, it would have shown a dangerous gap in my heart rate that afternoon.

He motioned for us to approach the guest microphone that faced his command center. Stuck between Catherine and Allison on one side and Heather on the other, I shuffled toward the malevolent-looking mic that would broadcast my inarticulacy across South African airwaves. "Let me give that some thought and get back to you by email" wasn't going to fly on live radio.

Really, though, the announcer was a total pro and made it easy for us. Long before I relaxed my clenched fists, we were into our groove, bantering back and forth about soccer in the United States and why it had failed to gain the same popularity it enjoyed in the rest of the world.

"Soccer has so much more *action* than your beloved baseball," our honey-voiced interviewer pressed.

You're preaching to the choir, pal. Baseball has never held my attention. American football hasn't, either. Those games are mostly waiting. Give me a fast-paced soccer match any day. (I diplomatically failed to mention to him that I'm not much of a professional sports person in general.)

The host nimbly turned the conversation to our favorite Vakhegula Vakhegula squad. "Beka now has eight teams of Granny soccer players, you know," I chirped eagerly—obviously warming to my international radio debut. "They're great role models for us in the US and for younger South African women too."

The radio announcer admitted that initially he had laughed at their attempts to play soccer. "But I grew to respect them," he told us, and now even encouraged his own grandmother to play with one of the Grannies' squads. To date, she hadn't yet laced up her cleats.

We vented about how hard it had been to get the team to the States and how through it all Beka had always maintained a positive attitude, convinced it would work out even when everything had looked like it was falling to pieces. "Mmm, yes," our host said, almost purring. "Mama Beka moves mountains with her positive attitude."

An aggressively blinking blue light yanked my attention to the command console. Perhaps a one-minute warning until commercial break? The announcer took note and put to us one final question: "We in South

Africa have seen the Grannies play soccer. You women look quite fit. Tell us, please—how did the Grannies win a trophy?"

Another gap in my heart rate.

Clustered around the microphone, Catherine, Allison, Heather, and I exchanged raised eyebrows. Fighting the urge to clear my throat, I leaned in close, shrugging my shoulder. "You saw the trophy, right?" I extemporized. "I mean, you can't question that. Your team of Grannies is inspirational."

My soccer buddies nodded, quickly, as if to say, *Yes, that.*

Saved by the flashing blue light, he let us get away with our nonanswer and wrapped up the segment, thanking us for stopping by.

We fled into the hallway.

"*Beka*," Heather chided, "you should have *warned* us that we were going to be on the *radio*."

"Did we do okay?" I asked.

Beka just laughed. "Thank you, thank you, my friends. That was perfect. Everyone in South Africa needs to hear about our Soccer Grannies. I so want them to get the respect they deserve. I love the Grannies. I want everyone to know them like I do."[4]

In retrospect, I realized that if Beka had told us in advance that we were going to do live radio publicity for the Grannies, I might have booked an early flight back to Boston. Her methods were effective.

Our last minutes with Beka ticked away far too quickly.

All the next morning, the day of our departure, my slumped posture spoke my sorrow; I didn't want to be separated from my friend again. Meanwhile, as we were ostensibly gathered to make our farewells, she was talking without stopping for a breath—perhaps a strategy to delay the inevitable.

She was telling us all about her grand idea to protect the older women of South Africa, especially those suffering from dementia. Her plan was to build a senior residence where vulnerable seniors would be cared for and could thrive. A plot of land was already in her hawk-eyed view. She was confident she could readily assemble building supplies and secure the labor to build houses; after all, this was nothing more than an expansive house, and how many houses had she already built? She could hire care workers with support from aid organizations and government subsidies. She practically had a blueprint in her head. I could already see the sign out front—"Mama Beka's Home for the Aged." If anyone could make it happen, Beka Ntsanwisi could.

"I'm just trying to do what I can, as much as I can," she said with a sigh. "The retirement home will come, but not for some time. For now, I teach the people about dementia. I tell people to take their mothers to the doctors." And she badgers and wheedles her Grannies onto soccer fields; she knows that a little bit of regular physical exercise will make them that much less likely to develop dementia, that much less likely to be targeted by a mob unable to see the Grannies like she does.

I wished we'd had more time to learn from Beka while we were in South Africa—to spend more time with the Grannies, to see more of their beautiful country. I promised myself that I would return to South Africa. But until then, I would stay in touch with my dear friend. I would assist her in any way I could from an ocean away. As I'd gotten to know her over the past year and a half, I'd taken a stake in her dreams. More than almost anything, I wanted to find a way to help her do her life's work—sheltering, feeding, protecting the vulnerable women of South Africa.

Our time was up. We had to start our drive to O. R. Tambo International Airport in Johannesburg.

"Beka," said Heather, taking her hands, "we need to say goodbye. Thank you—thank you *so* much for sharing your world with us. I can't tell you what a wonderful experience it's been."

"Very soon we will host a tournament, here in South Africa," said Mama Beka, never a pause in her scheming, planning, dreaming. "We'll have teams of grandmothers attend from every country in the world. We have started the preparations. You must return."

"Oh, we'd *love* to," I said.

"Everyone should join," Beka continued, "sit and visit, dance and sing with us. They don't even have to play soccer. If you can understand us and our life, that's what helps us. Yes, I want to have a World Cup for Grannies. I want to host this before I die."

I didn't want her to talk about dying. I wasn't ready to confront this woman's mortality.

I held on to our goodbye embrace. With tears welling up, I forced a smile on my face. "It's been just wonderful, Beka," I choked. "Really wonderful. Thank you so much."

We had one final stop to make before heading to the airport. Beka had told us we must visit a particularly venerable baobab tree. A hand-painted signpost marked the turnoff. We traveled the last mile down a rust-colored dirt road, pulling over to watch ostriches grazing in the scrub. Further on, a giant tree loomed into view on the horizon. The towering, barrel-shaped trunk was capped with an expanse of wildly angled branches. As legend has it, the devil yanked the baobab tree out of the earth and thrust it back in upside down, leaving its roots dangling in the air.

We pulled into the deserted parking area and piled out of our cars. Karen and I stood next to the massive trunk and stared upward, marveling at its canopy.

"How tall is it?" she asked.

I imagined the floors of a building and guessed this one was about forty feet tall. And who knew how old; some live to be two thousand years old.

The baobab is found in thirty-two countries across Africa. As a succulent, it stores water in its trunk during the rainy season to help it survive the upcoming dry season. It's been called the Tree of Life, and for good reason. The leaves are rich in iron and can be eaten like spinach. The seeds can be roasted or pressed for oil. The pulp of the gourd-like fruit, which people use to make juice, jams, and even beer, has six times the vitamin C of an orange. The tree provides shelter, food, and water for the animals of the savanna. Sometimes you can find scars in the bark where elephants have scraped their tusks to get to the moisture-laden wood under the bark.

I took a few steps back and admired this tree's grandeur. With a plane to catch in Johannesburg, we couldn't linger, so after too few minutes, we loaded back into our cars. Heather led our caravan as we departed from the site of the mighty baobab.

We had driven only twenty minutes when I rounded a sharp curve and spotted her car pulled over by two policewomen. I slowed to a stop, parked along the side of the road, and walked back, nervous about what I would learn.

"I was going too fast," Heather explained. "And since I'm not from South Africa, the officer says she can't write me a ticket; I have to stop at the police station in the next town." She looked worried. "I'm scared we're gonna miss our flights. Maybe you guys should go on ahead."

I didn't like the idea of splitting up.

The police officer, now with a pad of paper in her hand, strolled back toward us. Suddenly Heather's face lit up. "Do you by any chance know Beka Ntswanwisi?" she asked.

"The radio personality?" asked the officer, puzzled. "Everyone knows Mama Beka."

I felt a glimmer of hope.

Heather rushed on: "Have you heard of the Soccer Grannies?" The officer raised her eyebrows and nodded. Now Heather was bubbling with excitement. "I'm one of the Americans who helped bring the team to the United States. We're here visiting Beka and the Grannies and your beautiful country."

The officer excused herself and went to confer with her partner. They returned with broad smiles on their faces. Beaming, the second officer asked, "Do you remember the overweight Granny who came to America, the one who had trouble walking?"

That description fit a few of them, I thought. "I do!" Heather enthused, diplomatically.

"That's my grandmother," the officer said, "and I can't tell you how excited I was for her. It was the trip of a lifetime for her. She'd never been out of Limpopo before. She will never forget that experience. We're so proud of her. Thank you for helping her."

The first officer added in a lowered voice, "We don't want to delay your travels. Feel free to continue on your way."

We thanked them effusively and made our way back to our cars.

We shouldn't have been surprised. *Of course* everyone knows Mama Beka.

My friend's reach brings to mind the canopy of the baobab and the sustenance and shelter it provides. Imagine its massive root system, out of sight: The biggest and oldest of trees are the most highly connected under the ground. Within a forest, the network of trees and other flora nurture each other—sharing nutrients, sending word to one another over long distances about threats, and working together for the future health of the entire forest. Above the ground, the trees appear to be separate, but under the surface they are joined in a community.

I had become part of Beka's community. She'd offered, and I'd embraced the chance to share her dreams of a South Africa that is stronger and safer for its mothers.

Strong, resilient, and lifesaving—Mama Beka is just like the baobab tree, an icon of South Africa.

EPILOGUE

Sisters in Soccer

If we come together with love, we can change the world and be one. Soccer brings us together. —Rebecca "Beka" Ntsanwisi, founder of the Soccer Grannies[1]

IT IS SUMMER 2022. A DOZEN YEARS HAVE PASSED SINCE THE GRANNIES' visit to the United States; it's been eleven years since I've hugged my friends. But our hearts are still connected.

Across an ocean, on their practice field in Nkowankowa, they still dribble their soccer ball, weaving between orange cones and taking shots on goal. Beka sends me video snippets of the game-time action, and I scan the screen for familiar faces, *so* wishing I could join them on the field. Their joyous mix of determination and laughter has only seemed to strengthen with age and experience.

The Lexpressas also still meet several times a week, although we whine a little more about aching joints. I admire my teammates who have returned to the field after hip replacements—seemingly more of us each season. I live by the motto of athlete Lynn Naftel, septuagenarian soccer player from California: "You don't quit playing soccer because you get old," she says. "You get old *because* you quit playing soccer."[2]

Back at home in Limpopo, Beka has been busy, busy. Thanks to the allure of her creative soccer initiative, she now has eighty-four soccer teams playing the beautiful game across all nine provinces of South Africa. The Grannies are changing the way their people look at older folks: These grandmothers are increasingly appreciated as a vibrant, integral part of their communities—admired for remaining strong and healthy, having fun. One game after another, one soccer team after another, Vakhegula Vakhegula sets a direction for others to follow.

Beyond the borders of South Africa, the Grannies have continued to forge international connections. Each subsequent World Cup has brought on a frenzy of Soccer Granny mania. In 2014, when Brazil hosted the tournament, Coca-Cola showcased the Grannies in a commercial celebrating the power of sport and aging with grace. Beka and several of the Grannies traveled to Rio, where they attended numerous games. Four years later, they were in Russia for the 2018 World Cup.

Africa? North America? South America? Asia? Check, check, check, check.

Next up: Europe.

In advance of the 2019 Women's World Cup, Beka held tryouts across her South African squads, choosing the best of the best for a national team to play in France. Bull and Lizzy won well-deserved spots. And when Khune learned she'd been chosen among all the teams as Vakhegula Vakhegula National's keeper, she squealed. "*Heeeeeeee!*" She may have missed the trip to the States, but she would not miss this one. "The day we departed for France, I was so excited to board the fly machine," she says. "People were asking if I was not scared. I replied that I was not scared of anything; so many people have traveled by fly machines and were able to come back safely. I told them in the name of Jesus that I would also come back safely."[3]

From Charles de Gaulle Airport and the Paris Métro, Beka sent me videos of Grannies dancing and singing. Without a doubt they earned a few curious looks from bystanders, but I know firsthand the fond enthusiasm they inspire. In France they played a game with Les Mamies Foot, their host team of French grandmothers. The seasoned South African players scored ten goals and traveled home with medals around their necks and another trophy to add to the growing collection.

Beka's dreams of hosting a Grannies' World Cup was put on hold by the onset of the global COVID-19 pandemic. As worldwide cases grew exponentially, I was afraid to imagine how the virus would affect my community; when I thought of Nkowankowa, I was *very* afraid. From my computer screen in Massachusetts, I examined maps tracing the contagion and worried about how long it would take for vaccines to reach rural South Africa.

Beka has been great about sending me updates during this anxious time. South Africa's president, Cyril Ramaphosa, has done his best to explain the government actions taken to curb the worst of the pandemic and asked for patience with the economic fallout. He has provided vital leadership in a time of fear, uncertainty, and risk.

Even so, the reality of life in South African under COVID-19 is sobering. As businesses began shuttering to protect their workers and clients, the town of Nkowankowa, unfortunately, was hit hard. "The pandemic has made me lose my job," Granny Omo says.[4] When it became too unsafe to continue operations, the children's nursery where she worked closed down, depriving her of needed income. Many, many households like Omo's find the added burden heavy.

While the shutdowns have been critical from a public health perspective, they've only exacerbated long-term problems throughout South Africa. Declining grain and fruit production, already impacted by severe droughts in 2018 and 2019, have escalated food insecurity. Millions more people have become dependent on government subsidies and food donations. Beka, ever the activist, began soliciting donations for fifty-pound bags of maize and organized deliveries to the people in her community who were most in need.

Each solitary act of kindness is a candle in the darkness. And when things seemed darkest and her people were weary, South Africa danced.

The song "Jerusalema," composed by a Limpopo musician, was first released as a catchy club hit in late 2019. By the summer of 2020 its upbeat gospel cry for salvation and home had captured the attention of a world yearning for hope. "Celebrate our South African heritage," President Ramaphosa urged that September. Join the #JerusalemChallenge spreading globally, he said, and "demonstrate our good music, good dance, and good moves."[5] The Soccer Grannies heeded the call and soon shared a video of themselves, arms waving, hips shimmying, to the song.

I loved seeing the Grannies—some in traditional Tsonga attire, some in soccer kit—move with synchronized steps on the very field where we had played our friendly game, except now most were wearing masks and staying six feet apart. This virtual connection in a time of separation tugged on my heartstrings, and when Mama Beka challenged us to respond with our own video, my fellow Lexpressas and I eagerly accepted.

At the time, we had only just made it back onto our Massachusetts soccer field after a long, lonely lockdown. It was fantastic to be back together. Our footwork was perhaps less than fantastic—at least compared to our South African sisters'—but we twirled a message of love back to them.

As treatment protocols have stabilized and vaccines make travel safer, Beka has begun talking again of hosting a Grannies' World Cup. Teams from Benin, Togo, Zimbabwe, Guinea, Mozambique, Ghana, and Malawi, all inspired by Vakhegula Vakhegula, are slated to participate. Les Mamies Foot will be there, and of course the Lexpressas will too.

Coach Abraham is excited to welcome the guest teams. "We will show the world what we do."[6]

I am exceedingly grateful that Beka's cancer has remained in remission, allowing her to train her mind and energies on helping others. Sadly, in the intervening years, we have lost some of our beloved soccer friends. In 2016, we mourned the passing of Granny Ennie Moyo, who died at age sixty-five. Beka sent me photos of Beatrice speaking at the graveside service; Bull was there too, dressed in a smart skirt and hat. On our side of the Atlantic, we grieve Anne Strong, who did so much to open soccer pitches to women and girls and was the first to suggest inviting the Grannies to the States. She passed away in 2013, at age sixty-eight, after a battle with lung cancer.

Our lives are finite. With this realization, we endeavor to appreciate each day. We take nothing for granted. We move our bodies. We foster our friendships. We find joy where we can. As eighty-six-year-old Granny Gingirikani Mirriam Mushwana says, "the secret to live to this age is to take care of oneself." Exercise. Eat healthy foods. Keep the indulgences to a minimum. Respect yourself. "Take care of your body until God decides to take you."[7]

I often marvel at the turn my life has taken since that first chance video encounter with the Grannies. I became a passionate fundraiser, driven to stand up and speak out where before I might have remained silent. To advocate for the people and causes I hold most dear, I've had to confront my aversion to the limelight. The Grannies have opened my heart to a bigger world, and I want to share their story as far and wide as possible.

My South African friends have fun, feel their power, approach their lives with gratitude. When their burdens grow heavy, they are

The venerable baobab, Tree of Life, provides shelter, food, and water to all living things on the South African savanna. Limpopo, August 11, 2011. *Photo by Catherine Steiner*

philosophical: *Eh, life goes on.* They understand that life is bigger than them, that they are part of a whole, so they come together and support one another and create something beautiful. They hold one another up, giving each other the courage to dream of bigger things. Every time an eighty-year-old Granny kicks a soccer ball along that pitch, she stakes a claim: *I belong.* Soccer isn't just a man's sport, their confidence tells us; it's a sport big enough for everyone. Athleticism doesn't belong only to the young; bodies of all ages and sizes and abilities can do beautiful things.

They are teachers, my Grannies, showing us how to live life more fully, joyfully, meaningfully. And they, in turn, have come to this place of flourishing through the gentle coaxing of Mama Beka.

I have come to see Beka as a role model of fearless generosity. She recognizes, catalogues, and uses her every advantage, her every gift and privilege, to protect and nurture, to revive those with less. Granny Makoma Selina Matwalane couldn't have said it better: "I would like to thank Mama Beka so much for her sense of humor and her encouragement. I love her so much."[8]

As I write, I am optimistic about COVID risks waning; I can hardly wait to return to South Africa for the Grannies' World Cup. We will have so much fun together. Our relationship is just beginning.

Life? *Eish!* It is so good.

Acknowledgments

Writing is a uniquely solitary experience, but in the twelve years during which this story unfolded and found its way to the page, I was never alone. An outpouring of thanks goes to the following:

Rebecca Ntsanwisi—"Mama Beka"—who over the years I have known her has been generosity itself, sharing with me her wisdom, insights, and recollections for the asking. She has inspired, enriched, and soothed countless lives. Without her there would be neither Soccer Grannies nor *Soccer Grannies*. *Inkomu*, Beka.

The women whose stories are the core of this book—the Grannies who move me with their candor, selflessness, and humor. In particular, I thank Annah Masesa Vuma, Beatrice Tshabalala, Gingirikani Mirriam Mushwana, Maka Rossina Mathe, Mamalia Chauke Novela, Makoma Selina Matwalane, Modjadji Mdaka Gayisa, Nkhensani Nyavani Florah Baloyi, Nora Mtileni, Uyazi Asnath Shibiti, and Grannies coach Abraham Sevor Kwabina for sitting down for formal interviews. I also thank Happiness Maake for conducting, translating, and transcribing those interviews and providing invaluable situational and cultural context.

My publication team—Christen Karniski, editor at Rowman & Littlefield, who previously played soccer professionally and shared my enthusiasm for telling the story of the Soccer Grannies. Gillian MacKenzie, agent at Gillian MacKenzie Agency, provided essential connections and guidance and is a recreational footballer just like me!

My collaborative editors—E. B. Bartels, who first suggested I conduct research to better understand what's at stake for the Grannies, and Debbie Justice, whose insightful and heartfelt guidance, creative flair, and attention to detail got me over the finish line.

My first creative writing teacher—Mindy Pollack-Fusi, who taught with equal measures of fun and encouragement. Just what I needed.

My guiding light on South Africa's history and the issues that impact the lives of my friends who live there—Meghan Healy-Clancy of Bridgewater State University, who directed me to enlightening books and articles, pointed out holes in my research, and shepherded me through cultural sensitivity issues. Her counsel and insight have proven invaluable.

My amazing Lexpressas soccer teammates—Catherine Steiner, Heather Broglio, and Allison LaClaire, who helped make miracles happen, and to all the rest of my fellow Pinkies who eagerly helped host our South African visitors and continue to nimbly dash and scoop up my bad passes on the soccer field.

The Massachusetts soccer pioneers—Lois Kessin and Anne Strong, who championed soccer in Massachusetts and made it possible for so many women and girls to find our way to the pitch.

The photographers—Tessa Frootko Gordon, whose unforgettable photographs grace these pages. Please check out her beautiful work on Instagram (@frogorfoto) or contact her by email (frugorfoto@gmail .com). Mike Broglio of MDB Sports was with us in South Africa and snapped some great candids of our time together (http://www.mdbsports .com). Catherine Steiner and Lafe LaClaire generously let me rifle through the many pictures they captured of the events narrated. Dineo Raolane was both an evenhanded referee for our Nkowankowa soccer scrimmage and a steady hand when taking the stunning photographs for the Grannies' profiles.

My cherished writing group—Laura Beretsky, Marcie Kaplan, Maggie Lowe, S. Schirl Smith, and Bev Stohl, who I met in a GrubStreet memoir writing class. We've convened regularly for five years and counting, and have lovingly held and nurtured each of our stories that so need to be told.

And finally, my family—daughters Karen and Kate, who have been rousing cheerleaders for me, and my husband, Mark, who edited several drafts even though there were no chase scenes. Love you guys, darn it!

Notes

Epigraph

1. Final stanza of "The Baobab Tree," by John Akanvariyuei Agandin, *Village Boy Impressions* (blog), April 3, 2017, https://villageboyimpressions.blogspot.com/2017/04/the-baobab-tree.html.

Prologue

1. Nelson Mandela, keynote address given at the inaugural Laureus World Sports Awards, Monte Carlo, Monaco, May 25, 2000, https://www.laureus.com/news/celebrating-the-legacy-of-a-hero-on-mandela-day.

2. Republic of South Africa, "National Anthem," accessed May 20, 2022, https://www.gov.za/about-sa/national-symbols/national-anthem.

Part I

1. Nelson Mandela, *The Long Walk to Freedom: The Autobiography of Nelson Mandela* (London: Little, Brown, 1994), 625.

Chapter 1

1. Abraham Sevor Kwabena, interview with Happiness Maake in Nkowankowa, Limpopo, September 18, 2021.

2. In this chapter, unless otherwise specified, quotations have been compiled from several sources: Pumza Fihlani, "S Africa's Football 'Grannies' Look to World Cup," BBC News, last modified December 3, 2009, http://news.bbc.co.uk/2/hi/africa/8389067.stm; Chris Murphy, "World Cup Fever Grips African Grannies," CNN, last modified October 25, 2009, http://edition.cnn.com/2009/SPORT/football/10/25/football.africa.world.cup/index.html; Reuters, "Grannies Take on the Beautiful Game," video, uploaded October 22, 2009, https://web.archive.org/web/20100614221553/https://www.youtube.com/watch?v=4yabcFLlTAA; Ndundu Sithole, "South African Grannies Catch World Cup Fever," Reuters, updated October 21, 2009, https://www.reuters.com/article/ozasp-soccer-world-grannies-idAFJOE59L01C20091022; and the author's personal correspondence.

3. Beka Ntsanwisi, as quoted in Fihlani, "S Africa's Football 'Grannies.'"

Chapter 2

1. Gingirikani Mirriam Mushwana, interview with Happiness Maake in Nkowankowa, Limpopo, September 18, 2021 (interview conducted in Xitsonga and translated into English by Mr. Maake).

2. Quotations in this chapter are compiled from multiple sources: the author's personal correspondence; Pumza Fihlani, "S Africa's Football 'Grannies' Look to World Cup," *BBC News*, last modified December 3, 2009, http://news.bbc.co.uk/2/hi/africa/8389067. stm; Robyn Dixon, "They Kick Like Grannies, Proudly," *Los Angeles Times*, June 21, 2010, https://www.latimes.com/archives/la-xpm-2010-jun-21-la-fg-soccer-grannies -20100622-story.html; Lara-Ann De Wet, dir., *Alive and Kicking: The Soccer Grannies of South Africa*, film (New York: Lazuli Film, 2015), https://www.soccergrannies.com; and Maka Rosina Mathe, Makoma Selina Matwalane, and Nkhensani Nyavani Florah Baloyi, interviews with Happiness Maake in Nkowankowa, Limpopo, September 18, 2021 (interviews conducted in Xitsonga and translated into English by Mr. Maake).

Chapter 3

1. Abraham Sevor Kwabena, as quoted in Lara-Ann De Wet, dir., *Alive and Kicking: The Soccer Grannies of South Africa*, film (New York: Lazuli Film, 2015), https://www .soccergrannies.com.

2. Lisa Lindahl, as quoted in Allison Keys, "How the First Sports Bra Got Its Stabilizing Start," *Smithsonian*, March 18, 2020, https://www.smithsonianmag.com/smithsonian -institution/how-first-sports-bra-got-stabilizing-start-180974427/.

3. This snarky reportage courtesy of the *Glasgow Herald*, May 9, 1881, as quoted in Patrick Brennan, "'England' v 'Scotland'—1881: First Attempt to Establish Women's Football Disrupted by Hooligans," *Donmouth* (blog), last modified March 9, 2020, http:// www.donmouth.co.uk/womens_football/1881.html.

4. "Nettie Honeyball" in the *Daily Sketch*, as quoted in Anton Rippon, "From the Press Box: England's Women Footballers Deserve More Recognition," Sports Journalists' Association, July 19, 2018, https://www.sportsjournalists.co.uk/view-from-the-pressbox/ view-from-the-press-box-why-englands-women-footballers-deserve-more-recognition/.

5. In this chapter, quotations from Anne Strong are as recounted by her husband, Charlie Allen, in an interview with author, January 24, 2018.

6. In this chapter, quotations from Lois Kessin are from an interview with the author, August 28, 2018.

Chapter 4

1. Abraham Sevor Kwabena, as quoted in Lara-Ann De Wet, dir., *Alive and Kicking: The Soccer Grannies of South Africa*, film (New York: Lazuli Film, 2015), https://www .soccergrannies.com.

2. This and following quotations from Beka Ntsanwisi are pulled from private correspondence with the author.

3. "Betsy" is a pseudonym. The following quotations are taken from her private correspondence with the author.

4. This wisdom is universally attributed to the late, great Archbishop Desmond Tutu, but I have not been able to ascertain where and when he originally said it.

CHAPTER 5

1. Makoma Selina Matwalane, interview with Happiness Maake in Nkowankowa, Limpopo, September 18, 2021 (interview conducted in Xitsonga and translated into English by Mr. Maake).

2. Beka's quotations in this chapter are assembled from the author's private correspondence and from Beka Ntsanwisi's presentation "Alive and Kicking," Ashoka Fellows Round Table on Aging, Zoom conference, streamed live July 8, 2020, https://drive.google.com/file/d/1rFt374TAoJhxY_olgwABbriuR6dnr_Ot/view.

3. Times Editors, "The Land Question Must Be Handled with Extreme Sensitivity," *TimesLive*, February 28, 2014, https://www.timeslive.co.za/news/south-africa/2014-02-28-the-land-question-must-be-handled-with-extreme-sensitivity/, as quoted in Cherryl Walker, "Critical Reflections on South Africa's 1913 Natives Land Act and Its Legacies: Introduction." *Journal of South African Studies* 40, no. 4 (2014): 655.

MAMA BEKA

1. In this chapter, quotations from Beka Ntsanwisi are compiled from three sources: an interview with author on July 15, 2010; Beka Ntsanwisi, "Alive and Kicking," Ashoka Fellows Round Table on Aging, Zoom conference, streamed live July 8, 2020, https://drive.google.com/file/d/1rFt374TAoJhxY_olgwABbriuR6dnr_Ot/view; and Rebecca Ntsanwisi, speech given at the 6th International Women's Conference, Bangaluru, India, February 7–9, 2014, video, https://www.youtube.com/watch?v=RL6fLIdQWJs.

CHAPTER 6

1. This evocative quote was found among a collection of African proverbs at Kalima-Quotes.com, https://www.kalimaquotes.com/quotes/192457/by-pounding-the-dough.

2. All excerpts from this news story are found in William C. Rhoden, "For the Love of Soccer and a Lasting Sisterhood," *New York Times*, June 6, 2010, https://www.nytimes.com/2010/06/07/sports/soccer/07rhoden.html.

3. In this chapter, this and other emails and messages are pulled from the personal correspondence of either the author or Catherine Steiner.

4. All excerpts from this news story can be found in Robyn Dixon, "They Kick like Grannies, Proudly," *Los Angeles Times*, June 21, 2010, https://www.latimes.com/archives/la-xpm-2010-jun-21-la-fg-soccer-grannies-20100622-story.html.

PART II

1. This quotation is attributed to Nelson Mandela, purportedly from a 2001 speech he gave; further sourcing is unavailable.

Chapter 7

1. Makoma Selina Matwalane, interview with Happiness Maake in Nkowankowa, Limpopo, September 18, 2021 (interview conducted in Xitsonga and translated into English by Mr. Maake).

2. This narrative and the following quotations from Tessa Frootko Gordon are pulled from her interview with author on July 22, 2019.

Granny Rossina

1. In this chapter, quotations from Maka Rossina Mathe are taken from her interview with Happiness Maake in Nkowankowa, Limpopo, September 18, 2021 (interview conducted in Xitsonga and translated into English by Mr. Maake).

Chapter 8

1. Nkhensani Nyavani Florah Baloyi, interview with Happiness Maake in Nkowankowa, Limpopo, September 18, 2021 (interview conducted in Xitsonga and translated into English by Mr. Maake).

2. Beatrice Tshabalala, as quoted in Mark Goodman, "Lexpressas Host 'Soccer Grannies' from South Africa," *Wicked Local*, July 23, 2010, https://www.wickedlocal.com/story/lexington-minuteman/2010/07/23/lexpressas-host-soccer-grannies-from/39094522007/.

3. In this chapter, quotations from Beka Ntsanwisi are pulled in part from Beka Ntsanwisi, "Alive and Kicking," Ashoka Fellows Round Table on Aging, Zoom conference, streamed live July 8, 2020, https://drive.google.com/file/d/1rFt374TAoJhxY_olgwABbriuR6dnr_Ot/view.

4. Beatrice Nyeleti Tshabalala, interview with the author via email, January 30, 2022.

Granny Khune

1. Unless otherwise noted, quotations from Mamaila Chauke Novela in this chapter are pulled from her interview with Happiness Maake in Nkowankowa, Limpopo, September 18, 2021 (interview conducted in Xitsonga and translated into English by Mr. Maake).

Chapter 9

1. Beka Ntsanwisi, "Alive and Kicking," Ashoka Fellows Round Table on Aging, Zoom conference, streamed live July 8, 2020, https://drive.google.com/file/d/1rFt-374TAoJhxY_olgwABbriuR6dnr_Ot/view.

2. Robyn Dixon, "They Kick Like Grannies, Proudly," *Los Angeles Times*, June 21, 2010, https://www.latimes.com/archives/la-xpm-2010-jun-21-la-fg-soccer-grannies-20100622-story.html.

Chapter 10

1. Abraham Sevor Kwabena, interview with Happiness Maake in Nkowankowa, Limpopo, September 18, 2021.

2. This and the following news coverage from David Abel, "Kicking up Their Heels: Soccer Grannies Find Their Way from South Africa," *Boston Globe*, July 17, 2010, http://archive.boston.com/news/local/massachusetts/articles/2010/07/17/kicking_up_their_heels/.

3. Lara-Ann De Wet, dir., *Alive and Kicking: The Soccer Grannies of South Africa*, film (New York: Lazuli Film, 2015), https://www.soccergrannies.com.

GRANNY BULL

1. In this chapter, all quotations from Annah Masesa Vuma are pulled from three sources: her interview with Happiness Maake in Nkowankowa, Limpopo, September 18, 2021 (interview conducted in Xitsonga and translated into English by Mr. Maake); Lara-Ann De Wet, dir., *Alive and Kicking: The Soccer Grannies of South Africa*, film (New York: Lazuli Film, 2015), https://www.soccergrannies.com; and her interview with Tessa Frootko Gordon in Nkowankowa, Limpopo, October 2, 2020 (interview conducted in English and Xitsonga with interpretation by Abraham Sevor Kwabena and English translation by Nkhensani Ntsanwisi).

CHAPTER 11

1. I first encountered this beautiful African proverb in Risenga Maluleke, *Grandparenthood in the Context of Ageing in South Africa*, report no. 03-00-12 (Pretoria: Statistics South Africa, 2018), 4, http://www.statssa.gov.za/publications/Report%2003-00-12/Report%2003-00-122016.pdf.

GRANNY NORAH

1. In this chapter, quotations from Norah Mtileni are from two primary sources: her interview with Happiness Maake in Nkowankowa, Limpopo, September 18, 2021 (interview conducted in Xitsonga and translated into English by Mr. Maake); and her interview with Tessa Frootko Gordon in Nkowankowa, Limpopo, October 2, 2020 (interview conducted in English and Xitsonga, with interpretation by Abraham Sevor Kwabena and English translation by Nkhensani Ntsanwisi).

CHAPTER 12

1. Mamaila Chauke Novela, interview with Happiness Maake in Nkowankowa, Limpopo, September 18, 2021 (interview conducted in Xitsonga and translated into English by Mr. Maake).

2. Mark Goodman, "Lexpressas Host 'Soccer Grannies' from South Africa," *Wicked Local*, July 23, 2010, https://www.wickedlocal.com/story/lexington-minuteman/2010/07/23/lexpressas-host-soccer-grannies-from/39094522007/.

3. Anna Masesa Vuma, interview with Tessa Gordon in Nkowankowa, Limpopo, October 2, 2020 (interview conducted in English and Xitsonga with interpretation by Abraham Sevor Kwabena and English translation by Nkhensani Ntsanwisi).

4. Rebecca Ntsanwisi, as quoted in Goodman, "Lexpressas Host 'Soccer Grannies.'"

Part III

1. While I cannot locate the original sourcing for this quotation, it is commonly attributed to Nelson Mandela. See, for example, Bathandwa Mbola, "The Game That United a Nation," South African Government News Agency, July 5, 2011, https://www .sanews.gov.za/south-africa/game-united-nation.

Chapter 13

1. Beatrice Nyeleti Tshabalala, interview with the author via email, January 30, 2022.

Granny Omo

1. In this chapter, quotations from Uyazi Asnath Shiviti are from her interview with Happiness Maake in Nkowankowa, Limpopo, September 18, 2021 (interview conducted in Xitsonga and translated into English by Mr. Maake).

Chapter 14

1. Attributed to Bill Shankly. His actual words were, "Somebody said that football's a matter of life and death to you; I said, 'Listen, it's more important than that,'" in an interview with Shelley Rohde on *Live from Two*, Granada TV, May 20, 1981. Per Mark Jones, "Bill Shankly's Famous 'Life and Death' Misquote and What Liverpool Icon Really Meant," *Mirror*, last modified March 31, 2020, https://www.mirror.co.uk/sport/football/ news/bill-shanklys-famous-life-death-21784583.

2. Lizo Sitoto, as quoted in Jeré Longman, "Origins of Tournament in an Infamous Prison," *New York Times*, July 5, 2010, https://www.nytimes.com/2010/07/06/sports/ soccer/06robben.html.

Granny Gayisa

1. In this chapter, quotations from Modjadji Mdaka Gayisa are pulled from two sources: her interview with Happiness Maake in Nkowankowa, Limpopo, September 18, 2021 (interview conducted in Xitsonga and translated into English by Mr. Maake); and her interview with Tessa Frootko Gordon in Nkowankowa, Limpopo, October 2, 2020 (interview conducted in English and Xitsonga with interpretation by Abraham Sevor Kwabena and English translation by Nkhensani Ntsanwisi).

2. Desmond Tutu, "The Ancestor Cult and Its Influence on Ethical Issues," *Ministry: A Quarterly Theological Review for Africa* 9, no. 3 (July 1969): 103–4.

Chapter 15

1. The origins of this saying are discussed in Joel Goldberg, "It Takes a Village to Determine the Origins of an African Proverb," *Goats and Soda*, July 30, 2016, https://www .npr.org/sections/goatsandsoda/2016/07/30/487925796/it-takes-a-village-to-determine -the-origins-of-an-african-proverb.

2. Beka Ntsanwisi, "Alive and Kicking," Ashoka Fellows Round Table on Aging, Zoom conference, streamed live July 8, 2020, https://drive.google.com/file/d/1rFt-374TAoJhxY_olgwABbriuR6dnr_Ot/view.

3. Translation per South African History Online, "The 1956 Women's March in Pretoria," last modified August 6, 2021, https://www.sahistory.org.za/article/1956-womens-march-pretoria.

4. Winnie Madikizela-Mandela, as quoted in South African History Online, "The Role of Women in the Struggle against Apartheid, 15 July 1980," last modified June 11, 2019, https://www.sahistory.org.za/archive/role-women-struggle-against-apartheid-15-july-1980.

5. Annah Masesa Vuma, as quoted in Lara-Ann De Wet, dir., *Alive and Kicking: The Soccer Grannies of South Africa*, film (New York: Lazuli Film, 2015), https://www.soccer-grannies.com.

CHAPTER 16

1. Beka Ntsanwisi, interview with the author, Lancaster, Massachusetts, July 15, 2010.

2. As archived at Matthew Knott-Craig, "2010 Bid Announcement," video, uploaded August 28, 2008, https://www.youtube.com/watch?v=R72Zwxx0WbI.

3. Beatrice Tshabala, interview with the author via email, January 30, 2022.

4. Ntsanwisi, interview with the author.

EPILOGUE

1. Beka Ntsanwisi, as quoted in Jean Duffy, "When We Couldn't Meet on the Soccer Field, We Danced—8,000 Miles Apart," *Cognoscenti*, May 5, 2021, https://www.wbur.org/cognoscenti/2021/05/05/covid19-south-africa-soccer-grannies-jean-duffy.

2. Lynn Naftel as quoted in Maddi Davidson, *Kicking Grass Taking Games: Women Fight for Their Right to Play the Beautiful Game* (Scotts Valley, CA: CreateSpace, 2018), 237.

3. Mamaila Chauke Novela, interview with Happiness Maake in Nkowankowa, Limpopo, September 18, 2021 (interview conducted in Xitsonga and translated into English by Mr. Maake).

4. Uyazi Asnath Xibiti, interview with Happiness Maake in Nkowankowa, Limpopo, September 18, 2021 (interview conducted in Xitsonga and translated into English by Mr. Maake).

5. South African president Cyril Ramaphosa, in News 24, "Ramaphosa Urges SA to Do 'Jerusalema' Dance Challenge on Heritage Day," video, uploaded September 16, 2020, https://www.youtube.com/watch?v=zJGcq9DGb5c.

6. Abraham Kwabina Servile, interview with Happiness Maake in Nkowankowa, Limpopo, September 18, 2021.

7. Gingirikani Mirriam Mushwana, interview with Happiness Maake in Nkowankowa, Limpopo, September 18, 2021 (interview conducted in Xitsonga and translated into English by Mr. Maake).

8. Makoma Selina Matwalane, interview with Happiness Maake in Nkowankowa, Limpopo, September 18, 2021 (interview conducted in Xitsonga and translated into English by Mr. Maake).

Bibliography

Abel, David. "Kicking up Their Heels: Soccer Grannies Find Their Way from South Africa for Tournament, Fun." *Boston Globe*, July 17, 2010. http://archive.boston.com/news/local/massachusetts/articles/2010/07/17/kicking_up_their_heels/.

Abel, Martin. "Long-Run Effects of Forced Resettlement: Evidence from *Apartheid* South Africa." Working paper. Harvard University, March 4, 2016. https://oconnell.fas.harvard.edu/files/abel/files/abel_homeland_social_capital.pdf.

Adler, David. "Stories of Cities #19: Johannesburg's Apartheid Purge of Vibrant Sophiatown." *Guardian*, April 11, 2016. https://www.theguardian.com/cities/2016/apr/11/story-cities-19-johannesburg-south-africa-apartheid-purge-sophiatown.

Aduna. "The Baobab Tree: Africa's Iconic 'Tree of Life.'" Aduna, accessed May 22, 2022. https://aduna.com/blogs/learn/the-baobab-tree.

African Studies Center at Michigan State University. "The Defiance Campaign: Summary." *South Africa: Overcoming Apartheid, Building Democracy*, accessed June 2, 2022. https://overcomingapartheid.msu.edu/multimedia.php?id=65-259-9.

African Travel Canvas. "Iconic South African Women and Their Role in the Struggle against Apartheid." African Travel Canvas, August 6, 2019. https://africantravelcanvas.com/experiences/history-and-politics/iconic-south-african-women-and-their-role-in-the-struggle-against-apartheid/.

Agandin, John Akanvariyuei. "The Baobab Tree." *Village Boy Impressions* (blog), April 3, 2017. https://villageboyimpressions.blogspot.com/2017/04/the-baobab-tree.html.

Alegi, Peter. *Laduma! Soccer, Politics, and Society in South Africa, from Its Origins to 2010*. Scottsville, South Africa: University of KwaZulu-Natal Press, 2010.

Alegi, Peter, and Chris Bolsmann, eds. *Africa's World Cup: Critical Reflections on Play, Patriotism, Spectatorship, and Space*. Ann Arbor: University of Michigan Press, 2013.

Ally, Yaseen. "'Burn the Witch': The Impact of the Fear of Witchcraft on Social Cohesion in South Africa." *Psychology in Society* 49 (2015): 25–45. http://www.scielo.org.za/pdf/pins/n49/03.pdf.

Alzheimer's Society. "Physical Exercise and Dementia." June 7, 2022. https://www.alzheimers.org.uk/about-dementia/risk-factors-and-prevention/physical-exercise.

Arthur, Adelaide. "Africa's Naming Traditions: Nine Ways to Name Your Child." BBC, December 30, 2016. https://www.bbc.com/news/world-africa-37912748.

Ashforth, Adam. *Witchcraft, Violence, and Democracy in South Africa*. Chicago: University of Chicago Press, 2005.

Ashoka. "Beka Ntsanwisi: Ashoka Fellow." Accessed May 21, 2022. https://www.ashoka
.org/en-us/fellow/beka-ntsanwisi.

Augustyn, Adam. "Bantustan." *Britannica*, last modified August 26, 2020. https://www
.britannica.com/topic/Bantustan.

Bauer, Pat. "Bantu Education Act: South Africa (1953)." *Britannica*, last modified July 22,
2020. https://www.britannica.com/event/Bantu-Education-Act.

BBC World Service. "Southern Africa: Collapse of Apartheid." In *The Story of Africa*.
BBC News, accessed March 3, 2022. https://www.bbc.co.uk/worldservice/africa/
features/storyofafrica/12chapter11.shtml.

Bell, Claire L. "South Africa's Female Tribal Chiefs Often Rule in Fear." *Time*, June 7,
2010. http://content.time.com/time/world/article/0,8599,1994210,00.html.

Best, Alan C. G. "South Africa's Border Industries: The Tswana Example." *Annals of the
Association of American Geographers* 61, no. 2 (June 1971): 329–43.

Blakemore, Erin. "The Harsh Reality of Life under Apartheid." History, last modified
September 10, 2021. https://www.history.com/news/apartheid-policies-photos
-nelson-mandela.

Brennan, Patrick. "'England' v 'Scotland'—1881: First Attempt to Establish Women's
Football Disrupted by Hooligans." *Donmouth* (blog), last modified March 9, 2020.
http://www.donmouth.co.uk/womens_football/1881.html.

Brown, Luke. "The Mopane Worm—A Popular African Delicacy." *Infobwana*, October 31, 2013. https://medium.com/the-best-of-zambia/the-mopane-worm-a
-popular-african-delicacy-2aa2c20ec630.

Bureau of Diplomatic Security. "Carjacking—Don't Be a Victim." US Department of
State publication no. 10863. August 2020. https://2009-2017.state.gov/m/ds/rls/
rpt/19782.htm.

Butler, Jeffrey, Robert I. Rotberg, and John Adams. *The Black Homelands of South Africa:
The Political and Economic Development of Bophuthtswana and Kwa-Zulu*. Berkeley:
University of California Press, 1977. http://ark.cdlib.org/ark:/13030/ft0489n6d5/.

Campbell, Derryn. *Awesome South Africa*. Edited by Siobhan Gunning. Cape Town:
Awesome South African Publishers, 2010.

Chazan, May. *The Grandmother's Movement: Solidarity and Survival in the Time of AIDS*.
Montreal, QC: McGill-Queen's University Press, 2015.

Chimere-dan, Orieji. "Apartheid and Demography in South Africa." *African Population
Studies* 7 (April 1992): 26–36. https://doi.org/10.11564/7-0-419.

City of Polokwane. "Peter Mokaba Stadium." Accessed June 7, 2022. https://www.polo
kwane.gov.za/Pages/peter-mokaba-stadium.aspx.

Claassens, Carina. "10 Things to Know about Hillbrow, Johannesburg's Notorious
Neighbourhood." Culture Trip, June 14, 2017. https://theculturetrip.com/africa/
south-africa/articles/10-things-to-know-about-hillbrow-johannesburgs-notorious
-neighbourhood/.

Collinson, Mark, Brent Wolff, Stephen Tollman, and Kathleen Kahn. "Trends in Internal
Labour Migration from the Rural Limpopo Province, Male Risk Behaviour, and
Implications for Spread of HIV/AIDS in Rural South Africa." *Journal of Ethnic
and Migration Studies* 32, no. 4 (May 2006): 633–48. https://www.ncbi.nlm.nih
.gov/pmc/articles/PMC2854811/pdf/ukmss-28918.pdf.

Cultural Atlas. "South African Culture: Etiquette." Accessed June 7, 2022. https://cul turalatlas.sbs.com.au/south-african-culture/south-african-culture-etiquette.

———. "South African Culture: Religion." Accessed March 3, 2022. https://culturalatlas .sbs.com.au/south-african-culture/south-african-culture-religion.

Cuní Sanchez, Aida. "Baobab Trees Have More Than 300 Uses but They Are Dying in Africa." *The Conversation*, June 24, 2018. https://theconversation.com/baobab-trees -have-more-than-300-uses-but-theyre-dying-in-africa-98214.

Davidson, Maddi. *Kicking Grass Taking Games: Women Fight for Their Right to Play the Beautiful Game*. Scotts Valley, CA: CreateSpace, 2018.

Davis, L. "An Application of the Rational Choice Perspective on Vehicle Hijacking." *Acta Criminologica: African Journal of Criminology and Victimology* 14, no. 3 (January 2001): 102–13. https://hdl.handle.net/10520/EJC28692.

De Wet, Lara-Ann, dir. *Alive and Kicking: The Soccer Grannies of South Africa*. Film. New York: Lazuli Film, 2015. https://www.soccergrannies.com.

Dinkelman, Taryn. "The Effects of Rural Electrification on Employment: New Evidence from South Africa." *American Economic Review* 101, no. 7 (December 2011): 3078– 108. https://doi.org/10.1257/aer.101.7.3078. August 2010 version available at https://rpds.princeton.edu/sites/rpds/files/media/dinkelman_electricity_0810.pdf.

Dixon, Robyn. "They Kick Like Grannies, Proudly." *Los Angeles Times*, June 21, 2010. https://www.latimes.com/archives/la-xpm-2010-jun-21-la-fg-soccer-grannies -20100622-story.html.

Drewes, J. Ernst, and Mariske van Aswegen. "National Planning in South Africa: A Crit- ical Review." Paper presented at the 6th International Conference on Sustainable Development and Planning, Kos, Greece, May 27–29, 2013. Published in *WIT Transactions on Ecology and The Environment* 173 (2013): 193–204. https://www .witpress.com/Secure/elibrary/papers/SDP13/SDP13016FU1.pdf.

Duffy, Jean. "The Lexpressas Soccer Team Joins the Jerusalema Challenge." Video. Uploaded December 9, 2020. https://www.youtube.com/watch?v=QtyUCEDC 5yQ.

———. "When We Couldn't Meet on the Soccer Field, We Danced—8,000 Miles Apart." *Cognoscenti*, May 5, 2021. https://www.wbur.org/cognoscenti/2021/05/05/ covid19-south-africa-soccer-grannies-jean-duffy.

Elphick, Richard, and Rodney Davenport, eds. *Christianity in South Africa: A Political, Social and Cultural History*. Berkeley: University of California Press, 1997.

Encyclopedia Britannica Editors. "Mswati III: King of Eswatini." *Britannica*, last modi- fied April 15, 2022. https://www.britannica.com/biography/Mswati-III.

Engh, Mari Haugaa. "Tackling Femininity: The Heterosexual Paradigm and Women's Soccer in South Africa." *International Journal of the History of Sport* 28, no. 1 (2010): 137–52.

EntoMarket. "Edible Mopane Worms." Edible Insects, accessed March 3, 2022. https:// www.edibleinsects.com/product/edible-mopane-worms/.

Evans, Laura. "Forced Relocation in Apartheid South Africa: The Impact of 'Separate Development.'" *Modern History Review* 20, no. 2 (November 2017). https://

www.hoddereducation.co.uk/media/Documents/Magazines/Sample%20Articles/
November%202017/ModHisRev20_2_Nov2017_sample.pdf.

Facing History and Ourselves. "Africans Resist White Control." In *Confronting Apartheid*, chapter 1, reading 5. Accessed February 7, 2022. https://www.facinghistory
.org/confronting-apartheid/chapter-1/africans-resist-white-control.

———. "Women Rise up against Apartheid and Change the Movement." In *Confronting Apartheid*, chapter 2. Accessed June 7, 2022. https://www.facinghistory
.org/confronting-apartheid/chapter-2/women-rise-against-apartheid-and-change
-movement.

Faul, Michelle. "What Life Was Like in South Africa during Apartheid." Associated
Press, December 9, 2013. Reprinted at https://www.businessinsider.com/what-life
-was-like-in-south-africa-during-apartheid-2013-12.

Fihlani, Pumza. "S Africa's Football 'Grannies' Look to World Cup." BBC News, last
modified December 3, 2009. http://news.bbc.co.uk/2/hi/africa/8389067.stm.

Fitzpatrick, Liseli A. "African Names and Naming Practices: The Impact Slavery and
European Domination Had on the African Psyche, Identity and Protest." Master's
thesis, The Ohio State University, Columbus, Ohio, 2012. http://rave.ohiolink.edu/
etdc/view?acc_num=osu1338404929.

Goldberg, Joel. "It Takes a Village to Determine the Origins of an African Proverb." *Goats
and Soda*, July 30, 2016. https://www.npr.org/sections/goatsandsoda/2016/07/30/
487925796/it-takes-a-village-to-determine-the-origins-of-an-african-proverb.

Goodman, Mark. "Lexpressas Host 'Soccer Grannies' from South Africa." *Wicked Local*,
July 23, 2010. https://www.wickedlocal.com/story/lexington-minuteman/2010/07/
23/lexpressas-host-soccer-grannies-from/39094522007/.

Gould, Kayley. "The White Savior Complex: The Dark Side of Volunteering." Video.
Filmed March 2019 at TEDxLAHS, Los Altos, CA. https://www.ted.com/talks/
kayley_gould_the_white_savior_complex_the_dark_side_of_volunteering.

Griffin, Nicholas. "How Soccer Defeated Apartheid." *Foreign Policy*, June 7, 2010. https://
foreignpolicy.com/2010/06/07/how-soccer-defeated-apartheid/.

Gross, Daniel A. "How Should South Africa Remember the Architect of Apartheid?"
Smithsonian, September 14, 2016. https://www.smithsonianmag.com/history/how
-should-south-africa-remember-architect-apartheid-180960449/.

Hadithi Africa. "History of the Xibelani Dance of the Tsonga Culture." January 6, 2020.
https://hadithi.africa/history-of-the-xibelani-dance-of-the-tsonga-culture/.

Healy-Clancy, Meghan. "The Family Politics of the Federation of South African Women:
A History of Public Motherhood in Women's Antiracist Activism." *Signs: Journal
of Women and Culture in Society* 42, no. 4 (summer 2017): 843–66. https://www
.journals.uchicago.edu/doi/full/10.1086/690916.

Herbalife Ltd. "Vakhegula-Vakhegula: Herbalife Helps Bring South African Soccer
Grannies to Compete in Veteran's Cup." Press release, July 13, 2010. https://ir.herb
alife.com/news-events/press-releases/detail/552/vakhegula-vakhegula---herbalife
-helps-bring-south-african.

History.com Editors. "Apartheid." History, last modified March 3, 2020. https://www
.history.com/topics/africa/apartheid.

Hudson, Alexandra. "Robben Island Reminds of Liberating Power of Soccer." Reuters, last modified June 14, 2010. https://www.reuters.com/article/us-soccer-world -robbenisland/robben-island-reminds-of-liberating-power-of-soccer-idUSTRE65 D1EU20100614.

Hunter, Mark. *Love in the Time of AIDS: Inequality, Gender, and Rights in South Africa.* Bloomington: Indiana University Press, 2010.

Imray, Gerald. "South Africa Spent $3 Billion on 2010 World Cup." *Washington Times,* November 23, 2012. https://www.washingtontimes.com/news/2012/nov/23/south -africa-spent-3-billion-2010-world-cup/.

Johnston, Thomas F. "Secret Rites of the Tsonga Girls' Initiation School (Khomba)." *Papers in Anthropology* 17, no. 1 (spring 1976): 15–36. http://www.fcsh.unl.pt/ mozdata/files/original/6/3191/MOZ_304.2.pdf.

———. "Tsonga Musical Performance in Cultural Perspective (South Africa)." *Anthropos* 70, nos. 5–6 (1975): 761–99. http://fcsh.unl.pt/mozdata/files/original/6/3239/ MOZ_71.1.pdf.

Jones, Mark. "Bill Shankly's Famous 'Life and Death' Misquote and What Liverpool Icon Really Meant." *Mirror,* last modified March 31, 2020. https://www.mirror.co.uk/ sport/football/news/bill-shanklys-famous-life-death-21784583.

Junod, Henri-Alexandre. *The Life of a South African Tribe.* Part 1, *The Social Life.* Neuchâtel, Fr.: Imprimerie Attinger Frères, 1912.

Keys, Allison. "How the First Sports Bra Got Its Stabilizing Start." *Smithsonian,* March 18, 2020. https://www.smithsonianmag.com/smithsonian-institution/how -first-sports-bra-got-stabilizing-start-180974427/.

Knoema. "South Africa—Elderly (65+) Literacy Rate." Accessed May 22, 2022. https:// knoema.com/atlas/South-Africa/topics/Education/Literacy/Elderly-literacy-rate.

Knott-Craig, Matthew. "2010 Bid Announcement." Video. Uploaded August 28, 2008. https://www.youtube.com/watch?v=R72Zwxx0WbI.

Kyei, Kwabena A., and K. B. Gyekye. "Unemployment in Limpopo Province in South Africa: Searching for Factors." *Journal of Social Sciences* 31, no. 2 (2012): 177–85. https://doi.org/10.1080/09718923.2012.11893026.

Lam, Murray, Gloria Leibbrandt, and Vimal Ranchhod. "Labor Force Withdrawal of the Elderly in South Africa." In *Aging in Sub-Saharan Africa: Recommendation for Furthering Research,* edited by Barney Cohen and Jane Menken, chapter 7. Washington, DC: National Academies Press, 2006. https://www.ncbi.nlm.nih.gov/ books/NBK20294/.

Lehohla, Pali. *Census 2011: Census in Brief.* Report no. 03-01-41. Pretoria: Statistics South Africa, 2012. http://www.statssa.gov.za/census/census_2011/census_prod ucts/Census_2011_Census_in_brief.pdf.

Lewis, Michael. "Golden Memories: USA Kicks Off Olympic Women's Soccer in 1996." US Soccer, August 1, 2021. https://www.ussoccer.com/stories/2021/07/feature -golden-memories-usa-kicks-off-olympic-womens-soccer-in-1996.

Lin, Jami Nakaruma. "Seek Solidarity, Not Charity." Anti-Racism Daily, November 10, 2020. https://the-ard.com/2020/11/10/seek-solidarity-not-charity-anti-racism -daily-bt62d/.

Longman, Jeré. "A Bleating Soundtrack for Soccer." *New York Times*, June 8, 2010. https://www.nytimes.com/2010/06/09/sports/soccer/09horn.html.

———. "Origins of Tournament in an Infamous Prison." *New York Times*, July 5, 2010. https://www.nytimes.com/2010/07/06/sports/soccer/06robben.html.

Luiz, John M., and C. S. van der Waal. "Re-evaluating South Africa's Regional Industrial Development Programme: Case Studies from Brits and Nkowankowa." *Urban Forum* 8, no. 1 (1997): 61–79.

Maluleke, Risenga. *Grandparenthood in the Context of Ageing in South Africa*. Report no. 03-00-12. Pretoria: Statistics South Africa, 2018. http://www.statssa.gov.za/publications/Report%2003-00-12/Report%2003-00-122016.pdf.

Mandela, Nelson. Keynote address given at the inaugural Laureus World Sports Awards, Monte Carlo, Monaco, May 25, 2000. https://www.laureus.com/news/celebrating-the-legacy-of-a-hero-on-mandela-day.

———. *The Long Walk to Freedom: The Autobiography of Nelson Mandela*. London: Little, Brown, 1994.

———. "Nelson Mandela on South Africa Hosting the World Cup." Nelson Mandela Foundation, May 14, 2010. https://www.nelsonmandela.org/news/entry/nelson-mandela-on-south-africa-hosting-the-world-cup.

Moalusi, Karabo. "Best Tsonga Wedding Entrance Dance." Video. Uploaded April 6, 2019. https://www.youtube.com/watch?v=S1AHW2-gPfE.

Masondo, Sibusiso. "Ironies of Christian Presence in Southern Africa." *Journal for the Study of Religion* 31, no. 2 (2018): 209–31. http://dx.doi.org/10.17159/2413-3027/2018/v31n2a10.

Mass Adult State Soccer (MASS). "Hall of Fame: MASS Soccer; 2003." Accessed May 21, 2022. https://www.mass-soccer.org/page/show/1700845-hall-of-fame-awards.

Mbola, Bathandwa. "The Game That United a Nation." South African Government News Agency, July 5, 2011. https://www.sanews.gov.za/south-africa/game-united-nation.

McCarthy, Joe, and Erica Sánchez. "4 Ways Nelson Mandela Championed Women's Rights." Exiger l'équité. Global Citizen, July 9, 2018. https://www.globalcitizen.org/fr/content/nelson-mandela-champion-for-womens-rights/.

M Convert. "1960 ZAR to USD or Convert 1960 South African Rand in US Dollar." Accessed June 3, 2022. https://zar.mconvert.net/usd/1960.

Medie, Peace A., Andriana Biney, Amanda Coffie, and Cori Wielenga. "Women Traditional Leaders Could Help Make Sure the Pandemic Message Is Heard." *The Conversation*, August 24, 2020. https://theconversation.com/women-traditional-leaders-could-help-make-sure-the-pandemic-message-is-heard-143033.

Mlaba, Khanyi. "3 Things That Have Increased Food Insecurity in South Africa This Year." Global Citizen, October 27, 2020. https://www.globalcitizen.org/en/content/issues-increase-food-insecurity-south-africa-covid/.

Mosoetsa, Sarah. *Eating from One Pot: The Dynamics of Survival in Poor South African Households*. Johannesburg, South Africa: Wits University Press, 2011.

Mothibe, Mmamosheledi E., and Mncengeli Sibanda, "African Traditional Medicine: South African Perspective." In *Traditional and Complementary Medicine*, edited by Cengiz Mordeniz. London: InTechOpen, 2019. https://www.intechopen.com/books/traditional-and-complementary-medicine/african-traditional-medicine-south-african-perspective.

Murphy, Chris. "World Cup Fever Grips African Grannies." CNN, last modified October 25, 2009. http://edition.cnn.com/2009/SPORT/football/10/25/football.africa.world.cup/index.html.

National Museum of American History. "Infant Food, Nestle's Lactogen." Accessed June 3, 2022. https://americanhistory.si.edu/collections/search/object/nmah_717074.

National Today. "National Women's Day—August 9, 2022." Accessed April 30, 2022. https://nationaltoday.com/national-womens-day/.

News 24. "Ramaphosa Urges SA to Do 'Jerusalema' Dance Challenge on Heritage Day." Video. Uploaded September 16, 2020. https://www.youtube.com/watch?v=zJGcq9DGb5c.

Ngcobozi, Lihle. *Mothers of the Nation: Manyano Women in South Africa*. Cape Town, South Africa: Tafelberg, 2020.

Niehaus, Isak. "Moralising Magic? A Brief History of Football Potions in a South African Homeland Area, 1958–2010." *Journal of Southern African Studies* 41, no. 5 (2015): 1053–66.

Nkuna, Boshoff Mavutana. *The Rose amongst the Thorns: The Biography on Beka Ntsan'wisi*. Mpumalanga, South Africa: Ndzheko Publishers, 2007.

Ntsanwisi, Beka. "Alive and Kicking." Ashoka Fellows Round Table on Aging, Zoom conference, streamed live July 8, 2020. https://drive.google.com/file/d/1rFt374TAoJhxY_olgwABbriuR6dnr_Ot/view.

Ntsanwisi, Rebecca. Speech given at the 6th International Women's Conference, Bangaluru, India, February 7–9, 2014. Video. https://www.youtube.com/watch?v=RL6fLIdQWJs.

Nyandoro, Mark. "Defying the Odds, Not the Abuse: South African Women's Agency and Rotating Saving Schemes, 1994–2017." *Journal of International Women's Studies* 19, no. 5 (May 2018): 177–92. https://vc.bridgew.edu/cgi/viewcontent.cgi?article=2052&context=jiws.

Oates, Katelyn. "South Africa's Sports Lack Progress in the Post-apartheid Period." Global Sport Matters, April 16, 2019. https://globalsportmatters.com/culture/2019/04/16/south-africas-sports-lack-progress-in-the-post-apartheid-era/.

O, Chacha. "Tsonga People: What to Know about Their Culture, Language and Food." Answers Africa, accessed March 3, 2022. https://answersafrica.com/tsonga-people-what-to-know-about-their-culture-language-and-food.html.

Pearson, Michael, and Tom Cohen. "Life under Apartheid: Demeaning, Often Brutal." CNN, last modified December 6, 2013. https://www.cnn.com/2013/12/06/world/africa/mandela-life-under-apartheid/index.html.

Pelak, Cynthia Fabrizio. "Women and Gender in South African Football: A Brief History." *Soccer and Society* 11, nos. 1–2 (2010): 63–78. https://www.academia.edu/18736139/Women_and_Gender_in_South_African_Football_A_brief_history.

Petruzzello, Melissa, with Gloria Lotha. "Baobab Tree Genus." *Britannica*, last modified September 12, 2021. https://www.britannica.com/plant/baobab-tree-genus.

Radiolab. "From Tree to Shining Tree." July 30, 2016. https://www.wnycstudios.org/pod casts/radiolab/articles/from-tree-to-shining-tree.

Republic of South Africa. Constitution of the Republic of South Africa, No. 108 of 1996. Promulgated December 18, 1996, commenced February 4, 1997. https://www.gov .za/sites/default/files/images/a108-96.pdf.

———. "National Anthem." Accessed May 20, 2022. https://www.gov.za/about-sa/ national-symbols/national-anthem.

———. "Progress Report on Declaration of Commitment on HIV and AIDS: Republic of South Africa; Reporting Period: January 2006–December 2007." Prepared for the UN General Assembly Special Session on HIV and AIDS. April 3, 2008. https://www.gov.za/sites/default/files/gcis_document/201409/prog-rpthiv -aids0607.pdf.

Republic of South Africa, the Presidency. "Rebecca Beka Ntsanwisi (1968–): The Order of the Baobab in Bronze." Accessed February 16, 2022. http://www.thepresidency .gov.za/national-orders/recipient/rebecca-beka-ntsanwisi-1968.

Reuters. "Grannies Take on the Beautiful Game." Video. Uploaded October 22, 2009. https://web.archive.org/web/20100614221553/https://www.youtube.com/watch?v =4yabcFLITAA.

Rhoden, William C. "For the Love of Soccer and a Lasting Sisterhood." *New York Times*, June 6, 2010. https://www.nytimes.com/2010/06/07/sports/soccer/07rhoden.html.

Rikhotso, Daniel Khazamula. "Industrial Development at Nkowankowa: A Geographical Analysis." Master's thesis, Rand Afrikaans University, November 1997. https://ujcontent.uj.ac.za/vital/access/manager/Repository/uj:9176?site_name =GlobalView&view=list&f0=sm_identifier%3A%22http%3A%2F%2Fhdl.handle .net%2F10210%2F5628%22&sort=ss_dateNormalized+asc%2Csort_ss_title+asc.

Rippon, Anton. "From the Press Box: England's Women Footballers Deserve More Recognition." Sports Journalists' Association, July 19, 2018. https://www.sports journalists.co.uk/view-from-the-pressbox/view-from-the-press-box-why-englands -women-footballers-deserve-more-recognition/.

Ross, Fiona. "What Nelson Mandela Ate for Breakfast." Food52, June 7, 2016. https:// food52.com/blog/17024-what-nelson-mandela-ate-for-breakfast.

RunRepeat and the IAFF. "The State of Running, 2019." September 21, 2021. https:// runrepeat.com/state-of-running.

SaferSpaces. "Gender-Based Violence in South Africa." Accessed April 30, 2022. https:// www.saferspaces.org.za/understand/entry/gender-based-violence-in-south-africa.

SAMSREC TV. "Jerusalema Challenge—Vakhegula Vakhegula & Vakhalabye Vakhalabye." Video. Uploaded September 23, 2020. https://www.youtube.com/watch?v =yFsMget-Tzo.

SA-V. "About Louis Trichardt." Accessed April 4, 2022. https://www.sa-venues.com/ attractionslm/louis-trichardt.php.

ScamWatch. "Nigerian Scams." Accessed May 21, 2022. https://www.scamwatch.gov.au/ types-of-scams/unexpected-money/nigerian-scams.

———. "Spot the Scam Signs." Accessed May 21, 2022. https://www.scamwatch.gov.au/about-scamwatch/tools-resources/online-resources/spot-the-scam-signs.

Selby, Daniele. "9 Trailblazing South African Activists, Past and Present." Global Citizen, August 6, 2018. https://www.globalcitizen.org/en/content/south-african-activists-ntshona-muholi-naidoo/.

Sithole, Ndundu. "South African Grannies Catch World Cup Fever." Reuters, last modified October 21, 2009. https://www.reuters.com/article/ozasp-soccer-world-grannies-idAFJOE59L01C20091022.

Smith, Nicholas Rush. *Contradictions of Democracy: Vigilantism and Rights in Post-apartheid South Africa.* New York: Oxford University Press, 2019.

Smith, Whitney. "Flag of South Africa." *Britannica*, last modified April 24, 2017. https://www.britannica.com/topic/flag-of-South-Africa.

Solomon, Ben C. "Musangwe Fight Club: A Vicious Tradition." *New York Times*, February 26, 2016. https://www.nytimes.com/2016/02/27/sports/musangwe-fight-club-a-vicious-venda-tradition.html.

South African History Online. "Defiance Campaign Time Line 1948–1952." Last modified November 12, 2021. https://www.sahistory.org.za/article/defiance-campaign-timeline-1948-1952.

———. "The Native Land Act Is Passed: 19 June 1913." Last modified September 30, 2019. https://www.sahistory.org.za/dated-event/native-land-act-passed.

———. "The 1956 Women's March in Pretoria." Last modified August 6, 2021. https://www.sahistory.org.za/article/1956-womens-march-pretoria.

———. "The Role of Women in the Struggle against Apartheid, 15 July 1980." Last modified June 11, 2019. https://www.sahistory.org.za/archive/role-women-struggle-against-apartheid-15-july-1980.

———. "Sophiatown." Last modified August 28, 2019. https://www.sahistory.org.za/place/sophiatown.

———. "When, Why and Where the First African Farmers Settled in Southern Africa." Last modified August 27, 2019. https://www.sahistory.org.za/article/when-why-and-where-first-african-farmers-settled-southern-africa.

———. "Women and the Struggle against Apartheid." Last modified August 27, 2019. https://www.sahistory.org.za/article/women-and-struggle-against-apartheid.

South Africa Online. "Marriage in Tsonga Society." Accessed June 3, 2022. https://southafrica.co.za/marriage-in-tsonga-society.html.

———. "Social Organisation of the Tsonga." Accessed June 1, 2022. https://southafrica.co.za/social-organisation-of-the-tsonga.html.

———. "The Traditional Economy of the Tsonga." Accessed June 13, 2022. https://southafrica.co.za/the-traditional-economy-of-the-tsonga.html.

———. "Traditional Tsonga Political Structures." Accessed June 7, 2022. https://southafrica.co.za/traditional-tsonga-political-structures.html.

Statistics South Africa. *Census 2001: Primary Tables South Arica; Census '96 and 2001 Compared*, report no. 03-02-04 (2001), 25–28. Pretoria: Statistics South Africa, 2004. https://www.statssa.gov.za/census/census_2001/primary_tables/RSAPrimary.pdf.

———. "Five Facts about Poverty in South Africa." April 4, 2019. http://www.statssa.gov.za/?p=12075.

————. "Greater Tzaneen." Accessed March 3, 2022. http://www.statssa.gov.za/?page _id=993&id=greater-tzaneen-municipality.

Tawfeeq, Mohammed, Bukola Adebayo, and A. J. Davis. "South Africa Makes History as Women Make Up Half of Cabinet for First Time." CNN, last modified June 1, 2019. https://www.cnn.com/2019/05/30/africa/south-africa-gender-balanced -cabinet-intl/index.html.

Taylor, Paul. "Keepers of Afrikaner Flame Scorn De Klerk." *Washington Post*, March 16, 1992. https://www.washingtonpost.com/archive/politics/1992/03/16/keepers-of -afrikaner-flame-scorn-de-klerk/e3087ad0-b726-4d7b-bab5-727e0217e276/.

Time and Date. "Climate and Weather Averages in Limpopo, South Africa." Accessed June 2, 2022. https://www.timeanddate.com/weather/@1085597/climate.

Times Editors. "The Land Question Must Be Handled with Extreme Sensitivity." *Times Live*, February 28, 2014. https://www.timeslive.co.za/news/south-africa/2014-02 -28-the-land-question-must-be-handled-with-extreme-sensitivity/.

Torres Burtka, Allison. "More Female Athletes Take on Formerly Male-Only Sports." Global Sport Matters, January 7, 2020. https://globalsportmatters.com/culture/ 2020/01/07/female-athletes-male-only-sports/.

Tutu, Desmond. "The Ancestor Cult and Its Influence on Ethical Issues." *Ministry: A Quarterly Theological Review for Africa* 9, no. 3 (July 1969): 103–104.

Union of South Africa. Bantu Education Act 1953 (No. 47). Enacted October 5, 1953. https://www.sahistory.org.za/sites/default/files/archive-files2/leg19531009.028 .020.047.pdf.

Walker, Cherryl. "Critical Reflections on South Africa's 1913 Natives Land Act and Its Legacies: Introduction." *Journal of South African Studies* 40, no. 4 (2014): 655–65.

Webster, Edward, and Rahmat Omar. "Work Restructuring in Post-Apartheid South Africa." *Work and Occupations* 30, no. 2 (2003): 194–213. https://www.research gate.net/publication/249690526_Work_Restructuring_in_Post-Apartheid _South_Africa.

Western Province Council of Churches. "State of Emergency: What Does It Mean?" *Crisis News*, no. 4 (December 1984): 2–3. https://disa.ukzn.ac.za/sites/default/files/ pdf_files/Cnn485.pdf.

————. "Zweletemba: Siege Intensified." *Crisis News*, no. 4 (December 1985): 1. https:// disa.ukzn.ac.za/sites/default/files/pdf_files/Cnn485.pdf.

Wikipedia. "Louis Trichardt." Last modified August 30, 2021. https://en.wikipedia.org/ wiki/Louis_Trichardt.

————. "Pencil test (South Africa)." Last modified June 19, 2021. https://en.wikipedia .org/wiki/Pencil_test_(South_Africa).

Wolters Kluwer Health. "HIV/AIDS Deaths Are Down in South Africa, but Most Are Still Unacknowledged." *ScienceDaily*, October 29, 2015. https://www.sciencedaily .com/releases/2015/10/151029134646.htm.

World Wide Fund for Nature in partnership with the United States Agency for International Development. *Literature Review: Crime Prevention and High-Value Poaching*. Washington, DC: USAID, 2020. https://pdf.usaid.gov/pdf_docs/PA00XGJM.pdf.

INDEX

221

Cup games; Veterans Cup
preparations; *and specific
Grannies*
Venda chief's role, 175–76, 179,
182–83, 184
Verwoerd, Hendrik, 66–67
Veterans Cup activities: banquet,
105–8; first morning
breakfast, 81–84; opening
ceremonies, 56–57; post-
game celebrations, 88–89,
101–4; television coverage of,
104–5; trophy, 136–38, 189.
See also Veterans Cup games;
Veterans Cup preparations
Veterans Cup games: Bay State
Breakers versus Grannies,
79–81, 84–87; Hawai'i versus
Grannies, 110–13; San Diego
versus Grannies, 99–101. *See
also* Veterans Cup activities;
Veterans Cup preparations
Veterans Cup post-tournament
activities: goodbyes, 138–41;
Lexpressas scrimmage,
85–86; post-tournament
cookout, 113–16; thank-you
notes for donations, 141–42
Veterans Cup preparations:
airline tickets, 55–56;
donations, 28–29, 34, 55–56,
107; invitations to Soccer
Grannies, 18; promises of
help, 21; rearranging game
schedule, 56. *See also* Veterans

Cup activities; Veterans Cup
games; visa applications
vigilantism, 40
violence: abusive husbands,
183; carjackings, 146–47;
lawlessness, 128; threats of,
127–28, 159, 166–67, 183;
vigilantism and justice, 40
visa applications: difficulty of
securing, 29–31, 35–36;
fundraising for, 49–50;
invitation letter before
applying for, 18; obtaining,
51–55
Vuma, Annah Masesa. *See* Granny
Bull
vuvuzelas, 54, 62, 101, 103,
104, 112

weddings, 93–94, 108, 151–53
witchcraft and mental illness, 39,
40, 42, 44–46, 133
women of South Africa: female
chiefs, 182–83; first soccer
clubs, 19–20; in government,
183; initiation into
womanhood, 93; men taking
precedence over, 82, 182;
power of, 183; savings groups
of, 129
Women's Professional Soccer
league game, 135–38
Women's World Cup, 23
work opportunities for men:
under apartheid, 67, 72,

About the Author

Jean Duffy is a nonfiction writer who has published with the *Boston Globe*, the *Concord Monitor*, the *Packingtown Review*, the *Somerville Journal*, the *Stamford Advocate*, and WBUR's *Cognoscenti*. *Soccer Grannies* is her first book. She is grateful that going into this project, she didn't understand how long it actually takes to write a book.

Duffy worked for twenty-six years as an engineer and manager and is now retired. These days she frequents the soccer fields of Lexington, Massachusetts, where her team, the Lexpressas, have been playing for some twenty years.

When not pounding her fingers on the keyboard or flubbing a shot on goal, Duffy can be found consulting with nonprofits; helping people downsize; or spending time at home in Somerville, Massachusetts, doing crossword puzzles with her husband at the kitchen table. There's finally room to spread out the newspaper now that their two grown daughters have fanned their wings and flown the coop.

Duffy has not eaten a mopane worm since 2011; she is, however, determined to enjoy one (just one) at the upcoming Grannies' World Cup.

Follow her online at https://jeanduffy.com, on Twitter @Jean_G_Duffy, on Facebook @SoccerGranniesBook, and on Instagram @SoccerGranniesBook.

CPSIA information can be obtained
at www.ICGtesting.com
Printed in the USA
BVHW031733300123
656818BV00002BA/3